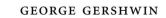

GEORGE GERSHWIN

MUSIC IN AMERICAN LIFE

A list of books in the series appears at the end of the book.

Walter Rimler

George GERSHWIN

An Intimate Portrait

UNIVERSITY OF ILLINOIS PRESS
URBANA AND CHICAGO

© 2009 by the Board of Trustees
of the University of Illinois
All rights reserved
Manufactured in the United States of America
C 5 4 3 2 1
♾ This book is printed on acid-free paper.

Library of Congress Cataloging-in-Publication Data
Rimler, Walter.
George Gershwin : an intimate portrait / Walter Rimler
p.   cm. — (Music in American life)
Includes bibliographical references and index.

ISBN 978-0-252-03444-2 (cloth : alk. paper)

1. Gershwin, George, 1898–1937.
2. Composers—United States—Biography.
I. Title.
ML410.G288R55   2009
780.92—dc22 [B]   2008047508

For Peg Rimler
And in memory of
Mark Trent Goldberg

Just seven years tomorrow (my birthday) since George wrote
"Plenty O' Nuttin'" and I took it down as he played it. My "Porgy"
lecture honestly wowed the people last night—the music is absolutely sure-fire in *any* group whatsoever. The whole audience
left feeling proud that so important a work has been done in this
country. And I left with a ghastly sense of the grayness of a world
without George, a profound personal and universal sense of loss.
For I believe his music is a force for strong Americanism, in the best
sense, that it strikes a powerful blow against the evils that besiege us
by giving people a magic lift and a strengthening touch. No wonder
Hitler hates it so! It's so positive and confident—a people that hear
that rhythm in their ears can't be licked.

—KAY SWIFT IN A 1942 LETTER TO MARY LASKER

CONTENTS

Illustrations follow page 98

GEORGE GERSHWIN

From Street Kid to Wunderkind

He was a ten-year-old, hyperactive, scrappy street kid, as well as a petty thief and a habitual hooky player. If he was good at anything it was roller skating—he was the acknowledged champion skater of Seventh Street—although he may have been precocious at sex as well. He later told his friend and biographer Isaac Goldberg that he "had a girl at the age of nine."[1] He was the second of four children and the opposite of the first, Ira, who was the dutiful good boy. George was pegged by his parents as the one most likely to end up in perpetual trouble, probably in jail.

But then one day as he played ball on the yard at Public School 25 at Fifth Street and Second Avenue—he was avoiding the school assembly—he heard a fellow student, Max Rosenzweig, playing Dvorak's *Humoresque* on his violin in the auditorium and the music mesmerized him. Later that day he waited in the rain outside the school entrance to meet the young musician, who soon became his best friend. It was not long after that that George's Aunt Kate bought a piano and George's mother, Rose, not to be outdone by her younger sister, got one too. The heavy upright was hoisted by straps from the Second Avenue sidewalk up in the air and into the Gershwin living room, at which point George walked over and played a tune. No one in the family knew, but he had been practicing at a friend's house and was already good enough to knock out a couple of pop songs, his left hand rocking back and forth rag piano style. Ira had been the designated piano student, but when Rose and her husband, Morris, saw that George had talent, they decided to let him take the lessons, first from Aunt Kate, then from a series of less than inspired instructors, and at last from an excellent teacher and musician, Charles Hambitzer.

Hambitzer was a tall, thin, disheveled, and, by all accounts, sweet-natured man, who was the first to recognize the enormousness of the boy's gift. In a letter to his sister he proclaimed, "I have a new pupil who will make his mark in music if anybody will. The boy is a genius, without a doubt; he's just crazy about music and can't wait until it's time to take his lesson. No watching the clock for this boy! He wants to go in for this modern stuff, jazz, and what not. But I'm not going to let him for a while. I'll see that he gets a firm foundation in standard music first."[2] Then he gave George that foundation, teaching him Chopin, Debussy, and Schoenberg—Hambitzer was one of the first American pianists to admire and perform the latter's music—and he was wise enough to broaden Gershwin's musical horizons without denigrating the world of dance music that he took to so naturally. Hambitzer himself had a foot in that world, having composed a series of light musicals for the Shubert organization. When his young wife died of tuberculosis, his own death came shortly thereafter at age thirty-eight, from the same disease exacerbated by his despondency over her passing. But by then he had introduced George to another teacher, Edward Kilenyi, a Hungarian-born composer and violinist who emphasized the fundamentals of music theory. Kilenyi, like Hambitzer, was familiar with both sides of the musical tracks, being another early admirer of Schoenberg as well as a player of light music with the Waldorf-Astoria Orchestra. While teaching George musical form, harmony, counterpoint, and orchestration, he did not shoo him away from popular music. On the contrary, Kilenyi encouraged him to pursue fame as a popular composer so that "conductors in due time would ask you for serious compositions."[3] There were additional lessons with Rubin Goldmark—the American-born nephew of

Hungarian composer Karl Goldmark—and courses in orchestration and music history at Columbia University. But he was also busy studying—it was more like inhaling—American popular music. As a young composer, his inclination was to emulate not Mozart and Beethoven but Irving Berlin and Jerome Kern. As a pianist, his idols were not Rachmaninoff and Paderewski; rather, he became a habitué of Harlem night spots, attaching himself to the great stride pianist Luckey Roberts, going to clubs to hear him play, sitting next to him, absorbing his technique. The best of the Harlem pianists—Roberts, James P. Johnson, and Eubie Blake—were amazed that, whatever pyrotechnics they displayed at the piano, Gershwin could match them.

Early on, he developed a carefully thought out professional trajectory. First there would be Tin Pan Alley–style popular songs, then Broadway theater music, and after that, when he had the necessary prominence and experience, he would compose serious pieces for the stage, probably opera. He was not much of an operagoer, but he had been born to and was surrounded by immigrants who considered opera a hallmark of civilization and who knew that every great European capital boasted as proof of its culture a glittering and opulent opera house. For a composer of theater music, there could be no higher aspiration. The great contradiction here was that opera was not an American form, and Gershwin very much wanted to be an *American* composer. He would spend many years resolving this quandary.

The first markers in his career plan were easily reached. At fifteen, he talked his parents into letting him leave the High School of Commerce—they were hoping he would be an accountant or maybe a lawyer—to take a $15 a week job with a music publisher, Jerome H. Remick and Company, demonstrating their songs to vaudevillians who stopped by his cubicle. In 1919, at twenty-one, he and lyricist Irving Caesar wrote a song, "Swanee," whose sheet music sold in the millions, as did Al Jolson's recording of it, earning them tens of thousands of dollars. He was twenty-two when showman George White hired him to write his annual Broadway extravaganza, *George White's Scandals*. It was while writing his third *Scandals* score that he made his first try at opera. For *George White's Scandals of 1922,* he and lyricist B. G. DeSylva gave White something loftier than the usual revue number. In five days, they turned out a half-hour work called *Blue Monday, Opera a la Afro-American*. It told the story of a Harlem gambler who, having been shot by his girlfriend due a misunderstanding, dies after singing a doleful aria called "I'm Going to See My Mother." Gershwin was so excited and nervous about this piece that, during its tryout in New Haven, he developed what turned out to be a permanent case of what he called his "composer's stomach"—a chronic combination of abdominal pain, nausea, and constipation. The New Haven performance went well enough. One critic wrote: "This opera will be imitated in a hundred years."[4] However, after witnessing the New York premiere, Charles Darnton, writing in the *New York World*, called it "the most dismal, stupid and incredible black-face sketch that has ever been perpetrated."[5] Other critics had other opinions—one called it "the first real American opera"[6]—but White took the piece out of the show, believing that, whatever its merits, it depressed the audience so much they could not get back in the mood for lighter fare, such as another Gershwin song, "I'll Build a Stairway to Paradise." Thus, his first attempt to move beyond popular song was a failure. He was determined to try opera again but was going to move cautiously.

Then, suddenly, the plan was turned upside down. Paul Whiteman, who had conducted and liked *Blue Monday*, asked him to write an extended instrumental piece—a jazz concerto—for his upcoming concert, billed as "An Experiment in Modern Music." Whiteman wanted to demonstrate the malleability of jazz and show that this new type of music was worthy of admittance to the concert hall. Gershwin demurred; he was working on a musical comedy, *Sweet Little Devil*, and did not have time to write the piece. The bandleader, however, went ahead and made plans for the concert. He did so hurriedly, toward the end of 1923, because he did not want to be beaten to the punch by Vincent Lopez, another bandleader who wanted to be the first to present jazz in a highbrow setting.

It was while playing pool on Broadway at Fifty-second Street that Ira showed his brother an article in the January 4, 1924, *New York Tribune* reporting that Gershwin had accepted the assignment and was at work on a jazz concerto to be presented on February 12 at a concert in Aeolian Hall. George called Whiteman to protest, insisting there was too little time to complete such a project. But Whiteman was persuasive, and George took the bait. While on a train to Boston for the out-of-town tryout of *Sweet Little Devil*, he began thinking about the piece. "There had been so much chatter about the limitations of jazz," he later wrote. "Jazz, they said, had to be in strict time. It had to cling to dance rhythms. I resolved to kill that misconception with one sturdy blow."[7]

On January 7, he selected a theme from his musical notebook (the one that opens the piece) and got to work. For the next three weeks, he wrote at breakneck speed in his flat at Amsterdam Avenue and 110th Street, which he shared with his parents, brothers, and sister. As quickly as the pages were completed, they were handed to Whiteman's arranger, Ferde Grofé, who turned the score, originally for two pianos, into one for piano and jazz band. Gershwin could have orchestrated the piece himself had he had time to do so. He had scored pieces in his studies and would just a few months later orchestrate several of the numbers for his London show *Primrose*. But Grofé was at that point the more accomplished orchestrator, and he was familiar with the strengths of particular Whiteman band members.

Ira suggested that a slow melody be included in the piece and recommended one he had heard his brother play. Thus, the majestic Andantino moderato became the heart of the work. Ira was also responsible for the title. At an exhibition of paintings by James McNeill Whistler, he noted the artist's fondness for using the names of colors in his titles (*Nocturne in Black and Gold*, for example) and suggested that George replace his provisional title, *American Rhapsody*, with *Rhapsody in Blue*. In rehearsal, clarinetist Ross Gorman jokingly turned the composer's opening seventeen-note run into a whoop. Gershwin loved the effect and asked Gorman to play it that way at the premiere.

Although the concert was called "An Experiment in Modern Music" it was not, prior to the rhapsody (which was next to last in a program of twenty-three numbers), particularly daring. Among the featured works were Edward MacDowell's "To a Wild Rose" from 1896 and Edward Elgar's *Pomp and Circumstance March No. 1* from 1901. The audience, which included Sergei Rachmaninoff, John Philip Sousa, and Jascha Heifetz, was restless and fidgety by the time George walked on stage. But then came the wild opening notes, bringing everyone to attention, and the audience remained rapt as the slender young pianist/composer played the new piece with élan and confidence, improvising some passages he had not had time to complete.

A quarter of an hour later, Gershwin and Whiteman were acknowledging the roars of the assembled. In the ensuing months, the rhapsody would make its way around the world. It was heard everywhere—played by orchestras, dance bands, bar room pianists, and by George himself at party after party as well as in subsequent concerts and in a studio recording. His worldwide fame had begun—only to be compounded when, ten months later, he had a huge triumph on Broadway—the musical *Lady, Be Good!*, which made stars of Fred and Adele Astaire, and for which he and Ira wrote "Fascinating Rhythm," "Oh, Lady Be Good!" and "The Man I Love," establishing themselves as a composer-lyricist team in the vanguard of those who were about to usher in the golden age of American popular song.

He had become wealthy, successful, and famous. He was now to America's music what F. Scott Fitzgerald was to its literature: a young man of solid accomplishment and limitless potential. Would he hold steadfast to his goal and write an opera—an American grand opera—one that would, as he had said to an interviewer in 1920, appeal "to the great majority of our people"?[8]

TWO

Falling in Love With Kay

Street urchin Gershwin had become genius Gershwin, and he was as bowled over by the phenomenon as everyone else. "I have heard him," wrote Goldberg, "while playing, come suddenly upon a beautiful tune. He would pause a moment, and in the most unaffected manner possible—for there was not the slightest room in George Gershwin's make-up for affectation—exclaim, 'Say, isn't that *good!*'"[1] His friend, the writer Alexander Woollcott, described him as a "slim, swarthy, brilliant young man who, with his dark cheeks that could flood with color, his flashing smile and his marked personal radiance, did, when serving at the altar we call a piano, achieve a dazzling incandescence."[2] In playwright Samuel N. Behrman's words, he "freshly oxygenated" any room he walked into and had "all the rush of the great heady surf of vitality."[3]

That vitality seemed limitless. He boxed, swam, played a good game of golf and an even better one of tennis. When away from the piano, his fingers would reach for the nearest surface and beat out complicated rhythms, paradiddles. When waiting for an elevator, he was liable to break into a tap dance.[4] Fred Astaire recalled that when he and sister Adele were stuck for an exit step during rehearsals for their "Fascinating Rhythm" routine in *Lady, Be Good!*, George jumped up from the piano and demonstrated a move that would work.

His was a rough background—he had been born in Brooklyn but raised mainly on the Lower East Side of Manhattan—and the fortunes of his family had always hovered just above the poverty line—yet he moved easily in society with faultless manners and impeccable tailoring. Cartier's executive Jules Glaenzer tutored him in table etiquette as well as other secrets of decorum such as the need for a gentleman to take the cigar out of his mouth when speaking to a lady. But he had a natural graciousness and a genuine interest in and liking for people—qualities that stood him in good stead, because he also, in Woollcott's words, always "said exactly what he thought, without window-dressing it to make an impression, favorable or otherwise."[5]

In April 1925, he was living in a newly acquired five-story, gray-stone townhouse at 316 West 103rd Street by Riverside Drive. He had just moved there, taking his parents and siblings with him. The new place, although bigger than the old flat, was no less a hive of activity. At any given time, George might be found in the penthouse with his musician friends; Ira a floor below with his literary crowd; the Gershwin parents, a younger brother, Arthur, and kid sister Frances (Frankie) sharing the second and third floors; and loiterers whom no one could identify in the ping-pong room on the first floor. Morris, who had struggled long and hard to support his family and whose wife treated him with contempt, had, with the coming of wealth through his sons, adopted an attitude of good-natured simplicity. The main status symbol at the Gershwin residence was the elevator, which Morris liked to operate himself, taking guests up and down, and it always pleased him to be mistaken for the butler.

On the afternoon of April 17, 1925, George went to the offices of the Symphony Society of New York. There, with the orchestra's conductor, Walter Damrosch, looking on, he signed a contract to write a piano concerto. It was to premiere in eight months at Carnegie Hall, and George was to be the soloist. That evening he went to a dinner party that James and Katharine Warburg were giving in honor of the young violin virtuoso Jascha

Heifetz. Gershwin went because he was dating Heifetz's sister Pauline. It was an on-again-off-again relationship that was going nowhere. Pauline talked of marriage but George was standoffish. Marriage, in his opinion, had to be perfection. A wife would need to satisfy in every way. Not only would she have to be adept in every social situation, she would have to be the ideal hostess, glamorous, an exciting lover, and a fan of music—his in particular. Also, she had to want motherhood—preferably many times over—*and* have a career and accomplishments of her own.

He had never been to the Warburgs' before and this was the first time he had met James and his wife Katharine. James—called Jimmy by his friends—was a tall, good-looking, and amiable young Harvard graduate who had been tapped by his father, Paul M. Warburg, to carry on the family's banking business. The Warburgs were one of the world's great banking families. They had been financiers in Germany as far back as the sixteenth century. In 1901, Paul M. Warburg and his brother Felix moved to New York City and became partners in the investment firm of Kuhn, Loeb, and Company. Their brother Max remained in Hamburg as head of M. M. Warburg and Company. Thus, the family was now influential on both sides of the Atlantic. In fact, Paul M. Warburg had helped design the U.S. Federal Reserve System. In an attempt to get away, at least temporarily, from his destiny as Warburg scion, Jimmy enlisted as a Navy flier during the war. But his father pulled strings in the Wilson administration to keep his son stateside. It was thus partly for spite that the young man married his non-Jewish girlfriend, Katharine Swift. Their June 1918 wedding took place not at the splendid Warburg residence but in the small Upper West Side apartment of Katharine's mother, a financially strapped widow. Not that it took her new in-laws very long to become smitten with her. She was, in the words of Gershwin biographer Robert Payne, "young and ebullient, wonderfully quick-witted as her mind bounced happily from one surprised idea to another."[6] An accomplished pianist and composer, she was also lovely—a five-foot-tall gamine with brown eyes and brunette hair worn in a chignon, who had, as James later recalled, "a provocative figure."[7]

In 1925, she and Jimmy were living in twin brownstone townhouses on East 70th Street in mid-town Manhattan. One had been a gift to them from the elder Warburgs. The other was purchased by the young couple themselves. They remodeled these buildings, knocking out the connecting upstairs walls but maintaining the downstairs separations so they could have a space on the ground floor apart from their children. They had three young daughters—the eldest was just six—who were cared for by servants and governesses in the upstairs portion of the home. Downstairs, Jimmy and Katharine lived a Jazz Age life, throwing all-night parties with glamorous Prohibition-defying guests. Among their friends were Algonquin Round Table regulars Robert E. Sherwood, Franklin P. Adams, and Alexander Woollcott. Jimmy wanted to be a writer like them, and some of his poetry had been published in *Century* magazine.

Although Katharine had not been born to wealth, she had, as a child, gotten used to being around people of renown. Her father, Samuel Swift, wrote music reviews for the *New York Tribune*, *New York Sun*, and *Evening Mail*, and he socialized with many of New York's most prominent musical and theater personalities. The Swifts were a musical family. Katharine's paternal grandmother, Gertrude Horton Dorr Swift, had been an accomplished pianist and a published composer of songs. Katharine's mother, Ellen Faulkner Swift, was also a fine pianist; she and her husband loved to play piano duets. Katharine had begun composing at the age of five. By twenty, she had toured as a pianist, playing chamber music by Beethoven and Brahms. Thus, she might have been blasé about the prospect of Gershwin as a guest—after all, she had been Albert Einstein's accompanist as he tried out a Stradivarius at the home of her in-laws. But the composer had, in both his bearing and music, a transfixing spark. That night, when he was asked to play the piano, he sat at one of the Warburgs' twin Steinway grands and dazzled everyone with impromptu variations on his show tunes. Swift would later recall that when he played at parties "people would rush to the piano, they couldn't even sit on a couch like this and be a little distance set from the piano; they rushed, they had to stand there and watch him. It was extraordinary; it really was. I've never seen anything like it." His music was "nourishing, and *he* was nourishing. Not only was the audience nourished, but so was he."[8]

Although she had tried using jazz in some of her own compositions, the classics were her mainstay. When she went to the theater, it was to the opera, not Broadway. But with Gershwin, the barrier between pop and classical came down, and the result was music brimming with personality—his personality—full of warmth, crackling with humor. Katharine could not help but be affected by this oddly handsome—he had a streamlined face, like a ram's, which he himself caricatured in drawings that showed him in profile, all jaw and nose—young musical house afire. She was particularly charmed when he suddenly jumped up from the piano bench, saying, "Well, I've got to go to Europe now,"[9] and raced out of the house. He was off to the docks to catch a ship to London where he would supervise the English production of his and Ira's current Broadway show *Tell Me More*.

She had been married to Jimmy for seven years. They had wedded in youth and inexperience only to find themselves in the midst of the Roaring Twenties, surrounded by people who made a point of being free from the constraints of the past. Taboos were crumbling, especially for women.

THREE

A Piano Concerto

George commenced work on the concerto in his penthouse atop the family residence, where he was awash in relatives, friends, and callers. He had always been able to compose in the middle of a crowded room. In fact, he preferred it that way. But now the commotion was getting in the way. He had written the *Rhapsody in Blue* amid the usual hubbub, but the new piece needed more planning and thought. When the critics delivered their verdicts, they were going to judge it by stricter standards than had been applied to the free-form rhapsody. They would compare it to concertos by Chopin, Beethoven, and Brahms. There was also going to be a sophomore jinx—a big one, given the success of the rhapsody. It was one thing to have a flop show—even Kern and Berlin sometimes had them. But a concert hall flop might well mean an end to the public's special ardor for him.

Although he appeared to be approaching both strands of his career with equal confidence, he knew that songwriting was, for him at least, the easier job. Though some of his tunes, such as "The Man I Love," were obviously the handiwork of the man who had composed the *Rhapsody in*

Blue, most of them, even some of the very good ones, could just as well have been written by some other Broadway craftsman. That would not be true of the concerto. In the new piece, he was revealing something of himself that had previously been withheld. In the struggle to get this right, he was for the first time in his composing career seeking solitude. First he retreated to the nearby Whitehall Hotel, and when visitors showed up there he traveled upstate to a cottage provided by the Chautauqua Institution—where music students inevitably knocked on his door and he, just as inevitably, opened it.

Before the official rehearsals began, he hired a fifty-piece orchestra to try the piece out, with his friend William Daly conducting. Daly, eleven years Gershwin's senior, was a tall, bespectacled Boston Irishman with a hedge of red hair that shot straight up from his skull. A musical prodigy in youth and a graduate of Harvard, he had, before settling on music as a career, had a stint out west as a laborer on the railroads and then a brief career as a literary editor, working with Lincoln Steffens on *Everybody's Magazine*. He had known Gershwin since working with him on a Broadway show called *Hitchy-Koo of 1918*. By that time, he was a sought-after conductor and orchestrator of Broadway music. He wielded the baton at many Gershwin shows, orchestrated some of Gershwin's Broadway work, and formed a duo-piano team with him at parties. Daly was also closely associated with Ira, having worked with him on songs as well as a never-produced show based on Chopin piano pieces. Daly and the Gershwins were personally and professionally very close. George called him "The Irishman," and he called George "Pincus."

That afternoon tryout of the concerto at the Globe Theatre was, Gershwin later wrote in *Theatre Magazine*, "the peak of my highest joy."[1] The sounds coming from the orchestra were those he had heard in his head. Apparently, just as there was a Gershwin piano style, there was also a Gershwin orchestral sound. Early in the first movement, the piano, upon making its initial entrance, presents a lonely, nocturnal theme that becomes more intense when, upon repetition, a countermelody is given to the English horn. In the second movement, a quiet melody played by a solo muted trumpet creates a lying-awake-in-the night stillness and restlessness. The third movement ends with the whole orchestra[2] sounding four exultant trills. Three years later, Ferde Grofé would rescore the concerto for Paul Whiteman, and a recording of this different instrumentation makes it clear that Gershwin was a better orchestrator than Grofé, at least for his own works.

Two weeks after the Globe Theatre tryout came the Carnegie Hall rehearsals with Damrosch conducting and with Gershwin playing, a pipe clenched between his teeth, as fellow songwriter Philip Charig turned the pages for him. At the December 3 premiere, the work was preceded by Glazunov's *Fifth Symphony*, Rabaud's *Suite Anglais*, and an intermission. Then came the first public performance of the *Concerto in F* and, with it, a split decision by the music critics. Samuel Chotzinoff—admittedly one of George's friends—writing in the *New York World*, said: "It was not luck that carried the composer of the rhapsody to success, and luck alone would never have created the *Concerto in F* heard yesterday afternoon. The truth is that George Gershwin is a genius—perhaps the only one of all the younger men who are trying with might and main to express the modern spirit."[3] On the other hand, Olin Downes of the *New York Times* said the concerto's themes were "denatured," that they lacked "inherent energy and physiognomy" and were "tinctured with a kind of harmony which frequently sounds forced and dry."[4] And Russian composer Sergei Prokofiev said the piece was nothing more than a lot of "32-bar choruses ineptly bridged together."[5] The concerto had not failed but it had not met with anything like the success of the *Rhapsody in Blue*. Three years would pass before Gershwin attempted his next orchestral work. Ten years would go by before he tackled anything so ambitious and grand as the *Concerto in F*.

Conductor Damrosch gave a party in honor of the concerto's premiere, and it was at his apartment that George and Katharine Warburg met again. Perhaps it was at this moment that the sparks really began to fly, although different chroniclers present different time lines. Some accounts put the affair off until the following March, when Gershwin again visited the Warburgs' apartment, this time at Katharine's invitation. Certainly it was in full bloom shortly thereafter, as he took to calling her Kay—a nickname that everyone else would adopt, including her husband—and as he and Ira named their new show *Oh, Kay!* "The Warburgs," one Gershwin biographer has noted, "were an enlightened couple who often went their separate ways without overt frictions or jealousies."[6] Thus Kay's affair was acceptable to Jimmy—at least, he gave that impression.

In addition to their residence on East 70th Street, the Warburgs had a Connecticut estate called Bydale, recently purchased by James.[7] The name of the property came from its geography—it was in a valley created by the Byram River. There was a colonial era house, a cottage, a millpond, and a forest—all this just thirty-six miles from New York City. When Jimmy was away on business trips—and sometimes even when he was present—George and Kay made it their playground. On the grounds were a stable and horses. She was an excellent rider, having spent time on a ranch in Colorado when she was eighteen. His only prior close-up experience with a horse occurred in his boyhood when one kicked him on the bridge of his nose. He now took the sport up avidly and, as with most everything else, he learned quickly. They would gallop across the landscape, ducking the hemlock trees, riding along the river, and over to the gorge. Then they would take a dip in the swimming pool or play tennis.

In Manhattan, they were seen about town together, frequently at his favorite jazz spots but just as often at the place she loved best: the Metropolitan Opera. As an opera devotee, she loved the Sturm und Drang kind, especially the ones that depicted the supernatural. It thrilled her to watch Gluck's Orpheus confront the Furies at the entrance to Hades. Gershwin was impressed by her knowledge of opera and by the fact that she had studied at the Institute of Musical Art (renamed Juilliard in 1926), given recitals, learned music theory from Percy Goetschius, and studied composition with Charles Loeffler. In her youth, she had actively pursued a musical career, especially after her father died, and at sixteen, she had helped her family out financially by giving piano lessons and by playing in a trio that hired itself out for swanky parties, which is where she met Jimmy. But after marrying she had become a mother and a socialite first and was less public in her music making. Now George Gershwin, impressed by her talent as a composer, was telling her that her melodies and harmonies were perfect for Broadway. Because of her tendency to look down on popular music, he gave her lessons in Irving Berlin, dissecting that master's songs, showing her how much thought had gone into making them so simple, straightforward, and right. She was intrigued by Gershwin's refusal to

A Piano Concerto

draw a line between light and serious music and by his insistence that it was wrong to believe that only gloomy music was profound. Once, when he was playing a progression of dark, misery-laden chords, she asked him what piece he was composing and he replied, "Oh, nothing. I was just working off some of the dreary music that lies near the top of a composer's mind. Then I'll dig down to the happier stuff, with any luck." It had not previously occurred to her that the joyous might lay a stratum *below* the sorrowful in music.[8]

GEORGE GERSHWIN

FOUR

Ira Takes a Wife

In the spring of 1926, Ira Gershwin, approaching his thirtieth birthday, had not yet had a serious romance. In fact, history knows of only one girlfriend, a high school sweetheart named Rose Eisen who, when he took her hand late one night as they rode a city bus, said, "Izzy, if you don't mean it, don't do it—and if you mean it, think of me."[1] He believed himself to be an unattractive man and could not imagine that any woman would really be interested in him.

No one had been particularly interested in him in his youth—not even his family. His father had been too busy trying to earn a living, and his mother too engrossed in card games, theatergoing, and the racetrack. When Rose and Morris did turn their attention to Ira, it was to use him. He was the one who in hard times was sent to pawn his mother's diamond ring. He was the one who went to Public School 25 to talk George's teachers out of expelling him. Although what he really wanted to do was stay at home and read (he started with dime novels such as the Hal Standish *Fred Fearnot* series but quickly moved on to books by Arthur Conan Doyle and Jules Verne), he was made to work at one and another of his father's innumerable businesses: a cigar store (with billiard parlor), a Turkish bath, restaurants, bakeries, a hotel. During this time, he began to write jokes, stories, and light verse for local newspapers. It seems inevitable that, given this bent, and with George making a living in Tin Pan Alley, he would gravitate there too. But he made it there on his own, writing with composers other than George and using a pseudonym (Arthur Francis, after his youngest brother and his sister) so as not to cash in on George's growing reputation. They each had successes with other collaborators before becoming a team, and they would not have been a team had not each seen in the other a significant talent. Nor is it likely they would have become close had songwriting not brought them together. All the Gershwin children had grown up ill attended and on their own.

In looks Ira was of fair complexion (brown eyes and blond hair according to his World War I draft card), bespectacled, stocky, almost as short as his father and with a similarly bland but kindly face. Although he had a powerful physique—his brother Arthur recalled him swimming the two miles from Coney Island to Brighton Beach—he was not fond of using it. He shunned not just the strenuous life but also, it seemed, the corporeal one. And he was shy—so shy he refused to drive a car out of a concern that other drivers might honk at him.

But now a woman was expressing interest. This was Leonore Strunsky, whom he had known for nearly nine years. He had first met her when George was working as a piano pounder for Jerome Remick and Company. Another pianist at the firm was Herman Paley, an older man who became George's friend, took him under wing, and brought him home to meet the Paley family. There George met Herman's brother Lou (who became, briefly, George's lyricist); his young cousin George Pallay; another young cousin Mabel Pleshette; Lou's girlfriend, Emily Strunsky; and Emily's younger sister Leonore. These people became the nucleus of George's and Ira's social lives. George always had a special place in his heart for Emily who was, he said, "as beautiful inside as out—her beauty comes from within."[2] But she was in love with Lou, a high school English teacher, and unavailable to either Gershwin brother except as a friend. He felt similarly about Mabel. But she too was engaged—to Robert Schirmer, whose father had founded the music publishing firm of G. Schirmer, Inc.

Leonore, however, was obtainable. Unlike Emily, who had soft features, laughed easily, and was an appreciative audience for people bubbling with ideas, Leonore—family and friends called her Lee—though pretty, had sharper features, an aggressive manner, and a predilection for saying exactly what was on her mind, the more outrageous the better. As a girl she had made a specialty of pulling the tablecloth out from under the dinner setting and watching with delight as the dishes fell to the floor. Unlike her sister, she was political. A devoted reader of the *Daily Worker,* she was a champion of the underdog—a concern that meshed nicely with a penchant for spotting people who needed mothering. She liked to find sad people and, while nurturing them, make them beholden to her.

She was interested in George but he kept her at arm's length. Ira, however, was a possible beau. The problem was his lethargy. When given the choice between doing something and nothing, he invariably chose the latter. He was slow to move, slow to make decisions, slow to get to work. George complained about how hard it was to coax him into writing a lyric, and how, when he finally put pencil to paper, he moved at such a measured pace. In romancing Leonore, the pace was glacial. Years passed and nothing happened between them. They saw each other every Saturday night at parties given by Emily and Lou who, after they married, held a weekly open house in their small Greenwich Village apartment. The Paleys had little money—the usual bill of fare was tea, cookies, and lychee nuts—but they were bright and hospitable, and these evenings became a must for, among many others, composers Vincent Youmans and Marc Blitzstein, playwright Behrman, and actors Sam Jaffe and Edward G. Robinson.

Ira loved these gatherings. He felt right at home at the Paleys', among clever, literate people with whom he could trade witticisms while discussing books, music, politics, and any other topic that came to mind. He joined everyone else as an appreciative audience for his brother, who would inevitably take to the piano and hold them all spellbound with his improvisations. There was no jealousy in Ira for George or for anyone else. He had no wish to be the center of attention. He was well aware of his own talent but knew that fine lyric writers abounded, as did good tunesmiths. George Gershwin was the singularity.

As time went on and as the Gershwin brothers became successful, Lee became more and more attentive to Ira. Sometimes he seemed responsive, sometimes not. It was hard to tell if he was hesitant about her or just hesitant in general. Finally, she came right out and popped the question, saying, "Well, how about it, kid? Can we get married?"[3] Apparently, she had just come downstairs from her own apartment, where she had found her boyfriend in bed with another woman.[4]

Faced with such directness, Ira did not have it in him to say no. Besides, it was gratifying to him that someone so intelligent and confident wanted him for a partner. He was fascinated by her quickness of mind, her love of new ideas, and her intense sociability—qualities they had in common.[5] Most of all, he was pleased at the prospect of having someone who would make a home for him. That he could marry a person whose reaction to the *Rhapsody in Blue* was "I don't get it. You can't dance to it"[6] puzzled his friends. But on September 14, 1926, they were wed. In commemoration, he wrote "Someone to Watch Over Me" for *Oh, Kay!*, portraying himself in the lines "Although he may not be the man some / Girls think of as handsome."[7] After the nuptials, it quickly became clear that their opinions about the rhapsody were not their only incompatibility. He wanted children but she did not, it being her belief that the dusk to dawn hours of theater people were inappropriate for good parenting. She also wanted a separate bedroom.

FIVE

Porgy

In the summer of 1926, during rehearsals for *Oh, Kay!*, Emily gave George a novel she had been reading, a best seller called *Porgy* written by the South Carolina poet DuBose Heyward. Gershwin was not much of a reader but this one kept him up all night. It was a tightly written, highly atmospheric story about a crippled, middle-aged black man who longed for love, found it, fought for it, and, finally, lost it. Its setting was a black tenement in Charleston, South Carolina—not so very different from the tenements of the Lower East Side. The potential of this book to become the basis of a powerful opera—*his* opera—jumped out at him. In the morning, he wrote to Heyward saying they ought to get together and discuss the idea.

Heyward was a courtly descendant of slaveholders, one of whom, Thomas Heyward, had signed the Declaration of Independence. The Heywards had once been wealthy but that was no longer so. DuBose's father had worked in a rice mill and was killed in an accident there when his son was two years old. To make ends meet, DuBose's mother took in boarders and did sewing. Heyward helped out by leaving school at fourteen (George had dropped out at fifteen) to work on Charleston's docks alongside African American stevedores, fishermen, and cotton checkers. At eighteen, he came down with polio, which permanently atrophied his right arm. During convalescence, he took up poetry. When he read a newspaper article about a crippled black beggar named Sammy Smalls who had tried to escape the police by means of a cart pulled by a goat, the pathos of the scene and his empathy for the cripple gripped him and it became the basis for his novel. In October 1926, he and Gershwin met in Atlantic City and talked excitedly about turning the book into an opera.

A few months earlier, in December 1925, Paul Whiteman had revived *Blue Monday*, presenting it in Carnegie Hall with, again, white actors in blackface. The work's original orchestration had been done by George's friend Will Vodery, a black man. Now it was reorchestrated for Whiteman by Ferde Grofé and renamed *135th Street*. This was a concert version of the opera, with just a few props in lieu of scenery, and there were only a couple of performances. Although no one mistook the opera for a masterpiece, the reviews were better than they had been in 1922. Olin Downes of the *New York Times* wrote that there was "in this work a potentiality for more than operetta, which is its main importance to Mr. Gershwin. With a properly fashioned libretto he might go far."[1] Now, having shown with *Concerto in F* that he could orchestrate, and having found in *Porgy* an appropriate story, George felt that the time might be right to try his hand at a real opera. Heyward liked the idea and talked about the need for black people to portray themselves on stage. That was fine with Gershwin—preferable, in fact—but in which opera houses could such a work be performed? The Metropolitan Opera Company had not yet hired its first African American singer, although there was hope that this policy might be changed, given that George had a friend on the Met's board, Otto Kahn, who could be of help in getting the work produced there.

But the idea fell through. Heyward's wife, Dorothy, unbeknownst to her husband, had been writing a stage play based on the book. When DuBose learned of this and told George that a nonmusical production was in the works, George graciously stepped aside while assuring the Heywards that their dramatized *Porgy* would not preclude a later operatic version. He was, he admitted to them, not sure he was ready to tackle so ambitious a project. In fact, it might be years before he could take on the task.

Instead, his next step was a Gilbert and Sullivan–style operetta, the antiwar musical *Strike Up the Band*, with lyrics by Ira and a script by George S. Kaufman. For Ira this was an opportunity to write the sort of satirical, intricate rhymes that W. S. Gilbert, his hero, had created fifty years earlier. For George, it was the chance to construct lengthy musical scenes, advancing them, as his biographer Howard Pollack has noted, with "various archetypes—the solemn hymn, the patriotic march, the recited pledge, the military drill, the folk song, the romantic waltz."[2] But Kaufman's script—in which hostilities erupt between the United States and Switzerland because of an argument about Swiss cheese—was second-rate, as Kaufman himself later admitted. "A composer of musical comedy is so horribly dependent on the quality of the book," he added, explaining this show's failure at the box office.[3]

If Gershwin were going to fulfill his potential as a stage composer, he would need better scripts. Like their fellow Broadway songsmiths, he and Ira would usually write independently of the plots and then wedge their songs into creaky storylines, usually about flaky socialites or lovable bootleggers. So far, none of his Broadway vehicles had had a good story, and his music for these shows was, more often than not, unremarkable. Of the nearly 250 songs he had composed by the end of 1926, only a handful were gems: "Swanee" for *Capitol Review* in 1919 (lyrics by Irving Caesar); "Do It Again" from *The French Doll* in 1922 (lyrics by B. G. DeSylva); "Tra-La-La" from *For Goodness Sake* in 1922 (lyrics by Ira using the pen name Arthur Francis); "I'll Build a Stairway to Paradise" from *George White's Scandals of 1922* (lyrics by DeSylva and Arthur Francis); "Somebody Loves Me" from *George White's Scandals of 1924* (lyrics by DeSylva); "Oh, Lady Be Good!," "The Man I Love," and "Fascinating Rhythm" from *Lady, Be Good!* in 1924 (lyrics by Ira); "That Certain Feeling" from *Tip-Toes* in 1925 (lyrics by Ira); "Someone to Watch Over Me" and "Clap Yo' Hands" from *Oh, Kay!* in 1926 (lyrics by Ira). The 1924 musical *Sweet Little Devil* is remembered now not for any of Gershwin's music but because it was while he was on a train to its out-of-town tryout that he imagined the *Rhapsody in Blue*. Similarly,

Porgy

Tip-Toes and *Song of the Flame* from 1925 are remembered mainly because he was working on them while writing the *Concerto in F*. As for *Strike Up the Band*, it certainly made greater demands on him as a composer than had his prior shows. But it was a higher aspiration for Ira to emulate Gilbert than it was for George to be Sullivan.

The true direction of the Broadway musical *was* revealed in 1927, but not by the Gershwins. Jerome Kern and Oscar Hammerstein II showed the way with *Show Boat*, which became a bellwether not because it was operatic but because its musical numbers furthered the plot—a serious, even tragic, story adapted from Edna Ferber's 1926 novel. It was also full of memorable songs: "Bill," "Ol' Man River," "Make Believe," "Can't Help Lovin' That Man," "You Are Love," and "Why Do I Love You?" The Gershwins' *Strike Up the Band* had only one outstanding tune, the title march.

The brothers spent the rest of 1927 writing a more typical Broadway show, *Funny Face*. Once again, they were working with Fred and Adele Astaire. In *Lady, Be Good!*, the Astaires had played a brother and sister evicted from their home in a ploy by their landlady to get Fred to marry her. In the new show, Fred was the guardian of his foster parents' three grown daughters, one of whom, Adele, convinces her boyfriend, an aviator, to steal her diary out of Fred's safe. These ephemeral plots were as different as could be from *Porgy*, but they became showcases for great Gershwin songs. *Funny Face*'s score included four new classics: "He Loves and She Loves," "Funny Face," "'S Wonderful," and "My One and Only." The Gershwins had returned to the winner's circle on Broadway, but with an old-fashioned musical comedy.

In the meantime, Kay, prodded by George, was beginning her own assault on Broadway. She had formed a songwriting team with Jimmy, who was writing her lyrics even while she was continuing her affair with George—all this while Jimmy continued his principal career, working for his father at the International Acceptance Bank. The elder Warburg had established that institution in 1921 to extend credit to Germany's businesses and rebuild its war-shattered economy. Toward that end, Jimmy made several trips abroad in the early 1920s, and he had become a prescient observer of international affairs, having seen at first hand what the vindictive terms of the Versailles Treaty were doing to Germany's finances.

When that part of his life came to the fore, the self-absorbed, hedonistic New York arts scene seemed inconsequential to him. But sometimes it was the other way around. On evenings when he returned home from work to find George Gershwin regaling Kay and their theater friends from the piano, German monetary trends seemed unexciting. And Gershwin was often in the Warburg living room. On one occasion, Jimmy walked in to find him at one piano and composer Sigmund Romberg at the other, with Kay and a group of admirers huddled around them. Jimmy watched as the two men traded musical quips. Romberg played his hit, "Lover, Come Back to Me," George said, "I'll show you where you swiped that melody, Siggie" and played a passage from one of Liszt's Hungarian Rhapsodies, at which point Romberg replied, "You're absolutely wrong, George! I'll show you where I got those eight bars!"[4] and played *another* Hungarian Rhapsody. Warburg, who had genially allowed himself to be pressed into service as the group's bartender, was as amused as everyone else by this interchange. But the basic situation was unstable: he was being cuckolded by a guileless man who seemed to be carrying the center of the world around with him.

By becoming Kay's lyricist, Jimmy had found a way of teaming up with her again, as well as a long-sought path into the literary world. He adopted the pseudonym Paul James (a reversal of his first and middle names) so that no one on Wall Street need know what he was up to. Kay joined the musicians union under her maiden name and became, at the age of thirty, Kay Swift. George gave the new team his blessing and tried to help them along. When Richard Rodgers needed a rehearsal pianist for his and Larry Hart's upcoming *A Connecticut Yankee*, George recommended Kay for the job. Rodgers knew and liked Kay from years before when they had been students together at the Institute of Musical Art, and he was happy to hire her. It proved to be the perfect entrée into the world of Broadway. In fact, it was the way Gershwin himself had gotten his start, working as a rehearsal pianist for *Miss 1917*, a show with music by Jerome Kern and Victor Herbert.

Kay's job was demanding—she was often in the theater day and night—but it brought her into the Broadway fold, showed her how a show was created, and made her feel professional, which fueled her enthusiasm for the songs she and Jimmy were now steadily turning out. That George looked with favor on her songwriting partnership with Warburg bode well for their venture. However, George's attitude also posed questions: Was his wish to see them together professionally a sign that he wanted them back together as husband and wife as well? Was he looking for a way out of his relationship with Kay? He was known for a brief attention span when it came to women. Lately, he had developed an interest in a seventeen-year-old girl, Rosamond Walling, a student at Swarthmore, who was a cousin of Emily and Leonore and perhaps the most beautiful of all the Paley-Strunsky women. George enjoyed playing the role of older man with her, taking her shopping, buying her clothes. It seemed as if he were grooming her for the day when, a little older, she would be ready for him. And there was another woman as well, Julia van Norman, who had written him a fan letter after hearing the *Rhapsody in Blue* and who, upon receiving a letter from him in reply, moved—with her husband and children—from Minneapolis to New York to be closer to him. Julia was a frustrated musician and writer who had an intense, melodramatic manner that intrigued him and contrasted sharply with Kay's irreverent New York–style drolleries.

And there were other complications. Kay did not get on well with George's mother, whom she found to be grasping and humorless—two qualities that George and Ira did not share. Yet George, unlike Ira, doted on her. Kay was later to recall that Rose was the source of George's "only completely nutty fantasy—he used to tell reporters she was 'the kind of mother the mammy songs were written about'—can you imagine that dame dashing up with a candied yam in her hand and a big smile on that tense, frowning face of hers?"[5] As Frankie remembered it, George naively believed that his mother adored him when she was actually "a woman who was interested just in what she wanted to do, and really didn't pay much attention to any of us."[6] Nor did Rose like Kay, whose money meant nothing to her because she only had it as Mrs. Warburg. That Kay was a musician meant even less; Rose was unmusical.[7]

Relations between Kay and Leonore were not much better. Kay found her to be a sinister woman,[8] and George felt the same way,[9] although there came to be what Leonore's nephew Michael Strunsky has called a "truce" between George and his sister-in-law.[10] What Lee really wanted was to become the family doyenne. This was impossible as long as her mother-in-law was alive but it would eventually happen if George did not marry or if he married someone flighty or feckless. Kay, however, was the perfect storm: as skilled a hostess as Lee and, like George and Ira, an artist. Thus, Lee was cool to her—although she was never very friendly to any of George's women friends.

There was also the question of religion. Although this never seemed to be an issue between George and Kay, there was no getting around the fact that the Gershwins, Strunskys, and Paleys were all Jewish. None was observant, but they did not hide from their origins or try to assimilate. George's best friend, William Daly, was an Irish Catholic, but most of his other intimates were Jewish, and there was an in-crowd quality to his social life that sometimes left Kay out of the picture. Although he had not spoken to her about marriage, he had popped the question to Rosamond, who was Jewish. That proposal, however, was made in a sudden, boyish outburst that was no declaration of love but, rather, a moment of keyed up daydreaming. "Let's have four children to begin with," he said, "and bring them up in the country. Greenwich, if you like. You can teach them to ride. We'll get six horses to start with."[11] Rosamond did not take the proposal seriously and had no intention of marrying George even if he became serious, because she did not love him in a romantic sense and knew he was not in love with her.

Kay was confident of George's love but would not have married him at this point, even had he asked, because doing so would have required a divorce from Jimmy, which might have meant losing custody of her children. It seemed wise not to ponder such questions for the time being.

SIX

Paris

In March 1928, New York City received a distinguished visitor—the composer Maurice Ravel. It was Ravel who, along with fellow Frenchman Claude Debussy, had steered European music away from the hefty works of Brahms and Mahler toward a more playful and sensual sonic world. Ravel would write his most famous piece, *Bolero*, later that year, but at this time, he was engaged in a tour of the United States and Canada, performing his works as both a pianist and as a conductor. In New York, he celebrated his fifty-third birthday and when asked what gift he wanted most he said he wanted to meet George Gershwin. This was immensely flattering to George, who had loved Ravel's music since he had been introduced to it by Hambitzer. A picture taken of him with Ravel shows the older man seated at a grand piano with Gershwin standing behind him, his head slightly bowed, looking uncharacteristically bashful.

This meeting seemed propitious to him. If he wanted to further his musical studies here was one of the world's great composers who admired his work. But when he asked Ravel to be his teacher, the latter gently dismissed his request, saying it was better to be a first-rate Gershwin than a second-rate Ravel. Instead, he provided George with a letter of introduction to the highly regarded Parisian piano and composition teacher Nadia Boulanger. "Dear friend," Ravel wrote to Boulanger, "there is a musician here endowed with the most brilliant, most enchanting, and perhaps the most profound talent: George Gershwin. His worldwide success no longer satisfies him, for he is aiming higher. He knows that he lacks the technical means to achieve his goal. In teaching those means, one might ruin his talent. Would you have the courage, which I wouldn't dare have, to undertake this awesome responsibility?"[1] Such praise from so esteemed a musician made George think seriously about an extended visit to Paris. He could, at least for a while, live the life of a serious composer, learning more about his trade while surrounded by the sounds of a city that had always been a haven for artists. He had been to Paris before, briefly, in 1925, and had at that time conceived the idea of a piece for orchestra that would depict the adventures of an American as he strolled about the City of Light. Now, with *Funny Face* safely launched, and with another equally old-fashioned musical comedy called *Rosalie* looking to be a hit (in it was the song "How Long Has This Been Going On?"), he decided to head for Europe to study and compose.

Paris of the 1920s was a lure for brilliant expatriates such as Joyce, Pound, Yeats, Picasso, Hemingway, and Diaghilev. It was also a haven for many of America's most experimental young composers, including Aaron Copland, Roy Harris, Marc Blitzstein, George Antheil, and Virgil Thomson, each of whom was living the traditional hand-to-mouth lifestyle of the Parisian artiste, and all of them were studying with Nadia Boulanger.

Kay and Jimmy gave George a going away party on March 9, 1928. Then he, Ira, Lee, and Frankie set sail for England. They spent some time in London, where *Oh, Kay!* was playing to packed houses, then traveled on to Paris, where they checked into the Hotel Majestic. Promptly, George, armed with his letter from Ravel, went to call on Boulanger. She listened to him play for ten minutes and then told him, echoing Ravel, that she had nothing to teach him. Because she said this without any of Ravel's affection, the remark was open to interpretation. Did she mean he was incapable of learning the secrets that she was so gladly dispensing to Copland and

Thomson? It was hard to know. But Gershwin took her rebuff as he did all others, without noticeable chagrin, and he went back to his hotel room and got to work.

Word soon got around that he was writing a piece about Paris and playing it to a steady stream of callers—in fact, to anyone who would listen. His friend Mabel Schirmer was in town and George went off with her one day to the Avenue de la Grande Armée. She was fluent in French and could help him ask shopkeepers at auto parts stores for taxi horns that honked specific notes. When he found what he wanted, he returned to his hotel and resumed work on the piece, only to be interrupted by a knock on the door. Standing outside his room were two young men—the duo pianists Jacques Fray and Mario Braggiotti, who had played in the 1926 London production of *Lady, Be Good!* Gershwin answered the door in his dressing gown. As Braggiotti remembered it:

> His hair was all sort of up, what I call "the composer's expression." He was busy writing his *American in Paris*. I went in, and I was the spokesman. I said, "Mr. Gershwin, my name is Mario, this is Jacques. We are music students, and we just would like to meet you."[2] "Well, boys that's fine. Just come right in!" He was very welcoming and very charming. We walked in and there was his Steinway piano, right in the middle of his room. And I noticed on the piano, a collection of taxi horns, those old fashioned ones they used on the Bataille de la Marne [*sic*] which you pressed, you know, you squeezed. There were about twenty of them, just laying there. I hadn't been to New York for a few years and I thought maybe this is a new eccentricity, or fad. I didn't know what to make of it.

Braggiotti remembered that when they asked Gershwin about the horns, he said:

> "Well, I'll tell you. In my opening movement of *American in Paris*, I'd like to get the traffic sounds of the Place de la Concorde during rush hour. I'd like to see if it works. I've just written the first two pages, the opening of *American in Paris*. Now Jacques, you take this horn. This is, I think, an A-flat and Mario take this, an F-sharp. Now, I'll sit down and play and when I go this way with my head you go: WACK!, WACK!,

WACK! Like that, in that rhythm." So, I took the horn. There we stood, very nervous, and excited. And for the first time anywhere, we heard the sound of the opening bars of *An American in Paris*. The lanky American walking down the Champs-Elysées. He captured the atmosphere, the feeling, the movement, the rhythm so perfectly. Since then it's been imitated. "Ump, ba, bum." You hear it in a lot of music.[3]

Meanwhile, the community of expatriate American composers was taking it as something of an affront that Gershwin would settle in Paris for a few weeks, stay at the best hotel, and attempt to capture the city with one of his crowd-pleasing compositions. Virgil Thomson, for instance, had been in Paris a lot longer than most of the others, knew every Parisian alleyway, and was still, at thirty-two, a long way from solvency, much less fame and fortune. The reaction to Gershwin from European composers was mixed. On the first leg of the trip, while in London, he had met William Walton and John Ireland, both of them admirers of his work. Ireland was heard to exclaim to a friend about "The Man I Love": "That, my boy, is a masterpiece—a *masterpiece*, do you hear? This man Gershwin beats the lot of us."[4] In Paris, George met with Ravel, Jacques Ibert, Darius Milhaud, Edgard Varèse, Francis Poulenc, Arthur Honegger, Serge Prokofiev, Igor Stravinsky, and Ernesto Lecuona.[5] It was during his stay in Paris that the *Concerto in F* had its European premiere there, whence Prokofiev described it as a succession of "32-bar choruses ineptly bridged together" and as a "drunken" concerto.[6] Not until *Porgy and Bess*, seven years later, would Prokofiev change his mind about Gershwin's abilities. Poulenc, on the other hand, was an ardent fan and would praise *An American in Paris* as one of the great works of the century. When George left Paris for a side trip to Berlin, he met with Kurt Weill, who had recently written *Mahagonny (Ein Songspiel)* with poet Bertolt Brecht and who was about to write *The Threepenny Opera* with Brecht, which would make them both famous. Weill and Gershwin got along amiably and appreciated one another's music, but years later, in 1935, when Weill and his actress-singer wife, Lotte Lenya, emigrated to the United States, they attended a party at Gershwin's apartment and were insulted when George, in praising a recording of *The Threepenny Opera*, complained to

Weill about the leading lady's "squitchadickeh" voice, not knowing that Lenya was that singer. After that, Weill spoke of Gershwin with derision, at least in his letters to Lenya, in which he described him as "stupid" and as a "bumpkin."[7] Gershwin had better luck with Alban Berg, whom he met in Vienna. There was something about Berg and his music that struck awe into Gershwin. He already knew of the man's music from his lessons with Hambitzer and Kilenyi, and now, upon attending a performance of Berg's 1926 *Lyric Suite* for string quartet, he was completely taken. When Berg asked him to demonstrate his own music, he became embarrassed by it; it seemed to him, at that moment, inadvisable to launch into the *Rhapsody in Blue*. "Mr. Gershwin," Berg said soothingly, "music is music."[8] When George returned to America, he brought the music of the *Lyric Suite* with him, as well as a signed photo of Berg, which he framed and displayed prominently in his apartment. ·

Back home, he continued work on the new orchestral piece at Bydale. There Kay heard it come to life and watched as he completed the orchestration. It was just as he had told her—he was digging beyond gloom to get to joy, and the resulting music, like the city it depicted, was radiant. Listening to *An American in Paris* was like revisiting the most intensely pleasurable moments of youth. In fact, although it depicts the experiences of a grown man in a city renowned for its sophistication, musically it has the feel of a return to childhood. There is the initial walking theme, which does not walk so much as skip, ending in a melodic tag that consists of a schoolyard-style "nyanny-nyah." The same spirit is in the nose-thumbing of the taxi horns and, later, in the staccato calls that make up the two other walking themes. It is even present in the blues, which has a comic edge: this homesick melody coexists with continuing jocular asides by the flutes.

The premiere had been promised to Walter Damrosch and the New York Symphony Orchestra, who had introduced *Concerto in F,* and the first performance took place almost three years to the day after the concerto's premiere, at the end of 1928. It was a joyous night. The whole Gershwin family was there, as was Kay. She did not, however, accompany the composer to Carnegie Hall. That honor went instead to Rosamond Walling. Gershwin was so excited that evening that he had his driver stop the car, took Rosamond by the hand, and told her he wanted to walk the rest of the way to Carnegie Hall. As they approached the concert hall, they saw a newsboy shivering in the cold. George bought a paper from him with a ten-dollar bill, refused to accept change, and when the boy recognized him, George was so happy he put one arm across his shoulders, the other around Rosamond, said "let's warm up this old sidewalk," and they tap-danced their way to Carnegie Hall.[9]

Shortly after the premiere, he took Kay to a matinee performance. He was no fan of Damrosch's conducting. The conductor gave the piece a sluggish, dragging tempo. On this occasion, the performance was so bad that George and Kay, who were in the standing area in the rear of the hall, left midway through. They went Christmas shopping instead. He bought her a pair of antique crown-shaped gold bracelets. Her gift to him was a golden fob for his pocket watch with an attached good luck charm consisting of a golden dove whose eyes were their birthstones (hers: a diamond, his: a sapphire). The bracelets became her most precious keepsakes, and he, from then on, never went on stage without the good luck charm.

SEVEN

"That Long Drip of Human Tears"

By 1929, Gershwin was once again thinking about opera. Several recent events had made him feel ready. One was the reception given *An American in Paris*. Although the reviews had been mixed—Herbert Francis Peyser, writing in the *New York Telegram*, called the piece "long winded and inane"[1]—it was favorably received on the whole. Leonard Liebling in the *American* described it as "merry, rollicking music."[2] In the *New York Times*, Olin Downes said he had enjoyed the piece and that it showed an improvement in technique and orchestration, although he warned that it was easier for Gershwin "to invent ideas than to develop them."[3] The *Musical Courier* said it was "in a class, atmospherically, with Berlioz's *Roman Carnival*, Svendsen's *Carnival de Venise* and Chabrier's *España*."[4] Audiences had no reservations; they immediately loved the piece because it was pure Gershwin and they loved Gershwin all the more for having written it. Most important, Gershwin was satisfied with it, especially with the structure and orchestration. There was a complete sureness of touch.

Shortly after the premiere, there was a celebratory party at Jules Glaenzer's Park Avenue apartment at which Otto Kahn, Gershwin's friend on the
board of the Metropolitan Opera Company (and one of its prime benefac-
tors), raised his glass and in an emotional toast that was later reprinted as
an article in the *Musical Courier*, compared George with Charles Lindbergh as a representative of the genius of American youth. Lindbergh and
Gershwin, Kahn said, both had the "the same engaging and unassuming
ways, the same dignity and dislike of show, the same absence of affectation,
the same direct, uncomplicated, naïve, Parsifalesque outlook upon life
and his task." Kahn went on to quote a line from Thomas Hardy's poem,
"On An Invitation to the United States," which talked about America as
a young nation, free of ancient European miseries—free of, as Hardy put
it, "that long drip of human tears." Although Hardy—and Kahn—were
conveniently forgetting a lot of tears, there was something about the exu-
berance of American life and culture in the 1920s that made it true. Kahn
continued, cautioning Gershwin about the need, as an artist, to understand
the value of tears. "They have great and strange and beautiful power,"
he said. "They fertilize the deepest roots of art, and from them flowers
spring of a loveliness and perfume that no other moisture can produce."
He then wished for George an "experience—not too prolonged—of that
driving storm and stress of emotions, of that solitary wrestling with your
own soul, of that aloofness, for a while, from the actions and distractions
of the everyday world, which are the most effective ingredients for the
deepening and mellowing and the complete development, energizing and
revealment, of an artist's inner being and spiritual powers."[5]

Actually, George was trying to live a life free from tears. Whenever an
unpleasant situation presented itself, his strategy was to quietly slip away.
Although he told his first biographer, Goldberg, that as a youth he had
itched like a terrier to get into street fights, and even though as an adult,
he liked to keep himself in fighting trim—going so far as to mention to
one reporter, "I have a forearm like a wrestler"[6]—he was always doing his
best to sidestep unpleasantness. That had been his way even as a teenager
when, after quitting his job as a song plugger at Remick's, he took on a
job as a pianist in a vaudeville house—the City Theater on Fourteenth

Street—accompanying the singers and dancers during the supper show. On his first—and, as it turned out, last—night on the job, he missed a cue, found himself playing one song while the chorus was singing another, and was then humiliated by the comedian who got a few laughs by throwing jibes at Gershwin from the stage, saying, "Who told you you were a piano player?" and "You ought to be banging the drums."[7] Gershwin remembered this as the most humiliating moment of his life. In response to the bullying comedian, he said nothing; rather, he simply stood up and walked away from the piano and the job. Now, past the age of thirty, he responded in a similar fashion whenever harsh criticism came his way. Paul Rosenfeld, a highly regarded music critic for *Vanity Fair, Modern Music,* and other publications, was typical of American reviewers when he described Gershwin as a "gifted composer of the lower, unpretentious order."[8] Gershwin pretended to ignore such statements but they obviously registered. When he gave a concert in Toronto in 1934, he told a reporter for the city's *Evening Telegram,* who had asked for a reaction to his critics: "I know my own place. I know I am small compared with the big fellows. But I know that what I have given is my own."[9] His reputed imperviousness to stage fright was also deceptive. In 1932, when the nineteen-year-old composer Burton Lane visited him in the green room just before he took the stage for the premiere of his *Second Rhapsody,* it was Gershwin who asked Lane if *he* was nervous, which made Lane laugh and reply, "Why should I be nervous? You're playing."[10] But Gershwin had, in fact, been sleepless for several days before that concert and his nerves were apparent during the opening moments of the piece.[11] Nor was he bulletproof when his mother derided him, which she sometimes did, asking why he could not write bigger-selling hits, such as those that the DeSylva, Brown, and Henderson team was coming up with so regularly like "Button Up Your Overcoat" and "The Best Things In Life Are Free." DeSylva, after all, had once been his partner. Rather than snap back at his mother, he would leave the room. And there was his meeting late in 1929 with the Russian composer Alexander Glazunov. The latter attended a concert where George played the *Rhapsody in Blue* under the baton of Ernest Schelling. After describing the piece to Mrs. Schelling as "part human and part animal,"[12] Glazunov was brought backstage to meet Gershwin who, thrilled that such an eminent musician had come to hear him play, said it was the dream of his life to go to Russia and study orchestration with him. Glazunov replied that such a thing would not be possible, that he would need to know theory before he could learn orchestration. Gershwin, who by then had written the *Rhapsody in Blue, Concerto in F,* the *Three Preludes,* and *An American in Paris,* listened dejectedly to the insult but said nothing. The next day, he phoned Glazunov at the latter's hotel to thank him for speaking so candidly and to ask his advice as to whom he might go to for lessons.[13]

He was known to be brash, even something of a braggart. In his 1928 meeting with John Ireland in England, he asked the older composer how many performances a year his rhapsody was receiving, and when Ireland said three, Gershwin replied, "Ah! *Mine* gets played two or three times a *day!*"[14] But such remarks were made so ingenuously they were endearing. There was nothing false about him, and he never spoke this way to puff himself up. Rather, he said what he thought—too often failing to filter what had popped into his mind—and when others said what *they* thought, he listened. He was never a bully. But he would not have been completely miscast as a bully's victim. Although he went his own way in his personal life, he tended, in his professional life, to take the line of least resistance, especially in choosing his Broadway projects, making the dreams of others come true while deferring his own. In late 1928, just before the premiere of *An American in Paris,* came the opening of his and Ira's *Treasure Girl,* about people finding romance during a beach party treasure hunt. The memorable "I've Got a Crush on You" came from this show, but the plot— banal even by the standards of the time—sank it. In mid-1929, there was *Show Girl,* which impresario Florenz Ziegfeld talked him—all but ordered him—into doing, and which was just as hackneyed and unsuccessful. It is remembered now for the song "Liza (All the Clouds'll Roll Away)" and for a Boston performance where Al Jolson stood up in the audience and sang it to his startled wife, Ruby Keeler, as she was on stage tap dancing to it.

With *An American in Paris* more satisfying and successful than his recent Broadway work, and having listened attentively to Kahn's speech, he now turned again to his goal of writing an opera. He knew what it would mean to take on such a task: a hiatus in his partnership with Ira, reduced income for more than a year, and critical assessments by the established arbiters of classical music—many of them already ill disposed toward him—on the value of several hours of intricately constructed music for soloists, chorus, and orchestra. It would also mean, should he try it and fall short, a tremendous professional failure. When writing musical comedies, he had no such fear of defeat. Despite some unsuccessful shows, he was an acknowledged master. Other songwriters longed for his approval. Duke Ellington was proud to hear that Gershwin admired his "Sophisticated Lady."[15] Hoagy Carmichael learned with pleasure that Gershwin, when he got a copy of "Washboard Blues," played it over and over. Fats Waller was befriended by Gershwin who went with him to Harlem "rent shouts" where admission fees paid rent for musicians down on their luck.[16] Many other songwriters, including Vernon Duke, Arthur Schwartz, Burton Lane, Ann Ronell, Dana Suesse, and Kay Swift, began their careers with his benediction. Although there were a lot of master songwriters at work in the late 1920s, the mystique was his. This was certainly helped by his simultaneous career in Carnegie Hall. But being a composer of orchestral works had not led him to write elaborate songs; rather, his best show tunes were marvels of economy, ingenuity, and understated power. In 1928, the year of *An American in Paris*, he wrote several for an aborted Ziegfeld show *East Is West*. One of them, "Embraceable You," would become the prototype for those he would compose in the coming decade: brief melodic phrases, a swaying beat, and chords to make the melody and rhythm tremble with feeling. He loved songwriting and songwriters. He was most at home among the group that lyricist E. Y. "Yip" Harburg called "our tribe of songsmiths." It was, Harburg added, "something like Fleet Street in Samuel Johnson's time—an artistic community where people took fire from one another."[17] This was his fraternity. But the fellowship involved more than songwriting; it was the theater. And for a theater composer in the days before the era of the Broadway book musical, opera was the end game.

He became intrigued by S. Ansky's play *The Dybbuk*, a Yiddish tale of the supernatural set in Poland. In that play, a poverty-stricken young mystic, upon learning that his intended's father has married her to another, wealthier, man, dies so he can inhabit her body as a demon. This project nearly came to fruition. A contract was drawn up between him and the Metropolitan Opera, and Gershwin began sketching ideas. He also made plans to go to Eastern Europe to study Chassidic music. Already he was well-versed in Jewish popular song, having, as a teenager, attended productions of New York's Yiddish Theater. When he was sixteen, one of the Second Avenue moguls, Boris Thomashevsky, asked him to collaborate with another young composer, Sholom Secunda, on a Yiddish operetta, and he would have gladly accepted the assignment had Secunda agreed to work with him. But Secunda (best known now as the composer of "Bei mir Bist du Schön") considered him too young and inexperienced, and the plan fell through. Now *The Dybbuk* appealed to him because it was an opportunity to go back to his musical roots in order to depict a poor, isolated, superstitious, and bullied community. In other words, it and *Porgy* attracted him for the same reason.

All of his Broadway musicals—even the ambitious *Strike Up the Band,* which satirized war—had the fluffiest of plots. Left to his own inclinations, however, Gershwin was drawn instead to stories about men who despaired of finding love while living in communities that suffered under the weight of prejudice. Despite all his success, he believed himself to be such a man. He was, after all, the son of people who had escaped the tsar's anti-Semitic regime. He knew about signs on Florida beaches that read, "No Jews or Dogs Allowed." In the mid-1920s, he was refused admission to the Lake Placid Club because he was a Jew. In 1934, on a concert tour, he would be denied a hotel room in Toronto for the same reason. When, in 1925, *Vanity Fair* magazine asked him and other celebrities to write their own epitaphs, his contribution was "Here lies the body of George Gershwin, American composer. Composer? American?"[18] There was abundant evidence in reviews of his concert pieces that uncertainty existed as to whether he really was a "composer." As for him being an American—that was questioned by people such as auto magnate Henry Ford who, in his magazine *The Dearborn Independent,* published a series of articles under the heading "The International Jew." One read: "The song pluggers of the theater, vaudeville and radio are the paid agents of the Yiddish song agencies. Money and not merit dominates the spread of this moron music which is styled Jewish, jazz and swing. Non-Jewish music is stigmatized as high-brow." Ford was not alone in this view. Columbia University professor—and American composer—Daniel Gregory Mason wrote, "Our whole contemporary attitude toward instrumental music, especially in New York, is dominated by Jewish tastes and standards, with their Oriental extravagance, their sensuous brilliancy and intellectual facility and superficiality, their general tendency to exaggeration."[19]

Gershwin never replied to such statements. But, in 1929, he became drawn to this idea of an opera about a Jewish shtetl, and he began composing some of the music. As he would later do in *Porgy and Bess*, he wrote choral prayers. Goldberg, who heard Gershwin play this music, described it as having a "slow lilt [that] gradually assumed a hieratic character, swinging in drowsy dignity above the drone. The room became a synagogue."[20] If there was any problem with such a text, it was that it was not an American story. Gershwin had from the beginning expressed his desire to write not just an opera, but one that was distinctly American. As it turned out, the rights to a musical version of *The Dybbuk* were unavailable, which forced him to abandon the idea. The music he wrote for that opera has been lost.

In the meantime, as he, the musical comedy king, pondered opera, Kay, the lifelong opera buff, was, along with Jimmy, making significant strides in musical comedy. In the summer of 1928, two of their songs were used in a show called *Say When*. Those songs, "Little White Lies" and "When the Lights Turn Green" were not published and went nowhere. But in 1929 came "Can't We Be Friends?," which, as performed by torch singer Libby Holman in *The Little Show*, was not only an immediate hit but a permanent one. Then, in 1930, the Swift and James team really came into its own. In February, two of their songs, "How Would a City Gal Know?" and "Up Among the Chimney Pots," appeared in the production *9:15 Revue*—the musical that launched Harold Arlen's career with "Get Happy." In June, there was an edition of the *Garrick Gaieties* that featured their song "Johnny Wanamaker" as well as music by Marc Blitzstein and Vernon Duke. On September 23 came the premiere of *Fine and Dandy*, whose score was entirely by them and included the songs "Fine and Dandy" and "Can This Be Love?," which were immediate hits and then classics. Kay Swift had thus become the first woman to compose a complete Broadway show, and a highly successful one at that.

They had made it to the top on Broadway. Yet neither was satisfied. James had not gotten what he wanted—he had not gotten Kay back. Kay did not have what she wanted—she did not have George. So, just as they were establishing themselves as a coming Broadway team, they decided to call it quits—not as husband and wife but as a songwriting partnership. James, in his 1964 autobiography, *The Long Road Home*, explained this turn of events by saying he had concluded that his true vocation lay not on Broadway but in international finance and world politics. By 1930, he had amply demonstrated his acumen in those areas. In the late 1920s, he had assessed world fiscal trends astutely enough to save his family's overseas assets by merging them with those of a U.S. bank. In 1930, while *Fine and Dandy* was playing to packed houses, he was in Bremen, Germany, watching Hitler rabble-rouse. As a result, he became one of the first Americans to voice alarm about the Nazis, who were still three years from power. James continued to have literary ambitions but could satisfy them by writing books about politics and finance.

Kay could have looked for another songwriting partner but she too chose to abandon Broadway. Just as fame and fortune were beckoning, she put her musical aspirations on hold and concentrated instead on George, becoming all things to him: lover, hostess, and musical confidante. The Gershwins had just written the musical *Girl Crazy*, which ran on Broadway concurrently with *Fine and Dandy*, and which introduced Broadway newcomers Ethel Merman and Ginger Rogers as well as an array of timeless songs, including "Embraceable You," "I Got Rhythm," "But Not for Me," and "Bidin' My Time." This great score was written for the last conventional Broadway musical that George would willingly write. There was something brewing in him: a restlessness that would no longer be satisfied by run-of-the-mill vehicles, an ambition that would no longer be put off for years at a time. Kay was attuned to this musical sea change. She was also aware of how his outward bravura and confidence masked a fear of failure. She knew other things as well. One was how much he loved the perks that came with life as a songwriter. Not only was there the approbation of critics, love from the audiences, big money, and deference from fellow practitioners of the art, there was also the fact that, songwriting being show business, it provided an unending supply of young, willing women.

Her mother, who had died in 1928, had been a mystic, and Kay felt a kindred capacity. She had a feeling about George—that he was vulnerable.

"That Long Drip of Human Tears"

41

There was a defenselessness in the way he went constantly from person to person seeking approval of himself and his work, seeking confirmation of the value of his interests and discoveries. He wanted everyone to share the childlike glee he took in being himself. To have such an exposed and overwhelming desire to be loved was to set oneself up for inevitable rebuff. George had thus far escaped that fate not just because he was talented but because his talent was so contagious. As Kay later observed, an audience would not only listen to his music but also feel that it was writing it along with him.[21] This was a most unusual attribute, one that let people believe they were in on the creation. It brought him fame, money, and a formidable name but in truth he was really just a slender fellow with thinning hair who fretted continuously that he was not doing the best work he could do, and who, whenever he tried to live up to his potential, received calumny from the appraisers of high culture. In 1930, given his dynamism and the way the world's doors always obediently swung open for him, it was not common to think about George as vulnerable. But Kay felt that way about him.

EIGHT

The Losing Streak Begins

In 1930, not only did George have a hit show in *Girl Crazy*, he signed a contract with Fox Film Corporation that paid him $70,000 and Ira $30,000 to come to Hollywood and spend six weeks writing the score for a movie called *Delicious*. The next year, 1931, was even better. *Of Thee I Sing* became the brothers' most successful Broadway show yet, and it was the first musical to win the Pulitzer Prize. It was a political satire in the vein of *Strike Up the Band* with a story, this time by George S. Kaufman and Morrie Ryskind, about a presidential candidate, John P. Wintergreen, campaigning on a platform consisting of one word—love—and picking a first lady via a beauty pageant. When the play was revived twenty years later, no one could figure out why it had been so popular, except for the songs, which included "Who Cares?," "Love Is Sweeping the Country," "Wintergreen for President," and the title song. But in 1931 it was immensely successful, and it ran longer than any other Gershwin musical.

It was at about this time that Babe Ruth, when asked how he could justify the fact that he was earning more than President Hoover, remarked,

"I had a better year than he did." In the years 1930 and 1931, George Gershwin was earning more than Ruth and Hoover combined. Big money was coming in not only from his songs but also from his classical compositions. In January 1929, he received $2,500 for the first radio performance of *An American in Paris*. *Rhapsody in Blue* brought in a check for $50,000 for its use in Paul Whiteman's 1930 movie, *The King of Jazz*. George picked up an additional $10,000 to promote that film by playing the piece daily for a week live on stage at the Roxy Theater, with Whiteman conducting. In late 1930, while he and Ira were in Los Angeles writing a handful of songs for the soon-to-be-forgotten film *Delicious*, he was making more than $10,000 a week from his movie contract alone, while he also soaked up the California sun; rented, along with Ira and Leonore, an opulent Spanish-style mansion near Griffith Park that had once belonged to Greta Garbo; assisted conductor Artur Rodzinski in rehearsing the Los Angeles Philharmonic for the upcoming Los Angeles premiere of *An American in Paris;* had a brief affair with silent screen star Aileen Pringle at her home in Santa Monica; and began an ambitious work for piano and orchestra that he initially called *Manhattan Rhapsody* and then *Rhapsody in Rivets* before deciding on the abstract title *Second Rhapsody*. Ostensibly, the new score was created to provide an instrumental backdrop that could be used in the film, but Gershwin's main purpose was to create a fourth orchestral concert work.

Back in New York, he had finally moved into quarters separate from his family. In the spring of 1929, he took a luxurious seventeenth-floor duplex apartment at 33 Riverside Drive at Seventy-fifth Street on the Upper West Side. One could step onto a wide wraparound terrace and look at the Hudson River or the New Jersey Palisades. Kay worked with professional decorators to give it a spare, modern look. The colors were subdued: gray, tan, silver, pale green. There were Japanese floor mats in the dining room and, in his bedroom, a sectional Japanese screen on which his cousin, Henry Botkin, had painted scenes as imagined from *An American in Paris*. In addition to all his other activities, Gershwin was now an enthusiastic art collector, and the walls of his new quarters were decorated with recently acquired works by Picasso, Modigliani, Utrillo, Soutine, and Rouault— the last his favorite. Not content to be a collector, he had also become a painter. As a youngster, his bent in that direction had been quashed by a schoolteacher who told him he did not have the gift. Ira had also been a compulsive sketcher in boyhood but his cartoons, drawings, and watercolors—which had the same low-key charm as his writings—were created for his own amusement, and he did not take them seriously enough to worry about what others thought of them. George, on the other hand, needed to believe that his work was important. Thus, when he finally returned to painting—at Ira's urging—he went into it with a will, as if to prove that bygone teacher wrong. He studied art intensively—mainly, as usual, as an autodidact although he did seek instruction from cousin Botkin. So it was that accompanying Picasso and the others on his penthouse walls were two originals by himself, both portraits: one of his grandfather and the other of a young black woman.

For a housewarming, he gave a party for a group of friends from the songwriting profession. Present were Richard Rodgers, Larry Hart, Buddy DeSylva, Joseph Meyer (DeSylva had written the lyrics and Meyer the music for "California, Here I Come"), and Gershwin's publisher, Max Dreyfus. For the occasion, George made place cards for each guest and every card had a musical quotation from a song written by that guest.[1] He might hobnob with society people and be thrilled by the company of concert hall greats, but he relaxed among those he knew best: the people who wrote words and music for Broadway.

Although he and Ira were living separately for the first time, they were not very far apart. Ira and Leonore had the penthouse next door, and the two apartments were connected by a passageway. As had always been the case, the brothers could pop in on one another without leaving the house. This was conducive to work, as George might come in late from a party, sit at the piano, come up with a good idea, and immediately take it to Ira—another night owl—who would allow himself to be coaxed into working on a lyric. Similarly, a gathering at George's might gravitate to Ira's, where the food was better. George was finicky about his stomach and tried to restrict himself to the simplest and blandest of diets. Leonore's cook, on the other hand, provided an ongoing horn of plenty, and it was at her house, not George's, that the new Gershwin salon took shape. In George's view, a woman who did not have children needed to have a career.[2] But

Leonore's life revolved around accumulating wealth and presiding over the Gershwins' social life. Gone were the days when everyone met at her sister Emily's Greenwich Village apartment. Now, it was Leonore who oversaw the gatherings of writers, musicians, actors, and wits, assisted by a staff that she ruled over like a benign despot. She could peremptorily fire an underling who disagreed with her but she might look the other way if a servant was stealing. She was like her parents in her concern for the underdog. Her father, Albert Strunksy, was known as Greenwich Village's most forgiving landlord. Her mother, Mascha, after her divorce from Albert, opened New York's first cafeteria-style restaurant, a Greenwich Village establishment called Three Steps Down, where Leonore and Emily worked as cashiers and where a young artist named Al Hirschfeld designed the daily menus in exchange for meals.

It was difficult for people to know where they stood with Leonore. Relatives as close as Frankie were permanently wounded by sudden, uncalled for remarks. Others became loyal to her because of unexpected acts of kindness. In early 1930, she was at the back of the Times Square Theatre during the second and more successful incarnation of *Strike Up the Band* (writer Morrie Ryskind had tempered Kaufman's script; now the war was not real but a dream and about chocolate, not cheese, and the Gershwins revised the score, adding many new songs, including "Soon") when she noticed Oscar Levant standing nearby. He had wandered over from the New Amsterdam Theater, where his own show, *Ripples*, was playing. It turned out that he liked Gershwin's music better than his own. In fact, he liked George a lot more than he liked himself. If anyone ever needed mothering, it was this twenty-five-year-old son of Russian-Jewish immigrants: a long-legged fellow with a pudgy torso and a boyish but weary face who had a notably quick and cutting wit and who, at age twenty-five, had already gone through middling careers as a dance band pianist, stage actor, screen actor, screenwriter, film scorer, pop songwriter, and highbrow music composer. Leonore understood his longing to be with George and Ira and sympathetically took him under her wing. Soon he was a self-described "penthouse beachcomber," moving from one Gershwin apartment to the other. For long periods, he would encamp at Ira and Leonore's.

George's staff consisted of a secretary, Nanette Kutner, and a man, Paul Mueller, who was a non-Jewish German immigrant who had formerly been a valet for the Warburgs and came recommended to him by Kay. Mueller continued to work for Gershwin until the end of the composer's life. When he married, his wife joined him in Gershwin's apartment. Later in life, after his service to Gershwin, he became a financial consultant. But now he was content to be what George called a man of all work. He was a loyal factotum who did any task George assigned him and who remained in close contact with Kay, keeping her apprised of what was going on in George's personal life.

This was how George Gershwin was living at the beginning of 1932 when, as he approached the age of thirty-four, he was at the pinnacle of his success. But it was then that things began to go wrong.

47

First, there was the failure of the *Second Rhapsody*. Although it was written as a stand-alone piece, Gershwin knew that its music would be used in the film *Delicious*, particularly in a scene in which Janet Gaynor was a Scottish immigrant escaping an immigration officer among the fast traffic and bright lights, clangs, jackhammers, and noisy ambience of the great metropolis. Thus, the rhapsody begins with an opening rivet theme, consisting mainly of repeated notes (the first eight notes are the same). This made for a determinedly minimal and intentionally monotonous start, and it is this idea that recurs most often and dominates the piece. Other themes arrive, including a delicate off-the-beat motif played high in the treble, a stately melody marked Sostenuto e con moto that is related (perhaps intentionally) to the Andantino moderato of the *Rhapsody in Blue*, and a noble anthem that Gershwin directs the orchestra to play "fervently." But the composer's principal concerns here are structure and orchestration. It is almost as if he wanted to see how much he could accomplish with less-than-stellar material. Critics of his prior concert works had praised the beauty of his themes but condemned the absence of development. Now he set out to prove that he could develop his motifs, play them against one another and, in doing so, create a real musical journey, one that would show that he was, in fact, a serious composer. By naming the piece *Second Rhapsody,* he invited a comparison with the *Rhapsody*

The Losing Streak Begins

in Blue in the hope that the contrast would show how much expertise he had gained and how much he had grown. This seemed to be the way to court the critics and get his foot in the door of the community of modern composers—perhaps even the League of Composers, which, led by Aaron Copland, had a membership that included Roy Harris, Virgil Thomson, George Antheil, and other well-regarded if poorly paid contemporaries.

Because the *Second Rhapsody* was the first Gershwin concert work not to have been commissioned by a conductor, George had to shop for one. He began by going to the top—to Arturo Toscanini, who led the New York Philharmonic. Toscanini was a man of elegant looks, incorruptible ideals, and impeccable taste who had been masterfully leading opera and concert orchestras for nearly fifty years. In 1896 (the year of Ira's birth), he had conducted the premiere of Puccini's *La Bohème*. It would have been a coup for Gershwin to get him to conduct the *Second Rhapsody*'s debut, and for a moment, he thought that this would also be a coup for Toscanini. They met at the home of music critic Samuel Chotzinoff, who was a friend of the composer as well as the conductor, and who, six years earlier, had delivered that loving review of the *Concerto in F* in the *New York World*. To play second piano at what was tantamount to an audition, George brought along Oscar Levant.

But it unsettled Toscanini to have the cigar-chomping George and his rumpled, wisecracking sidekick demonstrating music that was not only modern in sound—Toscanini disliked most twentieth-century music—but smacked of show business. George, in turn, was disturbed to learn that Toscanini was unfamiliar with his oeuvre. Not only had he never heard the *Rhapsody in Blue*, he had never heard *of* it. Gershwin and Levant demonstrated that piece for him as well as the *Second Rhapsody* but Toscanini politely refused to conduct the premiere.

The first performance went instead to Serge Koussevitzky, the conductor of the Boston Symphony. Koussevitzky was receptive to contemporary work and knew and admired Gershwin's music. After George's death, he would call him "this extraordinary being too great to be real."[3] On January 29, 1932, he conducted the premiere of the *Second Rhapsody* in Boston with Gershwin as soloist. On February 5, the Boston Symphony came to Carnegie Hall, where Koussevitzky and Gershwin introduced the new piece to New York. The house was packed and the ovation huge, but the critics did not accept the work as proof that George was a real composer. In fact, they looked on it as more evidence to the contrary. On February 6, writing in the *New York Times*, Olin Downes faulted the new rhapsody for being less "individual and originative" than the first and for being "too long for its material." But Downes did find something to admire: he commended Koussevitzky for putting as much time and effort into this piece as would have been the case had he been premiering an important work, such as a symphony by Roussel or Myaskovsky. His judgment was typical of most critics. Even more upsetting to Gershwin was the indifference of the audience. Despite their applause, the new work did not have any of the heart-stopping moments people had come to expect in his music. It generated no buzz.

After the lukewarm reception given to the *Concerto in F* in 1925, nearly three years had passed before Gershwin's next orchestral work, *An American in Paris*. During that period, except for the publication of the *Three Preludes for Piano*, he had concentrated exclusively on musical comedy with *Oh, Kay!*, *Strike Up the Band*, *Funny Face*, *Rosalie*, and *Treasure Girl*. Then came *An American in Paris*, which received a warmer welcome, but it too was followed by a hiatus of several years, which he devoted to *Show Girl*, *Strike Up the Band* (the second, more successful version), *Girl Crazy*, *Of Thee I Sing*, and *Delicious*. Now, with the *Second Rhapsody*'s disappointing reception, he might have been expected to continue the pattern and return to Times Square, perhaps for an indefinite stay. But that is not what happened. Although he and Ira were talking about doing a new musical with the Aarons and Freedley team, which had produced *Lady, Be Good!*, *Oh, Kay!*, and *Funny Face*, it was only because Aarons and Freedley had fallen on hard times. Gershwin was determined to press on in the concert world.

In mid-February, he and some friends, including publisher Bennett Cerf and financier Emil Mosbacher, went on vacation to Havana. They were not accompanied by married man Ira, inasmuch as this was to be a bachelor's vacation. George spent every night in the cafés of Havana, sampling the music and the women. One evening he returned to the elegant Almendares Hotel at four in the morning to find that a sixteen-piece rumba band had dropped by to serenade him. Effusively, he promised them that he would try writing a rumba of his own. He had found Cuban music irresistible, with its tricky, insistent rhythms and adventurous harmonies that could be both brooding and playful. Just as he had brought Parisian taxi horns home with him in 1928, he now purchased bongos, maracas, claves, and a gourd. He was going to write an orchestral ode to this lush and sexy Cuban sound.

That was one project on his mind when he arrived back in New York. But he was also thinking again about opera. The idea of making one out of *Porgy* returned to him, and he wrote again to DuBose Heyward to see if the author/poet were still interested. It had been nearly six years since they had last discussed the idea. George had backed off then, and even now, he was not committing himself, only testing the waters. He knew that, should the music rights be available and should Heyward still be interested, the project would mean many months, even years of work. There would be no new musicals and no songwriting with Ira during that period. This would affect not only his income, but would mean abandoning the field of popular songwriting just when it was exploding with talent. In the early 1930s, Cole Porter, Richard Rodgers, Harold Arlen, and Harry Warren had come into their own, while Irving Berlin and Jerome Kern were still in their prime. In writing a grand opera, he would risk becoming passé in this most competitive field, especially given the scarcity of Depression-era dollars for new productions. At the same time, he would also be exposing himself to the most monumental sort of artistic failure. There were other considerations as well. Should he write it for the Met—assuming they would accept black singers—and should it fail there, there was no assurance that they or any other major opera company would give him a second chance. Yet there was danger in writing it for Broadway, where audiences, unused to opera, might reject it whatever its merits. And even if it was well received in New York, problems would arise elsewhere. The Theater Guild's production of Dorothy and DuBose Heyward's dramatic treatment of *Porgy* had been banned by the City of Charleston—the story's locale—because of the all-black cast. Such bans would certainly occur in other locations. These were all significant and foreseeable problems. What seems never to have occurred to Gershwin was the possibility that the opera would be poorly received by the African American community. One of the things that had caused the Heyward novel to be so celebrated when it was published in 1925 was that it was one of the earliest—if not the first—by a white southern writer to portray black people without degradation or condescension. Then came the stage play, which had been highly praised by black leaders, among them civil rights pioneer James Weldon Johnson who, with his brother J. Rosamond Johnson, had written "Lift Every Voice and Sing"—a song adopted by the National Association for the Advancement of Colored People as the "Negro National Anthem." In Heyward's own words, the book was about his "conception of a summer of aspiration, devotion and heartbreak across the color wall."[4]

George's letter to Heyward was written on March 29, 1932. On April 12, Heyward wrote back to say he was still enthusiastic and that the musical rights were available. He had been pleased to hear again from Gershwin for financial as well as artistic reasons. The Depression had hit him hard and he was hurting for money. Gershwin received the letter and then hesitated again. This time, however, there was more going on than simple vacillation. His father had fallen ill with lymphatic leukemia.

Shaken, George got in touch with the Johns Hopkins School of Medicine in Baltimore to ask doctors there about the latest treatments, and he made sure his father received the most up-to-date medications. "Papa," he said, "I would give everything in the world if I could do something for you to get well."[5] Although Morris had never been someone his children could go to for advice or confide in, he had been a gentle and tolerant presence in their lives. He had accepted his lot as the feckless husband of a bullying woman and had entered his years of financial independence, gained through George and Ira, with a mirthful serenity. As he lay dying, he removed his oxygen mask to ask Rose if she intended now to marry a taller man. She had never stopped reminding him that he was short. Her answer to him, if she gave him one, has not been recorded. She did not remarry, but there would be taller men whose interest was in her money and, unlike Morris's, not in her or, at least, in the pretty girl she had been in St. Petersburg. He died in New York on May 14, 1932, and was laid to rest in a plot at the Westchester Hills Cemetery in Hastings-on-Hudson, New York.

The Losing Streak Begins

Six days later, on May 20, Gershwin replied to Heyward's letter of April 12. As had been the case six years before, he was drawing back. He told Heyward he was glad the rights to an operatic version of *Porgy* were available but he had too many commitments to begin work any time soon. In fact, his commitments would be taking him through the rest of the year. For one thing, he was about to write his Cuban piece, *Rumba*, which would be introduced at the first all-Gershwin concert, scheduled to take place that summer outdoors in Lewisohn Stadium. There were also two new Broadway shows in the offing. One was the promised Aarons and Freedley vehicle, a goofy confection called *Pardon My English* that was uninteresting to George and Ira except as a favor to the producers. The other was yet another satirical operetta with a story by George S. Kaufman, this one a sequel to *Of Thee I Sing* entitled *Let 'Em Eat Cake*. It would be every bit as ridiculous as its predecessor was—President Wintergreen would be voted out of office and then lead a revolution by manufacturing blue shirts.

Morris's death was not dwelt on in letters or conversation, but shortly thereafter the brothers wrote a song, "So What?," that went:

> I once had a father
> Worry didn't bother
> He had been around
> He knew what it was all about.[6]

Then George wrote his orchestral rumba, whose slow middle section is a haunting lamentation punctuated by insistent, funereal Cuban percussion. When asked to describe the new piece, he did not talk about his father. Nor did he discuss his discovery of and love for Cuban music, except to say he had "endeavored to combine the Cuban rhythms with my original thematic material." Instead, he gave a determinedly cerebral description of it, calling the elegiac section "a gradually developing canon in a polytonal manner . . . with a climax based on an ostinato of the theme in the canon."[7] It was another attempt to demonstrate his credentials as a composer. Most recently, they had been questioned, if indirectly, by Aaron Copland and the League of Composers.

On April 30 and May 1, 1932, there had been a festival of music by modern American composers at an estate called Yaddo in Saratoga Springs,

New York. It had been organized by Copland who, at thirty-two, was the undisputed dean of American modernists. Like Gershwin, Copland had been born at the turn of the century in Brooklyn to Russian-Jewish parents. He too had spent the 1920s trying to incorporate jazz into his concert works. But his approach had been unwaveringly intellectual and his audiences small. He had not yet written *El Salón México, Fanfare for the Common Man, Appalachian Spring,* or any of the other pieces that would gain him wide public acceptance. Gershwin's visceral music had from the start brought in huge audiences. Copland had the respect of his avant-garde peers, which Gershwin envied, while Gershwin had the worldwide audience that Copland wanted.

In early 1932, Copland was at a gathering at Gershwin's apartment at 33 Riverside Drive. Later, he could not recall having said much to his host, but he went out of his way to befriend Oscar Levant. When Levant played his *Sonatina for Piano,* Copland invited him to premiere it at the upcoming Yaddo festival. Although Gershwin was standing nearby, Copland issued no such invitation to him. The Yaddo program showcased music by Copland, Roger Sessions, Charles Ives, Paul Bowles, George Antheil, Vivian Fine, Levant, and others. It was not a big success. It drew only a few hundred people and just a couple of music critics, who complained of jarring chords and notes struck seemingly at random. Dr. Wesley La Violette, president of the Chicago Musical College, called what he heard "unhappy music, flavored of a discordant world." Copland, in return, negatively reviewed the reviewers for "lack of sympathy and understanding."[8] Nevertheless, he had managed to get himself and his fellow American modernists heard.

Gershwin was not invited to Yaddo, but he had no problem getting his latest music heard. *Rumba* was premiered at Lewisohn Stadium—a Roman-style amphitheater with gigantic Doric columns and twenty-five-cent seats in the heart of New York City. On August 16, 1932, 17,000 people, including standees, attended this, the first all-Gershwin concert. It was a record crowd for the stadium—quite an achievement, given that no large venue concert had ever before been devoted to the works of a single American composer. On the program were two pianists: George, performing both of his rhapsodies, and Levant, playing the concerto. There were also two conductors. Albert Coates, who had conducted the premiere of Holst's *The Planets* in England, was on hand to conduct the *Rumba* premiere. He also served as conductor for the *Second Rhapsody*. Gershwin's good friend William Daly took the podium for the concerto, the first rhapsody, and selections from the composer's songs and theater music.

From backstage, Gershwin watched his two friends, Daly and Levant, give a magnificent reading of the concerto. That Levant performed at all was something of a miracle, as he suffered an attack of stage fright so severe that he would eschew large venue public performances for another five years (his return came on September 8, 1937, when he once again played the concerto, this time at a Gershwin memorial concert). Then George bounded onto the stage—young, lanky, charismatic, a star—to thunderous applause, and he delivered a high-powered reading of the *Rhapsody in Blue*. It was, he said later, "the most exciting night I have ever had." After the concert when a friend greeted him backstage with, "George, it was wonderful," he replied, "Just wonderful?"[9]

In the next day's (August 17) *New York Times*, music reviewer Howard Taubman noted the size of the crowd and the fact that Gershwin was the only composer other than Beethoven and Wagner to be granted a Lewisohn concert entirely to himself. Taubman wrote, "In the face of these statistics, the critical attitude cannot help but be humble. What would it profit us to inveigh against the manifest disproportionateness of singling out Mr. Gershwin as the one composer to be honored thus, or against Broadway, popularity, the Great God publicity and other equally elusive matters?" Taubman acknowledged the vitality of the *Rhapsody in Blue* but complained that its lively reading was because "most of the week's rehearsals were spent on this program to the detriment of Scriabine [*sic*] and Borodine [*sic*]." Gershwin, he continued, had done "his cause more harm than good in allowing so revealing a program to be presented. For if he has any pretensions to being considered a truly gifted composer, the almost unvarying sameness and formlessness of this body of music did not help him." The new piece, *Rumba*, was quickly dismissed. "Despite the addition of maracas, gourd, bongo and other Cuban instruments," Taubman continued, it "was merely old Gershwin in recognizable form."[10] Other reviewers, such as Olin Downes and Pitts Sanborn, found the piece at least interesting. But it had nothing like the success of the *Rhapsody in Blue* and *An American in Paris*. This was due, Kay believed, to the fact that the piece begins without an introduction—mid-sentence as it were—"so that the audience doesn't know what hit them and it doesn't digest it."[11] To her, *Rumba* (soon to be renamed *Cuban Overture*) was Gershwin's finest orchestral composition and also his sexiest. But it went all but unnoticed then, and it has never caught on.

Worse was to come. As the year drew to a close Gershwin and Daly appeared together again, this time at a benefit concert at the Metropolitan Opera House by and for the Musicians Symphony Orchestra. It was an ensemble of the unemployed, one of them a viola player, Allan Lincoln Langley—a gaunt man of forty with a pointy Van Dyke beard. Langley had graduated from the New England Conservatory of Music, played viola and violin with the Boston Symphony and the New York Philharmonic, and, after receiving a substantial inheritance in the early 1920s (his father was an eminent pianist), had quit the viola to try his hand as a composer. He wrote chamber music, symphonies, and numerous symphonic waltzes. At a 1931 Lewisohn Stadium concert, he had conducted one of his waltzes on a program that also included Gershwin playing the *Rhapsody in Blue*. By then Langley was broke, the stock market crash having taken his nest egg. Now, in late 1932, he was back to eking out a living with his viola, and jobs were scarce.

The first half of the program featured conductor Sandor Harmati leading a performance of Franck's *Symphony in D Minor*. In the second half, Gershwin played and Daly conducted the *Concerto in F*, George conducted what he now called the *Cuban Overture*, and then Daly took the podium for *An American in Paris* followed by his own orchestral arrangements of four Gershwin songs. During a rehearsal of the Gershwin song medley Langley had heard Daly say, "Did I write that there?"[12] This made him wonder if Daly might have ghosted and orchestrated every one of Gershwin's pieces. In the December 1932 edition of *The American Spectator*, Langley posed that question as he simultaneously slammed Gershwin's music ("the Concerto was a profoundly amorphous and meretricious work").[13] George had always—outwardly, at least—been nonchalant about insults. But Langley's assertions struck deeper. They were not the usual accusations of incompetence; they were about plagiarism. This made for one of the few times people saw him visibly angry. When the editor of *The American Spectator* offered him space to reply to Langley, he turned instead to his lawyer. He was on the point of suing when Daly defused the situation by writing an article in the *New York Times* in which he said, "I have never written one note of any of his compositions, or so much as orchestrated one whole bar of any of his concert works."[14] For a *coup de grâce*, he added, "I suppose I should really resent the fact that Langley attributes Gershwin's work to me, since Langley finds all of it so bad. But fortunately for my amour-propre, I have heard some of Langley's compositions. He really should stay away from ink and stick to his viola."

Langley rebutted Daly with a letter of his own to the *Times*, protesting that he had not called Gershwin's work bad or claimed that Daly had written it. His concern, he said, was "with the peculiar trend of circumstances which made Gershwin's rise so much easier than that of many more qualified composers." He was referring to himself. "As everyone knows," he continued, "I renounced the viola nearly six years ago for other purposes which circumstances made impossible to realize."[15] Middle-aged and unemployed, he recognized the obscurity into which he was heading and the inescapable truth that no one would ever take any of his compositions to heart. Gershwin's music, on the other hand, had, as composer-critic Frederick Jacobi later put it, "that high attribute of making people fall in love with it."[16]

People did still love Gershwin music but the year 1932 was one of consistent failure and personal loss. It was also the first year since 1919 that did not see a new Gershwin show on Broadway. He had spent the whole year on instrumental works, none of which had caught the popular fancy. His final project that year was a collection of piano transcriptions of eighteen of his most successful songs. Many of these pieces were impromptu variations he had played at parties. Some were fond tips of the hat to the styles invented by the ragtime and stride pianists he had idolized in his youth: Luckey Roberts, Zez Confrey, Les Copeland, and others. They were intricate, difficult piano pieces, many notated by Kay as George played them for her. He dedicated this work, entitled *George Gershwin's Songbook*, to her, just as Jimmy was making her the dedicatee of his second and final book of poetry, *Shoes and Ships and Sealing Wax*, written under his Paul James nom de plume.

There was another event in 1932: Rosamond Walling, at the age of twenty-two, married someone else. Just a year earlier George had written to her when she was in London, saying, "Often when I think of you I get the desire to fly over to where you are, swoop down like an eagle and steal you and bring you to a big rock on a mountain and there have you all to myself." But she had taken that line no more seriously than his more prosaic, "You could be good for my stomach."[17]

As bad as 1932 had been, 1933 was even worse. In January, George and Ira returned to Broadway in a venture they knew to be doomed. This was *Pardon My English*, which, as noted above, they wrote out of friendship for producers Aarons and Freedley. Its plot was about the marriage of an American kleptomaniac to the daughter of a German police commissioner. The script was filled with hoary, lewd gags tailored for the show's stars, each of whom had made a career out of mangling the English language. George was reduced now to composing specialty material for acts such as George Givoty (whose forte was a Greek accent), Jack Pearl (who was best known for repeating the German-inflected phrase "Vas you dere, Sheryl"), and Lyda Roberti (whose trademark was the odd way she pronounced the letter *h*, especially in the word "hot"). The comic dialogue by Herbert Fields (brother of songwriter Dorothy Fields) had such lame jokes as: "The coast is clear." "So who the hell cares about the weather in California?"[18]

When this show opened on January 20, 1933, it was panned by Broadway reviewers who were usually rapturous in their praise for George and Ira's songs. Brooks Atkinson of the *Times* dismissed the musical score as a collection of "Mr. Gershwin's blaring café tunes." In reference to the bawdier jokes, he wrote, "the smugness with which the dirt is sprinkled around draws attention to the odor."[19] This was quite a contrast to the welcome given *Of Thee I Sing* in 1931 when reviewers showed up in person at Kay's opening night party to read their raves. For *Pardon My English's* opening night, George and Ira both went home early, each complaining of a cold. The show did have some good music though. There was "Isn't It a Pity?" which eventually became a standard, and "Tonight," which was not published until 1971, and then as a piano piece entitled *Two Waltzes in C.* George and Kay loved to play it at two pianos. She would play the first waltz, he the second, and then they would play the two together. Ira called this charming concoction, "Her Waltz, His Waltz, Their Waltz."[20]

The fact that the two waltzes could be played simultaneously was no accident. Gershwin had finally found someone to teach him counterpoint. This was Russian-born pianist and physicist Joseph Schillinger, who had devised a mathematical system for manipulating rhythms and themes and who was giving George three lessons a week in form, counterpoint, and orchestration. Those lessons, which bore titles such as "Rhythmic Groups Resulting From the Interference of Several Synchronized Periodicities,"[21] delighted Gershwin, who completed them on graph paper and was able to use them in constructing polyphonic passages. He first did so in the melancholy section of the *Cuban Overture.* He would use these techniques in subsequent works, most importantly in *Porgy and Bess.*

With *Pardon My English,* the new year had gotten off to an even less auspicious start than 1932, whose initial failure, the *Second Rhapsody,* had at least been an ambitious one. But 1933 would see no new symphonic works, just one more attempt by the Gershwin brothers—their last, as it turned out—to regain their preeminence as writers of Broadway musical comedy. This was *Let 'Em Eat Cake,* the sequel to *Of Thee I Sing.* Unfortunately for ticket sales, it bore the same relationship to its predecessor as the *Second Rhapsody* had to the *Rhapsody in Blue.* Both sequels were darker, less playful, and unromantic. Where *Of Thee I Sing* had made fun of a presidential candidate running on a platform of love, *Let 'Em Eat Cake* got him mixed up in a fascist plot to take over the United States. Not that such material was untimely. When the show debuted in October 1933, the United States was in the deepest trough of its worst economic crisis, while American demagogues were arising from the left (Louisiana Senator Huey Long) and right (radio priest Father Coughlin), and fascist militarists were consolidating power in Germany, Italy, and Japan. Scriptwriters George S. Kaufman and Morrie Ryskind took these issues on but with an unappealing combination of morbidity and silliness. Where *Of Thee I Sing* had charmed audiences with a bumbling Vice President Throttlebottom who could not get the necessary personal references to qualify for a library card, in *Let 'Em Eat Cake*, they watched in horror as the charming fellow was led to the guillotine (albeit to some interesting Gershwin music).

There was another problem with *Let 'Em Eat Cake*. In *Of Thee I Sing*, even though there were entire scenes set to music that sounded more like Sir Arthur Sullivan than Gershwin, the best-known songs were in Gershwin's recognizable style. In *Let 'Em Eat Cake*, however, the only song in the Gershwin style was the breezy "Mine" (a double song with a countermelody, originally written as a Schillinger exercise). Otherwise, the emphasis was not on isolated tunes but on scenes. He was using this show as a testing ground for opera. The trouble was that it was lost on the audience. What they wanted was something immediately identifiable as Gershwin music, as the songs from *Of Thee I Sing* had been. Instead, they were offered proof that George and Ira were big fans of Gilbert and Sullivan. Reviewer Henry Taylor Parker advised, "Be yourself, George."[22]

Parker need not have worried. On October 17, 1933—four days before the premiere of *Let 'Em Eat Cake*—Gershwin had signed a contract with Heyward to write *Porgy and Bess*.

59

NINE

"Something Big"

Heyward had been thinking about opera since his initial meeting with Gershwin in 1926. His first post-*Porgy* novel, *Mamba's Daughters*, written in 1929, concluded with a scene that had the Met putting on the first all-black opera. When the soprano brings down the house with "Lift Every Voice and Sing," one member of the audience exclaims to another, "Can't you see it's new—different? Can't you feel it's something of our own—American—something . . . that Gershwin actually got his hands on in spots of *Rhapsody in Blue*."[1] The idea of writing such an opera would not leave him alone.

Thus, when he received Gershwin's letter of March 29, 1932, asking if he was still interested in a collaboration, he immediately telephoned to say yes and then he followed his verbal assent with a written confirmation on April 10. Six weeks later, he received George's disappointing reply, in which the composer said he could not begin work on the project any time soon. This left him frustrated and in a quandary. Gershwin was backing off again, and there was, it seemed, nothing to be done about it. That summer, however, Heyward heard from his agent, Audrey Wood, that Al Jolson was interested in doing a blackface musical version of *Porgy*. Jolson had been fascinated by the story for a long time. A few years earlier, he had done it on radio. Shortly after that, he had sought to star in a movie adaptation. He was the first great star of the talkies, having appeared in 1927's *The Jazz Singer*, which was the earliest feature length film to incorporate synchronized talking and music. For part of *The Jazz Singer*, Jolson sang in blackface. Thus, a filmed version of *Porgy* seemed to him a logical thing to do. He paid $30,000 for the film rights, and the Heywards accepted their share of this money, but Jolson could not get the picture made. Now he was returning to the idea of *Porgy*, but this time as a Broadway show.

Heyward tried to use this turn of events to scare George into making a commitment, but to his surprise, Gershwin greeted the news not just with equanimity but also with something more like relief. If Jolson was in, he was out—and, therefore, off the hook. As of the summer of 1932, he still did not feel ready to write an opera. Heyward, however, was convinced that he and Gershwin could create a masterpiece. A soft-spoken and unassuming man, much like Ira, he now resorted to some uncharacteristic conniving. He told George that Jolson's offer was tempting to him not just for financial reasons but because it might actually turn out to be interesting. "I cannot see brother Jolson as Porgy," he wrote, "but I have heard that he was casting about for something more artistic than his usual Sonny Boy line, and what his real potentialities are, I have very little idea."[2] In fact, as Heyward and Gershwin soon found out, Jolson was trying to bring Jerome Kern and Oscar Hammerstein II into the undertaking. If that happened, the resulting show might be very good, maybe something on the order of *Show Boat*, a musical play George greatly admired. Heyward told Gershwin that he would very much prefer working with him but that, given further hesitation, he would go with Jolson. Then he backpedaled, asking if the two of them might collaborate with Jolson. "Or," he added, "is that too preposterous?"[3]

To Gershwin that *was* preposterous. The idea of Jolson as Porgy in blackface seemed like an invitation to disaster. No matter how good the script was or how terrific the music, it would be *Blue Monday* again. And this time it was not going to be an inexpensive skit inserted into an otherwise profitable revue. This was going to be a major production requiring a lot of money—money from the backers, money from the ticket buyers, money that was not plentiful in the middle of the Depression. And he would be abandoning the one milieu where he was comfortable and where he still reigned supreme—Broadway musical comedy—for the highbrow world where he had found more scorn than praise. Moreover, this time his foray would not be into the concert hall, it would be into the opera house, where even the most successful of his highbrow contemporaries— Rachmaninoff, Ravel, Prokofiev—had had disappointments. It would also mean at least a temporary halt to a comfortable and proven partnership with his brother Ira, to collaborate with someone he hardly knew, who was not from New York or Jewish, and who had never before written a song lyric, much less a musical. When the critics had their say, they were not going to simply review it, they were going to pass judgment on his true worth as a composer—and the reviews would come from everywhere: from theater critics, music critics, opera critics. It would be *the* Gershwin opus that everyone had always known was coming. What if it failed? What then? He was in no hurry to hasten what might be the Waterloo of his career. "The sort of thing I have in mind for Porgy," he wrote Heyward on September 9, 1932, "is a much more serious thing than Jolson could ever do. Of course I would not attempt to write music to your play until I had all the themes and musical devices worked out for such an undertaking. It would be more a labor of love than anything else. If you can see your way to making some ready money from Jolson's version I don't know that it would hurt a later version done by an all-colored cast."[4]

To Heyward, this was both gracious and frustrating. Gershwin was obviously interested in doing *Porgy* as an opera—after all, he was the one who had conceived the idea in the first place—but he was ready to stand aside and allow a Jolson version to proceed, just as, in 1927, he had bowed out in favor of the stage play. Both times, he was, he said, doing this so the Heywards could earn a decent living. Though it is likely that generosity was a factor in his behavior, prudence was probably the larger motive. Oddly enough, when it came to visualizing the opera, should they write it, Gershwin had the firmer set of principles. He would not accept white actors portraying African Americans, especially not in blackface. He would not accept spoken dialogue. It would have to be sung throughout. Nor would he allow it to be called or advertised as a musical. It had to be labeled as an opera. Heyward was willing to compromise on all of these points but, then again, he was the one who was willing to actually write the show. To get a firm commitment, he traveled to New York for a face-to-face conversation. Did George have a producer in mind? If so, why not just sign a contract, preempt Jolson, and get to work? George told DuBose that he had sent out feelers to producers but was not interested in actually signing with any of them. His inclination was to find a production company *after* he wrote the opera—*if* he wrote it. Thus put off, Heyward returned to North Carolina convinced that George had decided against the venture and he gave his agent the go-ahead to talk to Jolson. He informed George of this in a letter dated October 17, 1932, explaining, "Upon my return here after my talk with you I learned of circumstances that have put me in a tight spot financially, and that alone has prompted me to write Miss Wood. Of course what I would like to be able to afford would be to wait indefinitely for your operatic version, and to work with you myself without the least thought of the commercial angle." He promised that he would not work on the Jolson musical, only sell the rights. And then he added, "Please let me tell you that I think your attitude in this matter is simply splendid. It makes me all the more eager to work with you some day, some time, before we wake up and find ourselves in our dotage."[5]

At that point, in October 1932, communications between the two men ceased. George went to work on *Pardon My English* and *Let 'Em Eat Cake*, while Heyward, awaiting further word from Jolson, accepted an assignment to write the screenplay for a film adaptation of Eugene O'Neill's play *The Emperor Jones*. O'Neill himself offered him the job, having admired the stage production of *Porgy*. In writing the screenplay, Heyward added new material to the story, including a crap game sequence such as the one that would be staged in *Porgy and Bess*. The film was not a box office success, but Heyward appreciated the salary. Next, he accepted another movie assignment, this time in Hollywood (filming for *The Emperor Jones* had been done on Long Island) working for Irving Thalberg at Metro-Goldwyn-Mayer on the screenplay for an adaptation of Pearl Buck's *The Good Earth*. He was picked for this assignment because to Hollywood's way of thinking, if a man could write about black people, then he could write about the Chinese as well. All the while, Jolson tried to get his idea of *Porgy* as a musical off the ground. But it did not work out for him. Heyward refused to have anything to do with the script, and then Kern and Hammerstein proved to be too busy with their own joint and separate projects.

It was in the summer of 1933, after the failure of *Pardon My English*, that George phoned Heyward to say, emphatically, that he had made up his mind and was ready for "something big."[6] Heyward did not believe him at first. But this time Gershwin was serious. Suddenly, it was settled. They would do it.

What had happened to change George's mind? On January 24, 1932, Paul M. Warburg died and it fell to Jimmy to get his father's business affairs in order. That meant spending most of the year in Hamburg working with the German wing of the family, whose bank, M. M. Warburg, was foundering. With James away, George and Kay were freer than ever to be together. Perhaps it was a coincidence but it was at this point that George became mainly a serious composer and only secondarily a pop songwriter. During these months, he wrote two orchestral works, a set of piano variations on eighteen songs (dedicated to Kay), and, in the summer of 1933, as he made the decisive phone call to Heyward, he was working on *Let 'Em Eat Cake*—a show in which he tried out the techniques he would have to master before proceeding to grand opera: choral sequences, leitmotifs, recitative. There was only one memorable tune, "Mine." It was one of just five songs in the score to be published, and none was conventional. The title song was a long march that moved from key to key and meter to meter. "On and On and On" was another march that became increasingly dissonant, even noisy. "Union Square" was a multisectional piece with a lyric written for downtrodden revolutionaries and a lilting middle section that quoted from Schubert's *C-Minor Quintet*. "Blue, Blue, Blue" could hardly have been expected to sell well: its lyric was about painting the White House blue, and its piano accompaniment looked like something that had escaped from a Rachmaninoff concerto. Only "Mine" had a chance at broad appeal, and it too was unusual, consisting of two separate melodic lines, sung individually at first and then in counterpoint. The rest of the music for the show was just as extraordinary. Its predecessor, *Of Thee I*

Sing, had opened with a presidential campaign song, "Wintergreen for President," that featured quotations from "The Stars and Stripes Forever," "Sidewalks of New York," and "Hail Hail the Gang's All Here" (by Sullivan). In the new show, the opening scene is again a presidential campaign rally, but this time a fellow named Tweedledee is running against incumbent Wintergreen, and after "Wintergreen for President" is played, the audience is given a new number, "Tweedledee for President," which incorporates quotations from other American favorites such as "The Battle Hymn of the Republic," "Over There," and "Dixie." Then, as if to show all of his critics that he really had learned a thing or two about counterpoint, Gershwin has two separate choruses simultaneously sing the two campaign songs with each "Wintergreen" section achieving congruence with each section of "Tweedledee." Even the quoted songs are sung in counterpoint, "The Stars and Stripes Forever" working just fine in conjunction with "Dixie." He felt more pride in his score for this show than in anything he had yet written for Broadway. It was, he said, his "claim to legitimacy."[7] When he was interviewed about *Let 'Em Eat Cake* just prior to its premiere, he made no attempt to whet the appetites of prospective ticket buyers by telling them how enjoyable it would be. Instead, he gave an off-putting technical analysis, as he had done with the *Cuban Overture*: "I've written most of the music for this show contrapuntally, and it is this very insistence on the sharpness of a form that gives my music the acid touch it has—which points the words of the lyrics, and is in keeping with the satire of the piece. At least, I feel that it is the counterpoint which helps me to do what I am trying to do."[8] He was talking about musical comedy here! But it was hardly an ordinary musical. *Let 'Em Eat Cake* had every ingredient that would go into *Porgy and Bess* except one: soul.

The first thing Gershwin and Heyward did after signing the contract was look for a producer, this despite George's protestations from a year earlier that he would like to write the work first and find a production company later. Getting down to business meant getting down to business. First, they weighed an offer from the Metropolitan Opera's Otto Kahn, who had been urging George for years to compose an opera and who now offered $5,000 for the privilege of allowing the Met to stage it. But nothing was said about the Met hiring black singers. Broadway's Theatre

Guild, on the other hand, had already produced the successful all-black stage version of *Porgy*. Heyward liked the Theatre Guild. Gershwin liked Broadway—where shows, unlike Met operas, did not run for just a few days but generally kept going as long as people kept buying tickets. It was a given that reviewers from all the newspapers would be present on opening night, no matter where opening night was. They might as well have that night on friendlier turf. Therefore, the contract was signed on October 17, 1933, with the Theatre Guild. On November 3, this was reported by the *New York Times,* which said that Gershwin would write the score, Heyward the libretto, and that Heyward and Ira would collaborate on the lyrics.[9] Ira, however, was not a signatory to the October 17 contract. He was at work on his own project, independent of George, a musical with Harold Arlen. Nevertheless, George and Heyward both wanted him close by. As for Kahn, he would not live to see the Gershwin opus he had so longed for. He died the following March of a heart attack at age sixty-seven.

Heyward preferred to work at home, so immediately after signing the contract in New York he returned to Hendersonville, North Carolina, and got to work. He had built a house there in 1928, bought with his and Dorothy's earnings from *Porgy* and with royalties from *Mamba's Daughters.* It was a stately two-story residence with double-decker verandas and a daily bath of morning sunlight that led them to name it Dawn Hill. Its construction had taken place during what turned out to be the Heywards' one brief period of prosperity. Shortly after it was finished, the stock market crash took most of their savings. In 1931, all three of Hendersonville's banks failed on the same day.[10] The Theatre Guild had not, unlike Kahn, offered an advance—in fact, Heyward had decided to join George and Ira as an investor in the opera—but with the contract in hand, he put everything else out of mind and began fashioning a libretto. He started with act I, scene I, paring away as much of the play's dialogue as possible but adding a new opening—he wanted the curtain to rise during the overture to reveal a man on stage (called Jasbo Brown after a character in one of his poems) playing a honky-tonk piano. He also wrote lyrics for the first time in his life: "Summertime," "A Woman Is a Sometime Thing," "Here Come De Honey Man," "They Pass by Singin'," and "Oh, Little Stars." On November 12, he sent scene I to George. Thus, in a little over three weeks, and with no prior experience as a songwriter, Heyward was well on his way to becoming, in Stephen Sondheim's words, "the author of the finest set of lyrics in the history of the American musical theater."[11]

In his November 12 letter, Heyward brought George up to date in several areas. He mentioned his idea for the opening, indicated his preference for spoken dialogue over sung recitative, and said that beginning on December 1, he and his wife and young daughter would be on Folly Island, off the South Carolina coast. The Heywards had recently purchased a place there—a "shack" Heyward called it—"to get back to the simplicities, and away from people."[12] On November 25, George wrote back to compliment him on the libretto thus far, saying he had done "a swell job, especially with the new lyrics." He was receptive to Heyward's conception of the opening but adamant about using recitative. He mentioned that he was planning a trip to Florida and wanted to stop off in Charleston where they could meet to discuss the work in progress and "see the town and hear some spirituals and perhaps go to a colored café or two if there are any."[13]

After spending some time with Heyward in Charleston, George traveled on to Palm Beach, Florida, where he vacationed at the home of his friend, the financier Emil Mosbacher. It was a working vacation, but the work was not *Porgy*. In typical Gershwin fashion, he had committed himself to a frenzied schedule over the next several months—one that did not seem to include any time for opera composing. At the request of an old friend, Harry Askins, he agreed to a partnership venture that would have him touring in January in celebration of the tenth anniversary of the *Rhapsody in Blue*. There would be twenty-eight concerts in twenty-eight cities in twenty-eight days. Moreover, he had also promised to write a new orchestral work for the tour. Thus, instead of composing *Porgy*, he was working on the *Variations on "I Got Rhythm"* for piano and orchestra. He finished a two-piano version of the piece in Palm Beach and worked on the orchestration back in New York. On January 6, 1934, he finished the score and dedicated it to Ira. It was a short, humorous piece, not without its complexities, based on the song that he, breaking the taboo about writers picking their best-loved brainchildren, readily acknowledged as his favorite. However, as he was composing the variations in Florida, he also wrote his first song for *Porgy*. Heyward's November 12 package had included a lullaby that began, "Summer time, an' the livin' is easy." It is not known if George set this to music or applied it to an already written tune. The fact that the original lyric, "Yo' Daddy's rich, chile, an yo' ma's good-lookin'," was changed to "Oh, your daddy's rich and your mama's good lookin'" may mean that the words were shaped to accommodate music that already existed. If that was the case, the editing was almost certainly done by Ira in New York, although he never sought to have his name attached to the song. In 1971, the great film composer Bernard Herrmann recalled Gershwin asking him to come over to "hear the song we now know as 'Summertime'—only it wasn't called 'Summertime' then."[14] That would indicate that the melody came first—although by that time Gershwin already had the lyric in hand. Not that any of this matters much. What counted was that George for the first time was working with a lyric that was more than a clever confection about infatuation. The baby to whom the mother, Clara, sings "With Daddy and Mammy standin' by" would lose both of his parents during the course of the opera. The lyric is serene yet it foreshadows the tragedies to come. Gershwin's accompanying harmonies are gentle but disturbing. He had created in this his first *Porgy* music what Heyward had created in his first lyric: a masterpiece. It was a good harbinger of things to come.

TEN

"Don't Make It Too Good, George!"

In the fall of 1933, George and Ira moved out of their adjoining apartments on Riverside Drive to East Seventy-second Street near Park Avenue on the Upper East Side, where they took apartments across the street from one another. This was as far as they would ever live apart, and it was as close as they ever got to having separate households. George's was a penthouse apartment consisting of fourteen rooms on two floors. He had changed decorating styles and was no longer interested in the *moderne* look or any one style but bought whatever furniture appealed to him.

The new place was even more sumptuous than the old one had been. There was a gymnasium, an art studio, a garden, and plenty of wall space for his growing art collection. For a piano studio, he had a replica made of his old song-plugger's cubicle. This apartment was his great extravagance, and he delighted in it—one could not visit him without getting the grand tour. It was also, he believed, a necessity, as he was continually going to parties at the homes of rich folk and wanted to reciprocate. Yet, as wealthy as he was, he still found it easy to be one of the boys. Duke Ellington remembered him at rehearsals of *Show Girl*, "dressed like a stagehand, who could get in the front or back stage door. In a sports shirt, with no tie, he would humbly take his place in the standing-room area. If you didn't know him, you would never guess that he was the great George Gershwin."[1] During the *Porgy and Bess* rehearsals, he would sit in the back of the darkened theater wearing an old hat and a tweed sports jacket, cracking peanut shells.[2] It was also during those rehearsals that he instructed the first Porgy, Todd Duncan, about what "I Got Plenty o' Nuttin'" was really about. It was not, as Duncan assumed, a happy-go-lucky song. "What you're doing," Gershwin said, "is making fun of us. You're making fun of people who make money and to whom power and position is very important."[3]

Gershwin was hoping that the upcoming concert tour would provide an infusion of cash that would tide him over during the writing of *Porgy*. Another source of income would be a twice-a-week radio program that he was set to host on NBC immediately after the tour ended. That would bring in a solid $2,000 a week. The concert tour was speculative; he was sharing its costs and, hopefully, its profits with promoter Askins. Shortly before the tour began bandleader Leo Reisman had to drop out due to a hip fracture and was replaced by Charles Previn. Thus, the ensemble's name was changed from Leo Reisman and His Orchestra to the Reisman Symphonic Orchestra. There were fifty-five pieces in the band, and Gershwin scored the *Variations on "I Got Rhythm"* specifically for it. This was good practice because he would be writing *Porgy* for a pit orchestra of similar size.

The concert schedule was grueling. Every evening for twenty-eight nights there was another show in another city. The performances were generally sold out, but some venues were too small to offer any chance of a profit. On January 24, when they played at the West High School Auditorium in Madison, Wisconsin, more than a thousand people were turned away.[4] Another problem occurred in Toronto where a hotel desk clerk refused to give Gershwin accommodations because he was Jewish. Paul Mueller, his valet, who was German, was welcome. According to a diary kept by Mueller, they ended up at the Royal York Hotel that night and found it to be a depressing place. It is not known if the Royal York was a second choice or if it had been the original choice and had finally relented and allowed

Gershwin to take a room. In any event, Gershwin did not make a fuss; as usual when faced with a slight, he just stepped around it.

The concert schedule was strenuous for everyone and herculean for George. Each night he played the *Concerto in F*, the *Rhapsody in Blue*, the *"I Got Rhythm" Variations*, as well as solo versions of "Fascinating Rhythm," "The Man I Love," "Liza," and "I Got Rhythm." He did this without showing any sign of fatigue—in fact, most evenings he could be found at post-concert parties playing the piano well into the night. It was not until many years later that someone remembered that it was during this period that he first complained of symptoms that were indicative of what, three years later, would be his fatal illness. Mitch Miller—later an executive at Columbia Records as well as the host of television's "Sing Along With Mitch"—was an oboist with the Reisman Orchestra. He remembered that after the train pulled into Detroit and as he was disembarking with George onto the platform, Gershwin said, "I smell burning garbage." Miller detected no such odor.[5] Apparently, this happened more than once. According to Miller, the composer was "constantly smelling garbage."[6] Had anyone thought much about this odd complaint—and no one did at the time—they would have considered it nothing more than hypochondria from a man who would without prompting keep people informed about the state of his digestive tract.

The concerts went well and were favorably received. Small-town critics oohed and aahed over having Gershwin in their midst, but they hardly noticed the new *"I Got Rhythm" Variations*. With recent reviews in mind, he had decided not to include the *Second Rhapsody* or the *Cuban Overture* on the program. In the end, the tour lost money, and he found himself $5,000 in the hole.

On the other hand, the radio program, called *Music By Gershwin*, was an unqualified success—this even though George read in a wooden manner from stilted scripts. The programs aired on Mondays and Fridays from 7:30 P.M. to 7:45 P.M. Each edition began with the orchestra playing "The Man I Love." Then came an orchestral arrangement of one of the composer's lesser-known works ("Limehouse Nights," "Cossack Love Song") followed by his "inside story" of how he had come to write one of his famous songs, which he would then play. After that, he would talk about

"Don't Make It Too Good, George!"

the work of some other composer, sometimes an established writer such as Kern, but often a young songwriter or concert composer who needed a plug. The orchestra would then serve up one of that composer's songs or instrumental compositions. The scripts were written by Finas Farr and Edward Byron, two writers from the William Esty agency, who visited George in his apartment, got his ideas about which songs to include, and wrote up the anecdotes he recounted to them. It was there that Byron met Kay, forming a friendship that would turn into something more a couple of years later. Kay was present not just for these conferences, but also for the rehearsals and the broadcasts themselves. When George returned to the air in the fall of 1934, it would be for a weekly half-hour show on CBS that featured live banter with guest composers. But during this first season on NBC, it was just Gershwin, the announcer, and the orchestra. Thus, the world missed its only opportunity to listen to George chat with Kay when, on April 6, he featured her music. "It isn't often that one finds a girl's name on successful music," he said that night. "However, there are one or two exceptions and I take great pleasure in asking the orchestra to play two songs by Kay Swift, who wrote all the music for *Fine and Dandy* and many other song hits. Miss Swift is a first-rate musician, and here's hoping she writes more tunes like the ones we are about to play: 'Can't We Be Friends,' from the *First Little Show* [*sic*], and the title song from *Fine and Dandy*."[7]

While Gershwin was on tour and then on the radio, Heyward was at Dawn Hill in North Carolina busily working on the *Porgy* libretto. George's non-*Porgy*-related activities were making Heyward impatient. He wanted the composer to come south so they could work together, while Gershwin tried to get Heyward to come north and stay in his apartment so they could collaborate George and Ira style. In a letter dated March 4, 1934, Heyward wrote to say that while listening to *Music by Gershwin* over the radio, he'd wanted to shout out, "Swell show, George but what the hell is the news about PORGY!!!"[8] This letter also contained the completed libretto for act II, scene III. He was more than halfway through the script and, so far as he knew, George had written next to nothing.

That was not so. Gershwin was not composing it straight through, but he was getting a feel for the work as a whole, plotting the music as Heyward had plotted the story. While DuBose fretted in North Carolina, George, having completed "Summertime," wrote the perpetual motion music of the orchestral introduction, "A Woman Is a Sometime Thing," Porgy's majestic first entrance, "They Pass by Singin'"(his lament about the lonely life of a cripple), Crown's commanding leitmotif, the fugue that would underscore the crap game as well as the two murders, Serena's harrowing "My Man's Gone Now," and Bess's joyous choral spiritual "Leavin' for the Promise Lan.'"

Ira had not yet been asked to work on *Porgy* and was using the interval to write songs with Harold Arlen for the upcoming Broadway show *Life Begins at 8:40*. But he was well aware of what his brother was writing, as was Arlen. At one point, as they worked, Arlen leaned out the window of Ira's apartment and jokingly shouted across the street, "Don't make it *too* good, George!"[9]

Kay was the one who was with George the most during this period. She was in his apartment as the music was written, not just listening and watching but helping with the notation, playing second piano as he worked out ideas for the orchestral accompaniments, and singing the melodies as he wrote them. Together, they tried out the duets. "I was forever at that second piano in his studio," she said many years later. 'Kay, you play the melody,' he would say, and as I played he would interpolate delicate counter-melody phrasings that seemed to orchestrate the work." Or he would call, "and tell me to rush over to play the orchestral part of a song. He couldn't sing. Neither could Ira. But we'd all sing Ira's or DuBose Heyward's lyrics sounding like a chorus of crows."[10] In April, Heyward came to New York as George had wanted him to, and Ira joined them. It was during one of these sessions that George, musing that Porgy needed a more light-hearted song, went to the piano and improvised "I Got Plenty o' Nuttin.'" Heyward watched this in amazement and then was doubly wowed when Ira immediately came up with the title as well as the answering line, "an' nuttin's plenty for me." He asked the brothers if he could try writing up the rest of the lyric—so far in his collaboration, he had written the words first and then George had set them to music. With George and Ira it was almost always the other way around. Thus, the song came to be written by all three men. Kay notated it as George played it for her at the piano.[11]

"Don't Make It Too Good, George!"

Many years later, when she was asked if she and George's other friends knew as it was being written that the opera would be a masterpiece, she replied that it was "like watching a pitcher who has a no-hitter going for him. He knows it and you know it; and, in the case of George Gershwin, as in that of the pitcher, nobody mentions the fact at the time."[12]

There was another woman who, like Kay, acted as a sounding board as the music took shape. In late 1933, shortly after the announcement was made that Gershwin was at work on an operatic version of *Porgy*, Anne Wiggins Brown, a willowy twenty-year-old Juilliard student, wrote him to ask if he might consider her for a role. Despite her youth and lack of stage experience, she got an audition. She was invited to his apartment one rainy day, was admitted by the butler, and was looking in the foyer for a place to stow her boots when George appeared and introduced himself. At that moment, she was checking out the area by the coat rack. When he asked her what she was looking for she joked, "Your roller skates."[13] For a moment, he did not get it but when he did he threw his head back in laughter. Anyone who had read up on him would know that he had been, as he liked to tell interviewers, roller skating champion of Seventh Street. She had obviously taken the time to do some research.

So began a professional association that was also a warm friendship— although the audition got off to a rocky start. After Brown sang an aria by Massenet as well as German lieder, Russian songs, and "The Man I Love,"[14] George asked for a Negro spiritual. "I was very much on the defensive at that age," she recalled. "I resented the fact that most white people thought that black people should or could only sing spirituals. 'I am very sorry,' I said, 'but I haven't any of *that* music with me.' And then I broke out, 'Why is it that you people expect black singers to sing spirituals?'"[15]

George Gershwin simply looked long at me and he said, "Ah huh, I understand." And I realized that he *did* understand and then I wanted more than anything else to sing a spiritual for him. How dumb I had been! Wasn't this to be an opera about Negroes? "I didn't bring any accompaniment for a spiritual," I said, "but I could sing one without accompaniment if you would like." "Oh, yes, please do," he said. So I sang a spiritual, "A City Called Heaven." And when I finished I knew that I had never sung it better nor would I ever sing it better. Instead of the half hour I had expected to be there, I stayed nearly two hours. George played as much of *Porgy and Bess* as had been written, including "Summertime," with which I was completely fascinated. He sang all the parts himself and then he asked me to sing "Summertime." It was not a difficult melody and it just rolled out of my throat, and he was very pleased.[16]

During the spring of 1934, as *Porgy* was being written, Anne Brown, like Kay, was constantly called to the Gershwin apartment to try out something he had just written. She was there to sing the arias for all the principal female characters, and they sang the duets together, he in a voice she described as "like a nutmeg grater." Each found the other endearing. She advised him on singers' ranges, how long high notes could be sustained, and which portions of the opera in progress she liked the most. During this period, he did not tell her if she had been chosen for a part in the production. She would come over; they would have lunch. He would occasionally "invite me into his bed";[17] she—a married woman—would always politely refuse, and they would continue on with no hard feelings. This went on for many weeks until finally, over lunch, he offered her the role of Bess. A little while later, he asked her to lunch again. He had another surprise for her. In the opera, "Summertime" was sung not by Bess but by Clara. He told her that he had rewritten part of act III so that she, as Bess, could reprise it.

At 7:45 P.M. on May 18, 1934, NBC announcer Ed Johnson told the *Music by Gershwin* radio audience: "Friends, we'd like to announce that this is the last of the current series of programs featuring George Gershwin. The programs will of course be resumed early in the fall after the vacation period. *And* I want to say right here that the folks who made this broadcast possible—Feen-a-mint—are extending congratulations to George Gershwin for what they feel was a really brilliant series of programs. Yes, sir—and the sponsors are wishing George a very happy vacation and a world of success in the new American opera which he is writing."[18]

On June 16, George, accompanied by his cousin Henry Botkin, boarded a train at Penn Station bound for South Carolina.

ELEVEN

Kay, Jimmy, and FDR

Kay and Jimmy were at this point in completely different worlds. After his father's death in January 1932, he had found it necessary not only to manage his family's U.S. finances, but also to go to Hamburg to deal with troubles besetting M. M. Warburg and Company, which, as run by his uncle Max, was heading toward insolvency. When Jimmy returned to New York in late 1932, Franklin D. Roosevelt had just been elected president. Warburg wanted to know how the new administration would handle the nation's escalating economic emergency. The banking system had failed, mortgages were being called in, the jobless rate was at 25 percent, and the United States was sliding into a barter economy. Warburg wanted Roosevelt to keep his campaign promises to balance the budget and support a strong noninflationary dollar. To get a sense of how things would be, he met with the president-elect's eldest son, James Roosevelt—an old friend—and with Raymond Moley, a former Columbia law professor who had become one of FDR's key advisors and a member of his soon to be famous "brain trust." Roosevelt's men were vague in response to Jimmy's questions, but they were impressed by him. Here was a straight-talking young man with intelligence, good humor, and excellent connections to Wall Street. Several days later, Moley asked him to work for the incoming administration on an agenda for the upcoming London World Economic Conference. Toward that end, in February 1933, Warburg met with FDR himself, who joked, "Ray Moley tells me that you are the white sheep of Wall Street."[1] Jimmy joked back that that had been his father's title and that white sheep did not necessarily beget white lambs. In a few months, his actions would bear this out—at least in Roosevelt's eyes—but for the moment he was one of the new president's favorites.

The day after the inauguration, FDR declared a "bank holiday" to stop what had become a nationwide run on the country's savings institutions. Warburg was asked to help devise the system by which the banks would be allowed to reopen—a task he handled so well that in mid-March 1933, a pleased FDR offered him the job of undersecretary of the treasury. This was a huge opportunity. Apparently, he was being groomed for a significant government career. Being well connected to the Democrats in power as well as to the Republicans on Wall Street, he was a rarity, and his prospects at that moment were very bright. But, he declined the offer. He did not want to have to divest himself of shares in the institutions he would be overseeing. Not that anyone was asking him to sell his stocks, but he felt that his integrity would be suspect should he fail to do so. Given the condition of the economy, any such sale would have resulted in a substantial loss with a resulting decline in his wealth and living standard. He chose instead to work for the administration without a salary and without a job title. That meant moving to Washington, where he took up residence at the Carlton Hotel. He came home to New York on weekends, but Kay was rarely around.

Then came a series of events that soured him on the New Deal. In April 1933, the president took the nation off the gold standard. Warburg believed, as had his father, that this would lead to disaster and he said so to Roosevelt, calling the policy harebrained and irresponsible.[2] Shortly thereafter, while he was at the World Economic Conference in London presenting the administration's plan to stabilize world currencies, the president undercut him by suddenly reversing his anti-inflation policies. Roosevelt had belatedly realized that currency stabilization would work against his goal of promoting higher farm prices, and he took what to James looked like a foolish, precipitous step. In return, Warburg made a precipitous move of his own, submitting his resignation on July 6, 1933—from a job that had no title and no pay—with a threat to campaign against the administration's policies. Roosevelt was not without a temper or a vindictive streak but there was something about young Warburg that made him indulgent or, at least, slow to anger. The fact was he respected the banker's judgment. In early 1934, he reversed course again, setting the price of U.S. currency at a solid thirty-five dollars per ounce of gold. In a conciliatory gesture, he invited Jimmy to meet with him at the White House, where they spent a

pleasant evening together. Roosevelt praised the deft way Warburg had, in public letters, taken on fascist radio priest Father Coughlin—undermining the demagogue's credibility by debunking his economic policies while avoiding a frontal attack on his virulent anti-Semitism, which might have appeared self-serving.

Despite this cordial meeting, Warburg refused to be reconciled with the president. In fact, he went on an anti-Roosevelt tear. He rebelled against him more vigorously than he had ever rebelled against his father. He stood up to him in a way that he had never stood up to Kay or George. While on a Caribbean cruise, he wrote a book, *The Money Muddle*, which he published under his real name, blasting the administration for its financial policies. Brashly, he sent a prepublication copy to the president, who replied with the following letter:

> Dear Jimmy—
>
> I have been reading *The Money Muddle* with plenty of interest.
>
> Someday I hope you will bring out a second edition—but will you let an old friend make a special request of you before you do it? Please get yourself an obviously second-hand Ford car; put on your oldest clothes and start west for the Pacific Coast, undertaking beforehand not to speak on the entire trip with any banker or business executive (except gas station owners), and to put up at no hotel where you have to pay more than $1.50 a night. After you get to the Coast go south and come back via the southern tier of States. . . . When you have returned re-write *The Money Muddle* and I will guarantee that it will run into many

GEORGE GERSHWIN

more editions! After the above insulting "advice to a young man"—do nevertheless run down and see me some day.

Always sincerely,

Franklin D. Roosevelt[3]

The president now saw Jimmy as a representative of the privileged rich, and Jimmy saw FDR as a budding dictator. He was shortly to publish more anti-Roosevelt books, including one, *New Deal Noodles* (again, using his real name), that ridiculed the president in verse. It was a period of resentment in his life, due not only to his disillusionment with the Democratic administration, but also to the complete deterioration of his marriage. In all ways except on paper, Kay had divorced him, while in all ways except the legal one, she had married Gershwin. The Warburg children were appropriately confused by this and, in the case of the eldest, April, now fifteen years old, deeply bitter. The question of a divorce was at long last coming to a head.

For Kay the problem was that her love for George—white-hot now as he wrote his grand opera—was, though not unrequited, not exactly returned in full either. He did not speak to her of marriage. Nor did he show the slightest inclination toward monogamy. Life to him was high adventure and women were a big part of that adventure. But bigger yet was music, and he was presently on the greatest adventure of his life, writing music of such power that he himself was taken aback. Great musical ideas had come to him throughout his life, but never before had they come in such profusion and for a project for which his ideas, vocal and instrumental, could grow as one and be so serious of purpose. All the strands in his musical life were knitting themselves together: melodies that soared and despaired, rhythms that jarred and thrilled, harmonies that were spicy and soulful. This music was lavished on soloists, chorus, and orchestra in service of a story guaranteed to bring tears of happiness and sorrow. He had always suspected that he could do this. Kay had always known it.

What she did not know was whether she and George had a future together. One option was to divorce Jimmy to make herself available. But, it was all too predictable that, should she do that, Gershwin would expect to continue on as before. That would be easy enough for him but not so easy for her. The social and financial comforts that went with being a Warburg would no longer be hers. Should she sue, she would not be getting—or even asking for—a big settlement. It was she, after all, who, in having the very public affair with George, had humiliated Jimmy, and although she hardly regretted her time with Gershwin, she was not without guilt about what she had done to her husband and daughters. The girls had been brought up in what was, to say the least, a baffling environment. A divorce might well set Kay permanently adrift not just from her social standing and income, but also from April, Andrea, and Kathleen. In all likelihood, Gershwin would remain disinclined to marry her. It was at around this time that Oscar Levant, seeing the two of them together, quipped, "Here comes George Gershwin and the future Miss Kay Swift."[4]

To sort all this out she turned to a psychiatrist. He was Dr. Gregory Zilboorg, whose opulent office on East Seventy-fifth Street had become a magnet for many in New York's artistic community. Dr. Zilboorg was a short, bespectacled fellow with a bristly mustache, a domineering personality, and a colorful background. He had been born in Kiev in 1890. He was of Jewish parentage but had converted to Christianity, first as a Quaker, later as a Catholic. During the world war, he had been a physician in the czar's army. With the February 1917 revolution, he became a minister in the Kerensky government. A few months later, when the Bolsheviks took over, he immigrated to America where he at first earned a living in literature by translating plays (he was a gifted linguist) and writing a book (*The Passing of the Old Order in Europe*). Then he received his MD from Columbia's College of Physicians and Surgeons, joined the staff of New York's Bloomingdale Hospital, and started a private practice as a Freudian analyst. He was not the most ethical of men. He took pleasure in revealing to some of his patients what others of his analysands were saying. Kay may not have known this before she began seeing him (she had been referred to him by Jimmy's sister Bettina, herself a psychiatrist), but she certainly became aware of it shortly thereafter when the doctor added Jimmy to his roster and then, not long after that, George as well.

The doctor advised her not to get a divorce. In fact, he insisted. According to one account, Zilboorg was so adamant that Kay and George not marry that he threatened to turn George *and* Jimmy against her if she went ahead with the divorce.[5] In another, he threatened to state publicly what George and Kay had told him as his patients if they went so far as to marry one another.[6] It seems hard to believe that any doctor—even one with Zilboorg's pinched ethics—could have considered going public about his patients' confidences without knowing that it would immediately destroy his own career. Yet he was not above having sexual relations with Kay during her office visits, telling her it was part of her therapy.[7] Apparently, those encounters took place despite the fact that Kay found him singularly unattractive, and they happened during the final six months of her eighteen months of therapy, in early 1936, which was more than a year after her divorce and months after George had stopped his analysis. Kay could not have been having sex with Zilboorg as a means of gathering intelligence on George, because the doctor no longer had any inside information to report to her. Yet, it is hard to imagine a woman of Kay's intelligence accepting the doctor's advances as a legitimate tactic of psychotherapy. Nor is it known just why, back in 1934, Zilboorg had inveighed so strongly against a George-Kay marriage. Possibly, he was speaking on Warburg's behalf. However, when the latter wrote his autobiography in 1964, he said that he had been all for the divorce, that it had, in fact, been his idea.[8] This is not hard to believe, given the state of his marriage and the fact that he remarried very soon after the split became final at the end of 1934. Perhaps Dr. Zilboorg was speaking for George. No doubt Gershwin was more comfortable with Kay being married than with the prospect of her as unattached and available. Although he is known to have spoken to friends about marrying her, he was also wary. His mother continued to be a formidable obstacle. She disliked Kay and the feeling was mutual. Nor could Kay and Leonore stand each other. His marrying Kay would have undoubtedly resulted in serious family tensions, and George had always been dependent on family togetherness and solidarity. Moreover—and probably more important—there was Kay's family to consider. Of her children, the younger girls, Andrea and Kathleen, had come to like him, especially Andrea. But the eldest, April, despised him. She was, so far as is known, the only person who ever met George Gershwin who hated him. He must have found this completely unnerving. In the end, all these reasons may have factored into his decision not to marry Kay, along with

Kay, Jimmy, and FDR

the simple, fundamental fact that he found it impossible to dissemble and knew that, should he marry, he would inevitably give in to temptation, break his marriage vows, and find himself living a lie.

In the fall of 1934, Kay decided to go ahead and file for a divorce. "I had a happy career, was fond of my husband, had three children," she told an interviewer many years later. "Everything seemed all right. But I didn't like being in love with somebody else while I was married."[9] At the same time as her decision to file for divorce came the resumption of her career as a composer. In late 1933, choreographer George Balanchine, whose fame had been established in the preceding decade with the Ballets Russes in Paris and the Ballets Russes de Monte Carlo, came to America at the urging of arts philanthropist Lincoln Kirsten, to form an American ballet company in New York. Preparatory to that, he founded a School of American Ballet, which, in 1934, performed several original Balanchine works. One of them, *Alma Mater*, had a plot by another of the company's financial backers, Edward Warburg, who was an old friend of Kirsten and a first cousin of James Warburg. The plot satirized the rah-rah days of 1920s Ivy League football teams. Balanchine wanted Gershwin to write the music, and Eddie asked him if he was interested but he turned the assignment down, as he was too busy with the opera. He recommended Kay instead. Eddie knew Kay well, of course, and liked her and her music. The fact that she and Jimmy were headed for divorce court did not bother him. It is likely that he knew all about their private lives, inasmuch as he too was a patient of Dr. Zilboorg. So it was that during the summer of 1934 she was working on her first composition in four years, as George headed for South Carolina.

TWELVE

The Heart of American Music

They were called Gullahs, a West African word perhaps derived from the name of their country of origin, Angola. They had been brought in chains to the coastal islands of South Carolina and Georgia, where they lived separately from mainland slaves and maintained a language all their own, a mixture of various African dialects and seventeenth-century English. Folly Island, eight miles off the Charleston coast, is a six-mile long, half-mile wide barrier island (so called because it bears the brunt of Atlantic storms, shielding the mainland) with wide stretches of beach and an interior jungle. Heyward's cottage there was a comfortable house surrounded by pine and palmetto trees, just a short stroll from the surf. In anticipation of Gershwin and Botkin's arrival, he had rented a separate, smaller cottage across the street. Thus, Gershwin moved from his opulent penthouse at 132 East Seventy-second Street to a four-room shack with a front porch that faced the sand, the surf, and an endless swarm of mosquitoes. The island, once a haven for pirates, was a primitive place. Alligators rumbled from the swamps. Sand crabs crawled at will over Gershwin's cot and sink.

Potable water arrived daily in five-pound earthen jars—or one could, as an alternative, swig the local "Hell Hole Swamp" corn whiskey. There was not a single telephone on the island. Not that George was entirely without the comforts of home. He had brought his valet, Paul Mueller, who had, in turn, brought Gershwin's Buick and painting gear. George did as much painting as composing during his stay on the island, turning out one canvas after another. One watercolor, entitled "My Studio—Folly Beach," captured the look of his workroom; so unlike his New York lodgings, it more resembled Van Gogh's room at Arles.

His stay there lasted from mid-June into July. During that time, he spent his hours working at a rented upright piano and at his easel, swimming in—and sometimes driving his car through—the Atlantic surf, counting turtle eggs (one nest on the beach had 160), futilely hunting by day for the source of the crickets that kept him awake at night, sitting on the porch in the evening—it was enclosed, and bugs regularly crashed into the window and then fell sizzling to the sand—with cousin Henry and valet Paul. They discussed, as George put it in a letter to Emily, "our two favorite subjects, Hitler's Germany [and] God's women."[1] There were occasional visits to Charleston, where he played the piano for society folk. But the main activity was the composition of *Porgy*, and he was well aware of just how good things were going. One day, as he was playing his latest creations, he noticed that Dorothy Heyward was heading out the door, on her way to Charleston. Astonished that she would leave at such a time, he asked her to stay and "listen to the greatest music ever composed in America."[2] The qualifier "in America" shows that this was said with at least a little humility. It also made the statement true. On another occasion, he invited two friends of the Heywards, a young widow, Mrs. Joseph I. Waring, and her mother, to come have dinner with him at his place. After the meal, he said to them: "Now I'm going to play these pieces for you that no one has ever heard before. I want you always to remember that you were the first to hear these songs. DuBose hasn't even heard them. You will someday be very proud of this, because this is going to be a classic, it's going to be terrific, something wonderful." On the way home Mrs. Waring's mother exclaimed, "That is the most conceited man I've ever known in my life." To which her daughter—whom Gershwin was trying without luck to romance—replied, "You know, I think he's right."[3] When a reporter from the Charleston *News and Courier* came to the island to interview him, Gershwin explained that he was attempting "to put into operatic form a purely American theme" and that if he was successful it would "resemble a combination of the drama and romance of *Carmen* and the beauty of *Meistersinger*, if you can imagine that."[4] This time he went beyond America for comparisons, although again a qualifier ("if you can imagine that") mitigated the hubris.

Despite all the distractions—the widow, the beach, the turtles, golf, his watercolors, the beauty pageant he was asked to judge—it was a time devoted to music. He and Heyward visited churches and schools in the area, especially on James Island, a few miles west of Folly Beach. South Carolina had been the first state to secede from the union, and it was from James Island that the Confederates had fired on Fort Sumter, beginning the Civil War. At one point, Gershwin found himself at a school playing the piano for black children under a painting of Robert E. Lee.[5] In a letter to a friend in New York—an amour named Kay Halle—he mentioned being ill at ease among southern whites who, he said, "are still talking about the war—the Civil War."[6] But he was completely at home among the Gullah population. Back in New York he had, despite a well-deserved reputation for extroversion, always maintained a certain reserve and wariness and was a careful shepherd of his dignity. When a friend was driving too aggressively for his taste, he leaned forward and said, "Careful, man, you have Gershwin in the car."[7] Wherever he went, and under whatever circumstances he found himself, he was always alert to maintain his poise because *he* always had "Gershwin in the car." Here in South Carolina, however, he allowed himself more slack. When visiting churches—these were mainly one-room shacks called praise houses—he did not hesitate to join in as the congregation sang and clapped their hands and engaged in a local ritual called shouting. It was an activity that involved not just the voice but also the slapping of one's chest, knees, and thighs in complex rhythmic patterns. It was a descendant of the "Pattin' Juba" dance that had been developed in the wake of the prohibition against drums, put into effect after slaveholders realized that blacks could communicate with one another—and, perhaps, foment rebellion—through rhythm. This love of intricate patterns was right up

The Heart of American Music

Gershwin's alley. In one church, he got into a contest with the champion shouter and, in Heyward's words, "stole the show" from this fellow to the "huge delight" of everyone in the congregation. "I think he is probably the only white man in America who could have done it," Heyward wrote.[8] Anne Brown, remembering how Gershwin described this to her, said that "after he had out-shouted the best of them, an old man clapped him on the back and said, 'By God, you can sure beat out them rhythms, boy. I'm over seventy years old and I ain't never seen no po' little white man take off and fly like you. You could be my own son.'"[9] This was nearly twenty years after Gershwin, as a kid in Harlem, had amused Luckey Roberts and Eubie Blake by daring to trade piano licks.

In Hendersonville, where he stayed at Dawn Hill for a period in July, he was taken by Heyward to a church service in a cabin out in the North Carolina hills. As they were about to enter, Gershwin stopped and held Heyward back. Rather than go inside he stood at the door listening. The music from this nighttime service in the middle of nowhere consisted, as Heyward later wrote, "of perhaps a dozen voices raised in loud rhythmic prayer. The odd thing about it was that while each started at a different time, they formed a clearly defined rhythmic pattern and that this, with the actual words lost, and the inevitable pounding of the rhythm, produced an effect almost terrifying in its primitive intensity."[10] To a writer the sound may have been primitive. But to Gershwin it was what he had for so long been looking and striving for: American counterpoint. Back in 1930 he had told a reporter that perhaps it had been "kind fate" that decreed that he not write *The Dybbuk*. "Who knows," he told his interviewer, "but that it will result in my using an American effort in composing my opera."[11] Now here, in southern black churches, he had arrived at the heart of American music. For act II of *Porgy and Bess*, he would emulate what he heard in Hendersonville, writing a multipart prayer to convey the feelings of people huddled together to face the onslaught of a hurricane.

THIRTEEN

Kay's Divorce

Back in New York in mid-July, the first thing on his agenda was getting ready for the second season of *Music by Gershwin*. Again the scripts were by Farr and Byron, who worked on them with George in his apartment. The novelty of the new program was that it featured in-studio guests. Thus, radio audiences could tune in to CBS at 6:00 P.M. on Sunday nights and hear Gershwin chatting with Harold Arlen (they discussed and played selections from the Arlen/Ira Gershwin show *Life Begins at 8:40*, then running successfully on Broadway); Billy Hill (composer of "Last Round-Up"); Dana Suesse (sometimes called "The Girl Gershwin" because she wrote symphonic pieces as well as songs; her best-remembered tune is "You Ought to Be in Pictures"); the songwriting team of Dorothy Fields and Jimmy McHugh ("I Can't Give You Anything but Love, Baby"); Herman Hupfeld ("As Time Goes By"); Milton Ager ("Happy Days Are Here Again"); Rube Bloom ("The Peanut Vendor"); Ray Henderson ("Varsity Drag"); composer Harold Spina and his lyricist Johnny Burke ("The Beat of My Heart"); Hoagy Carmichael (who sang his song "Judy" on the program); and Richard Rodgers (who played a piano version of—but did not sing—"Lover"). On other shows, Gershwin featured the music of Arthur Schwartz, Victor Herbert, and Cole Porter. On one program, he demonstrated the styles of the ragtime pianists he had admired as a youth, reminiscing about how he had once stood outside a café on Coney Island listening to Les Copeland play. There was plenty of Gershwin music too, much of it obscure material from his early days.

On the penultimate show, which aired on December 16, 1934, he had two in-studio guests. Richard Rodgers was one. The other was his sister Frankie, who sang "My Cousin in Milwaukee" from *Pardon My English* to George's piano accompaniment. She also sang two songs by brother Arthur (accompanied by the orchestra). Arthur was the Gershwin sibling who never seemed to get any traction. He had tried his hand, without success, as a stockbroker. Now he was about to become an equally unsuccessful songwriter. As for Frankie, she had done well enough in an intermittent singing career, and then, in 1930, against her mother's wishes, had married Leopold Godowsky, Jr., son and namesake of one of the twentieth century's great pianists. Leo, Jr., did not at first seem to be much of a prospect. He was a so-so violinist and a would-be inventor. He seemed so unpromising to Rose that she attributed her asthma to her distaste for him. Leo never did amount to much in the music world, but in 1935, he and his piano accompanist, Leopold Mannes, invented the Kodachrome color film process, which brought him all the wealth and position Rose could have hoped for.

On December 23, George told his listening audience that they were hearing his final program. This was so, he explained, because he was "finishing the composition of my first opera based on the book *Porgy* by DuBose Heyward and the task of orchestrating this work will require my time for three or four months."[1] Calling it his *first* opera meant that *Blue Monday* was not to be considered a part of the canon, and that he intended to write more operas after *Porgy*.

During the fall season of *Music by Gershwin*, Kay was constantly at George's side. Over the summer, there had been an interregnum in their relationship, as she had not gone with him to South Carolina. Living with him in an island shack would have been a very public declaration of their affair as well as a step into bohemian life that neither was prepared to take. Instead, she spent the summer of 1934 working on her ballet, *Alma Mater*. It was an ambitious undertaking—a twenty-minute piece of sustained concert music. Kay was unable to attend the first performance, which took place on December 6 in Hartford, Connecticut. She was in Reno, Nevada, waiting out the six-week residency period necessary for her divorce. Thus, she missed the premiere—her first in four years and the first ever of one of her concert works. People present for *Alma Mater*'s opening night included Katharine Hepburn, Salvador Dali, and Gershwin, who had journeyed to Hartford on a train with others from New York, bringing along an ample supply of champagne. It was emblematic that Kay, who had made parties for all of his premieres, missed hers, while he managed to be there and have a good time without her. Later that evening, he phoned to tell her that her ballet had been a success.

By that point, she had been in Nevada more than a month and had less than two weeks to go before her divorce was final. She had traveled west with her longtime friend Mary Reinhardt, who was also seeking a divorce. Kay and Mary tried to enjoy themselves. They stayed at the stately Riverside Hotel, which was the traditional lodge for wealthy divorce seekers. It offered suites designed for long-term stays, complete with kitchens. They rode horses, made side trips to San Francisco and Los Angeles (in Los Angeles, they caught the new Astaire/Rogers film, entitled, fittingly for them, *The Gay Divorcee*),[2] and visited the Truckee Bridge to engage in a Reno tradition—throwing their wedding rings into the Truckee River.[3]

In the following months, there were several additional performances of *Alma Mater*, including one on Broadway. But the music excited little interest in either the classical or popular music communities. Certainly, it was no source of income for Kay who was now on her own and in reduced circumstances. Although she was divorcing a very wealthy man, she received next to nothing from him in the settlement. Nor had she sought much, believing that doing so would have been improper because she was the main culprit in the break-up.[4] The court granted her custody of the girls, but she generously allowed a joint guardianship. Before long, the children were spending most of their time with their father, because that allowed them to continue living at home, as he had retained the New

York townhouses and Bydale. Moreover, he quickly remarried—just three months after the divorce became final—and they found it more homey to be with their father and stepmother than with their mother, who was now living alone in a small apartment on Eighty-sixth Street near the East River. Warburg's new wife was Phyllis Baldwin Browne, who had divorced Jimmy's friend Gilbert Browne. The new Mrs. Warburg proved to be a good stepmother to the children—at least to the younger two; the eldest, April, quickly went off on her own.

Phyllis was from an upper class Protestant family, and through her, Jimmy made the Social Register. At that point, he ended all connections to Judaism, eschewing not only Jewish holidays but Jewish friends and, eventually, going so far as to show displeasure when two of his daughters chose to marry Jewish men. Given that his parents had been unhappy when he married outside the Jewish faith, this made for quite an irony, as did the fact that Kay's principal source of income now came from the generosity shown her by those very same in-laws, who had, upon her marriage to their son, set her up with an independent, if insubstantial, trust fund.

She now had to think about earning her own keep, even as she continued on with George, making the rounds among the rich and famous. Her return to New York coincided with the holiday season, and she spent Christmas Eve not with her children but with Gershwin. They were both consumed with *Porgy*, whose music was nearly finished except for the orchestrations, and on Christmas Eve, they decided on the spur of the moment to go over to Richard Rodgers's apartment and play the score for him. Rodgers and his wife Dorothy were expecting their second child. It had been a difficult pregnancy for Dorothy, who was confined to bed. Nevertheless, George and Kay arrived without notice, bubbling and eager to play the score—more than three hours of music. Rodgers later wrote about the occasion, remembering how George and Kay arrived "like two irrepressible magi"[5] and that he and George carried Dorothy from her bed to the living room, where Gershwin played and—despite the cigar in his mouth—sang the entire score at the piano by the Christmas tree (Rodgers, born Jewish, was as assimilated as Warburg).

It is interesting to speculate about why George chose Rodgers to pop in on. Rodgers and Kay had been friends for a long time, and Rodgers had just the week before been on Gershwin's radio program. So the contacts were ongoing and the two men were friendly. In truth, though, Rodgers was the only one of Gershwin's great Broadway contemporaries who was a real rival. He had a distinct vision of where the Broadway musical was going and how to get it there. He and Larry Hart were gradually turning old-fashioned musical comedy, with its thin plots, chorus lines, and comedians, into the musical play. George and Ira had also been moving in that direction, most successfully with *Of Thee I Sing*. But their three political operettas were zany comedies by George S. Kaufman, who had also worked on Marx Brothers scripts. Rodgers was after weightier fare. His goal was to connect the idiom of American popular song to real drama, as had been done seven years earlier in *Show Boat*. Jerome Kern, the composer of *Show Boat*, had shown no sustained interest in such projects. Oscar Hammerstein, who had written *Show Boat*'s book and lyrics, was still very much interested in the idea, but did not as yet have the right partner. In the early 1940s, as Larry Hart, an alcoholic, became dysfunctional and then mortally ill, Rodgers and Hammerstein would find each other and usher in the era of the American musical, beginning with *Oklahoma!* in 1943. In the 1930s, Gershwin was just as anxious as Rodgers to create an indigenous style of high-class Broadway musical, but he was going the opera route. He was adamant about orchestrating his new work himself (had Wagner or Bizet ever hired an arranger?) and that it be sung all the way through, which meant using recitative. Rodgers never had and never would orchestrate his music. As for recitative, he felt that George's insistence on it was a blunder. Many years later, he wrote that George "made a mistake in writing *Porgy and Bess* as an opera, because I truly do not think it worked as such when the Theatre Guild produced it in 1935."[6] We do not know if he expressed these misgivings to George and Kay on Christmas Eve 1934. But, whatever was said, the reality was that one man held the future of Broadway in his hands while the other was on a quixotic, if far more ambitious, quest.

On December 29, 1934, George went to the White House. He was not accompanied by Kay—or, at least, not by Kay Swift. His date for the evening was Kay Halle, a slim, blonde, thirty-year-old heiress from Cleveland. She had been the intermission commentator for the Cleveland Orchestra's radio broadcasts when George met her after a concert there. Now she was living at the Hotel Elysée off Park Avenue in New York, where she was romanced by Winston Churchill's son Randolph as well as by the elder Churchill's future nemesis Joseph P. Kennedy (JFK's father). She was also a good friend of President Roosevelt, having campaigned for him in 1932. The president had said to her some months earlier, "Kay, there's one thing you could do for me. Could you bring George Gershwin to our New Year's party at the White House?" Roosevelt was, she recalled many years later, "George's hero, and when I told George about the invitation, I thought he was going to faint. . . . I remember that when I met George and brought him from the diplomatic entrance to the main lobby, he stood under the chandelier and said to me, 'If only my father could see me now.'"[7] That evening Gershwin played the piano for the president (the selections inevitably included "Wintergreen for President"), and some who were there recalled seeing FDR's crippled legs bounce in time to the music.

Two nights later, on New Year's Eve, George was back with Kay Swift again. They and her recently divorced friend Mary and Mary's date went to a nightclub to wait it out until midnight. Had Kay stuck with Jimmy and had Jimmy stuck with Roosevelt, they might well have become a Washington power couple. But Kay wanted to be with George, come what may. Mary remembered the evening as a dreary one.[8]

FOURTEEN

Todd Duncan

For some time, Gershwin had been thinking about who would play the role of Porgy. In early 1934, he told the press that he had Paul Robeson in mind.[1] The remarkable Robeson—the son of slaves, an all-American football star, a graduate of Columbia Law School, a renowned actor, and a great bass-baritone—had been associated with *Porgy* as early as 1926, when he was signed by Cecil B. DeMille's production team for a film version of the novel, then still in galleys. But that project was shelved when DeMille realized the movie would be banned in the South. Robeson was also in the 1927 stage play, appearing for a short time in the role of Crown. His wife had written Gershwin early in 1934 to tell him of her husband's interest in the operatic role. Gershwin wrote back on April 25 to say, "I have Paul in mind for the part of Porgy which I think suits him admirably. I am bearing in mind Paul's voice in writing it, and if there are some things which are out of his range, I am sure I can fix it up."[2] That was the sticking point. Robeson was not an opera singer, a fact that kept him from actively pursuing the role. Gershwin still had him in mind as late as October,[3] but it was becoming clear that he would have to look elsewhere. During the months after his return from South Carolina, he auditioned dozens of potential Porgys without finding the one.

Having already chosen a Juilliard student to be Bess, he was looking for someone with classical training to play Porgy. One thing working against all the applicants was their eagerness to give Gershwin what they thought he wanted. They inevitably sang Negro spirituals and "Ol' Man River" for him. Anne Brown had won him over by singing Massenet, German lieder, and Russian songs before he asked, to her initial annoyance, for a spiritual. "Weren't you satisfied with what I sang?" she'd asked. "Why do people always ask Negro singers to sing spirituals?"[4]

Late in 1934, he heard about a man who had been singing in an all-black New York production of Mascagni's *Cavalleria Rusticana*. There is some debate as to just who told him about the singer, Todd Duncan. According to Duncan, the tip came from Olin Downes, who spoke to Gershwin not only about him but also about Abbie Mitchell, a soprano who had sung opposite him in the production and who had taught at the Tuskegee Institute in Alabama. Mitchell was chosen to play Clara and, thus, would introduce "Summertime" to the world. As Anne Brown remembered it, Mitchell was hired first and she was the one who told Gershwin about Duncan.

Duncan was an elegant, thirty-one-year-old professor of music at Howard University in Washington, D.C. Born in Danville, Kentucky, he had been trained in music at Butler University and the College of Music and Fine Arts in Indianapolis, and then in New York at Columbia, where he earned his master's degree. He was mainly an academic, with only occasional appearances in operas and on the concert stage. But those appearances were impressive. When he sang, his baritone voice displayed, in the words of author Peter G. Davis, a "sweet, dreamy, aristocratic" sound. Upon hearing about him, Gershwin phoned to invite him to New York for an audition. Knowing that his job kept him in Washington during the week, Gershwin scheduled the audition for a Sunday. Duncan knew about the upcoming Gershwin opus but had no interest in it. To him, George Gershwin was the Tin Pan Alley author of "Swanee" and not a serious composer. Trying to demur, he said he would be busy singing in church that day. But Gershwin persisted and the singer finally agreed to come the following Sunday.

"So I went to New York," he remembered, "and went up to his apartment at one P.M. He came to the door himself and he asked, 'Where's your accompanist?' I didn't know anything about New York ways.[5] I didn't know that I was supposed to pay five bucks and bring an accompanist. And I said, 'Well, can't you play?' 'Well, he said, 'I play a little bit.' And I said, 'If you can't, I'll play for myself.'"[6] Gershwin had not been much of a sight-reader in his early days but had progressed markedly. He would often play four-hand versions of the classics with Kay, Bill Daly, and Oscar Levant. Kay remembered him as "a fantastic sight reader, far better than I and he would gallop along in the tempo prescribed by the markings without exception—vivace or presto or any time."[7] Duncan was holding the sheet music for "Lungi dal caro bene," an aria by the eighteenth-century Italian composer Giuseppe Sarti. "I'll try," Gershwin said, taking the music.[8] This interchange fed Duncan's preconception of Gershwin, but it stoked Gershwin's admiration of Duncan. He was immediately impressed by the latter's singing—so much so that he asked him to go to the bow of the piano and sing while facing him. He had heard the man's voice. Now he wanted to watch him as he sang. Duncan did as he was asked. He knew the piece by heart, so did not need to look at the music. Gershwin, to watch him sing, had to take his eyes off the notes, which proved to be no problem—he had already memorized the piece. A few bars into it, he stopped the proceedings and popped the question: "Will you be my Porgy?"[9]

"Oh, he loved to tell that story!" Duncan remembered. "He used to tell it at all the parties and he would say, 'I fell in love with that man then.'" Still, Duncan had his reservations. He did not give a direct answer but said he would have to hear the opera first. More than fifty years later, he remembered Gershwin's reaction to that. "Oh, he loved it! He just loved it!"[10]

When Gershwin asked Duncan to come back the following Sunday for a reverse audition, Duncan expressed concern about the expense of another journey to New York—he had already been stiffed by the producers of *Cavalleria Rusticana* and was not anxious to spend his money on these train rides. Gershwin offered to write a check to cover his expenses.

Todd Duncan

How much would he need? Duncan calculated the cost for two tickets—he wanted his wife, Gladys, to accompany him—and added five dollars for their lunch. George, who was making $2,000 a week from his radio show alone, happily wrote out a check for $30.

It was on Sunday, December 23, 1934, that the Duncans stepped into the elevator for their ride up to Gershwin's Upper East Side apartment. Quickly, they realized that things were not going to be as they had expected. First, they found themselves in the elevator with Lawrence Langner, the patent attorney/playwright who had founded the Theatre Guild in 1919 and who now looked crossly at Duncan and asked, "Who are you? Are you going to George's?" Duncan was angered by the tone but, as he later told an interviewer,[11] he held his tongue. "Yes, we are," he replied. "Well, you'd better be damned good," Langner replied. "George has made us all come out of the country to come hear this new genius he's just found. The entire Theatre Guild board will be here today so you'd better be good."[12]

So, Duncan, who had already been offered the part, was going to have to audition all over again, this time before a room full of people who, if they were like Langner, to whom he had taken an instant dislike, would be unsympathetic. Gershwin had had a similar reaction to Langner a couple of months earlier when he had gone to the Theatre Guild's offices on West Fifty-second Street to tell him and the other directors about his and Heyward's idea for the show's opening scene. On that occasion, Langner, as Gershwin put it in a letter to Heyward, "came through with some pretty stupid remarks. I have heard from several sources that he is on the dull and thick side so I shall probably have to ask him in the future to keep out of my way."[13]

The Duncans entered Gershwin's living room to find it filled with theater people, including Ira and Leonore, all of them expecting to hear him sing. If he was intimidated by this, it did not show. Accompanied by Gershwin, he sang for more than an hour—opera, lieder, spirituals. Then lunch was served—apparently, Duncan need not have asked Gershwin for the extra five dollars. During the meal, it became apparent that George's part of the audition had begun. Although the Theatre Guild had committed itself to the show, their approval was needed for everything—casting, direction, music—if the production was to be properly backed and promoted. During lunch, George and Ira spoke to the assembled about the opera. They were, in fact, pitching it.

Until August, Ira had not had much to do with *Porgy and Bess*. He and Harold Arlen had spent the summer working on their revue, *Life Begins at 8:40*, which was now enjoying a successful run. This was Ira's first success in three years, since *Of Thee I Sing*. All of George's post–*Of Thee I Sing* creations had met with failure. When Ira joined the *Porgy* project, it was to help out with some of the lyrics, particularly those to be sung by the one sophisticate among the characters, Sportin' Life. Ira and Heyward worked well together. In fact, they were very much alike, both of them shy, soft-spoken, and gentlemanly. When it turned out that Heyward might not get his name on enough separately published songs to entitle him to an American Society of Composers, Authors, and Publishers membership, Ira offered to let him take credit for "It Ain't Necessarily So." As this was one of Ira's greatest lyrics—and a song obviously destined for substantial royalties—it was not a token gesture. "Ira, you're very sweet," Heyward said in refusing, "but no one will ever believe that I had anything to do with that song."[14] The Gershwins and Heyward worked in an atmosphere of the greatest mutual respect. After George's death, Ira wrote to Heyward: "To the end of my days I shall never forget the exciting and thrilling period of *Porgy and Bess*. George had not only a great respect for you, but also a deep affection, and I assure you, though I believe you must have known, I felt the same way about you and considered it a great honor to be associated with you, however small my contribution."[15]

After lunch, everybody went upstairs to George's workroom to hear the new music. People sat wherever they could find a spot—some on the floor—as George went to the piano and Ira stood beside him. Then came a demonstration of the *Porgy and Bess* score. Duncan, listening, was immediately heartsick. "Oh, my God," he said to himself. "This is junk."[16] As he later told it: "When he started the opening music, I said to myself: 'All this chopsticks—it sounds awful.' I looked at my wife and said quietly, 'This stinks.' They went on and sang 'Seven Eleven' with those awful voices. He just kept playing; they kept singing."[17] Then Ira sang "Summertime and the living is easy" in his off-key voice while George looked at Duncan and smiled. George took over at "Fish are jumping" in his gravelly voice.

Todd Duncan

He and Ira traded off in this way and as they did, Duncan warmed to the music. By the time they got to "One of these mornings," he was thinking, "This is so beautiful. Where did this man get this from?" Seconds later, when George played the music for Porgy's first entrance, it was to Duncan as if "the royal gates had opened."[18]

(top) Gershwin rehearsing the Los Angeles Philharmonic in February 1937. Courtesy of the Ira and Leonore Gershwin Trusts.

(bottom) George Gershwin. George Grantham Bain Collection, Library of Congress Prints and Photographs Division, LC-USZ62–54141.

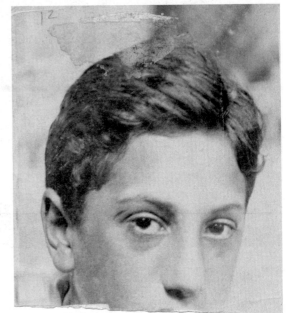

(top) George at around fourteen years of age. Courtesy of the Ira and Leonore Gershwin Trusts.

(bottom) George with pianist Josefa Rosanska at the beach, 1919. Courtesy of the Ira and Leonore Gershwin Trusts.

(top) Emily Strunsky Paley and Lou Paley on a beach boardwalk, 1924. Courtesy of the Ira and Leonore Gershwin Trusts.

(bottom) Leonore Strunsky beside a beach pier, 1924. Courtesy of the Ira and Leonore Gershwin Trusts.

(top) Mabel Schirmer, 1925. Courtesy of
the Ira and Leonore Gershwin Trusts.

(bottom) George at his newly purchased
townhouse at 316 West 103rd Street, 1925.
Courtesy of the Ira and Leonore Gershwin
Trusts.

George at home, 1925. Courtesy of the Ira and Leonore Gershwin Trusts.

(top) George and Kay Swift at Bydale in the late 1920s. Courtesy of the Ira and Leonore Gershwin Trusts.

(bottom left) Alban Berg gave Gershwin this inscribed photo in 1928. Library of Congress, Music Division.

(bottom right) Ira Gershwin and Leonore Strunsky Gershwin at the Chumleigh Farm near Ossining, New York, 1927. Courtesy of the Ira and Leonore Gershwin Trusts.

(top) George's apartment at 33 Riverside Drive, 1930. Courtesy of the Ira and Leonore Gershwin Trusts.

(bottom) Kay Swift and her husband/lyricist Paul James (James Warburg), 1930. Billy Rose Theatre Division, the New York Public Library for the Performing Arts, Astor, Lenox and Tilden Foundations.

(top) Frances Gershwin and Leopold Godowsky, Jr., 1930. Courtesy of the Ira and Leonore Gershwin Trusts.

(bottom) Posing at a 1931 Lewisohn Stadium concert rehearsal, left to right: Oscar Levant, Allan Lincoln Langley, George Gershwin, Robert Russell Bennett, Fritz Reiner, Deems Taylor, William Daly. Courtesy of the Ira and Leonore Gershwin Trusts.

(top left) Gershwin and William Daly at George's 33 Riverside Drive apartment, 1932. Courtesy of the Ira and Leonore Gershwin Trusts.

(top right) Harold Arlen. Courtesy of the American Society of Composers, Authors, and Publishers.

(bottom) Vernon Duke. Courtesy of the American Society of Composers, Authors, and Publishers.

(top) The four Gershwin siblings in May 1933 at the unveiling of Morris Gershwin's tombstone. From left to right: Ira, Frances, George, and Arthur. Courtesy of the Ira and Leonore Gershwin Trusts.

(bottom) William Daly and Kay Swift, 1934. Courtesy of the Ira and Leonore Gershwin Trusts.

(top) DuBose and Dorothy Heyward. Courtesy of the Ira and Leonore Gershwin Trusts.

(bottom) Todd Duncan. Courtesy of the Ira and Leonore Gershwin Trusts.

(top left) Ruby Elzy photographed by George Gershwin, 1936. Courtesy of the Ira and Leonore Gershwin Trusts.

(top right) Anne Wiggins Brown in *Porgy and Bess.* Museum of the City of New York, Theater Collection.

(bottom) At sea during a 1935 visit to Mexico. From left to right: Gershwin, an unidentified woman, Frank Morgan, Edward Warburg, and Gregory Zilboorg. Courtesy of the Ira and Leonore Gershwin Trusts.

(top) Gershwin in Mexico City, 1935. Courtesy of the Ira and Leonore Gershwin Trusts.

(bottom) Mabel Schirmer photographed by George Gershwin in New York, 1936. Courtesy of the Ira and Leonore Gershwin Trusts.

(top) Kay Swift photographed by George Gershwin in New York, 1936. Courtesy of the Ira and Leonore Gershwin Trusts.

(bottom) Jerome Kern photographed by George Gershwin in Beverly Hills, 1936. Courtesy of the Ira and Leonore Gershwin Trusts.

(top) Gershwin and Irving Berlin, in a time exposure photo by George Gershwin, taken in Beverly Hills, 1936. Courtesy of the Ira and Leonore Gershwin Trusts.

(bottom) Left to right: Harold Arlen and E. Y. "Yip" Harburg at 1019 N. Roxbury Drive, Beverly Hills, photographed by George Gershwin, 1936. Courtesy of the Ira and Leonore Gershwin Trusts.

(top) George and Ira flanking
their mother, Rose, in late
1936 or early 1937. Courtesy of
the Ira and Leonore Gershwin
Trusts.

(bottom) Leonore and Ira
Gershwin, 1953. Courtesy of
the Ira and Leonore Gershwin
Trusts.

FIFTEEN

Casting, Rehearsals, and an Omen

Although Gershwin had invited the Theatre Guild directors to hear Duncan sing and to hear his and Ira's rendition of the *Porgy and Bess* score, the producers never tried to exercise their veto power over his cast choices or music. This was to be the first and only time in his career that he was in charge of the whole show. Every prior musical had been someone else's idea, and he had taken those projects on as assignments, usually with enthusiasm, sometimes dutifully, but always without complaint. For instance, when problems arose in 1927 during the writing of *Funny Face,* producers Aarons and Freedley ordered him to rewrite the score, and he did so, discarding a dozen songs and composing a dozen more. Then he willingly complied when they insisted that *he* pay to have the new orchestrations copied. With *Porgy and Bess,* however, the Theatre Guild had not chosen him; he had chosen them. After he offered Anne Brown the role of Bess, she asked what he would do if the guild insisted on someone else. She was, after all, only twenty years old and without stage experience. His reply was, "Don't worry, Annie, George Gershwin will have the last word."[1] There was no way that he was going to let anyone else play Bess. In early 1935, prior to the beginning of formal rehearsals, she was often at his apartment singing what he had just written. It was during one such session that she witnessed what may have been the second—or, at least, the second known—presentiment of his coming illness. The first had been during his concert tour in early 1934 when he complained about phantom garbage smells. This time he was seized with a throbbing headache. It was so bad that she offered to leave and let him rest it out, but he said that would not be necessary, that he had been playing golf earlier in the day and had been hit in the head by a ball. So they continued to work, and he continued to rub his head.

Although he had the last word in choosing the production team and cast, the Theatre Guild held the purse strings and they could and did threaten to pull the plug on the entire venture. As 1935 dawned, they became worried as cost estimates went up and up. At one point, they fretted about a possible $100,000 tab. In the end, the Gershwin brothers and Heyward contributed their own money, buying 20 percent of a $40,000 estimate. George and Ira shared a 15 percent contribution, and Heyward purchased 5 percent.

One of the few disagreements between Gershwin and Heyward was over who would direct the show. Heyward wanted John Houseman, a thirty-two-year-old immigrant from Romania (his father was French, his mother English) who had become a man to watch when, in early 1934, he directed an African American cast in *Four Saints in Three Acts*. With music by Virgil Thomson and a libretto by Gertrude Stein, *Four Saints* had premiered in Hartford, Connecticut, and then gone on to a two-week engagement on Broadway. It was a New York cultural event, and Thomson, in his autobiography, recalled how during rehearsals "visitors from downtown—playwrights like Maxwell Anderson, reporters like Joseph Alsop, colporteurs of news like Mrs. Ira Gershwin—would come to watch the miracle take place."[2] Leonore was probably there as a scout for George, Ira, and Heyward, who were all worried that this black opera would lessen the novelty of *their* black opera. Novelty was one of the things they were counting on, as Gershwin knew that having a black cast would go a long way toward differentiating *Porgy* from all the other modern operas that were arriving with much promise and then quickly vanishing. The other side of the coin was that an all-black cast was going make it harder for *Porgy* to become a staple of the world's opera houses. It would have to survive via touring companies.

At the time of the *Four Saints* New York premiere, Thomson was still living hand-to-mouth, as had been the case in Paris in 1928 when Gershwin breezed into town for a stay at the Hotel Majestic. He was very pleased that on his opening night "everybody came from George Gershwin to Toscanini."[3] George was pleased too, but for a different reason. He quickly concluded that *Four Saints* was no threat. It had no drama. It did not even have a plot. As Stein explained it, "A saint a real saint never does anything, a martyr does something but a really good saint does nothing and so I wanted to have Four Saints that did nothing and I wrote Four Saints in Three Acts and they did nothing and that was everything. Generally speaking anybody is more interesting doing nothing than doing anything."[4]

Gershwin wrote Heyward, "The libretto was entirely in Stein's manner, which means that it had the effect of a 5-year old child prattling on. Musically it sounded early 19th century, which was a happy inspiration and made the libretto bearable—in fact quite entertaining."[5] It is not known if Thomson learned about this letter or about Gershwin's opinion of *Four Saints* during the year-and-a-half that separated its premiere and the *Porgy and Bess* opening, or if Gershwin's opinion, if he did know of it, played a part in his decision to deliver a critical slap to the Gershwin opera in the November/December 1935 issue of *Modern Music*. But Thomson was a connoisseur of musical gossip, and it is very possible that word of Gershwin's damning faint praise got back to him. If so, the *Four Saints* premiere was a bigger danger to *Porgy* than Gershwin and Heyward realized.

DuBose wanted Houseman to be the director but George preferred—and got—Rouben Mamoulian. The tall, dark bespectacled Mamoulian, an Armenian from Russian Georgia, had successfully directed the 1927 stage production of *Porgy* but had not been to Heyward's taste, possibly because he was always asking for script revisions. This tendency would come back to haunt *Porgy and Bess* as well. But Gershwin preferred Mamoulian because he had proven himself an innovative director of stage productions, operas, and movies. In the 1927 *Porgy*, for instance, his ingenious use of footlights to create eerie shadows had been a hallmark of the production. In his 1931 movie version of *Dr. Jekyll and Mr. Hyde,* he had transformed Frederick March from man to monster in a most creepy and seamless manner, apparently without film edits. In fact, no one could figure out how he did it until he himself revealed the secret (filters on lenses that rotated in conjunction with the makeup changes). In 1932, he made a movie musical, *Love Me Tonight,* that pioneered the technique of prerecording a song (in this case, Rodgers and Hart's "Isn't It Romantic?") so its screen performance could, via editing, be tossed from singer to singer and locale to locale. There was rhythm and musicality in his work. He was, in fact, an amateur musician—a violinist. Thus, Gershwin, backed by the Theatre Guild, got his way and Mamoulian became *Porgy's* director.

Gershwin may not have wanted Houseman but he, like Heyward, was eager to pick through the *Four Saints* troupe to create *Porgy's* lineup. He went backstage after the *Four Saints* premiere to ask its conductor, Alexander Smallens, to become *Porgy's* conductor. From the *Four Saints* production, he also found Edward Matthews (who became Jake the fisherman) and the Eva Jessye Choir. In these choices, he continued to show his preference for highly trained musicians. Eva Jessye, for instance, was, besides being a noted choir director and a leader of the Harlem Renaissance, the composer of an oratorio, *Paradise Lost and Regained.* Another composer in the cast was J. Rosamond Johnson who had, with his brother James Weldon Johnson, written "Lift Every Voice and Sing." Johnson joined the cast in the Lawyer Frazier role but was also the assistant choral director. The part of the widow Serena was played by Ruby Elzy who had come to Heyward's attention when he wrote and she acted in the film version of *The Emperor Jones.* She was a Mississippi-born woman who had washed dishes for a living while attending Ohio State University and then Juilliard. As Serena, she would be the first to sing "My Man's Gone Now"—a beautiful, hair-raising performance that was never formally recorded (she would die suddenly in 1943 at the age of thirty-five) but was captured on a 1935 rehearsal recording conducted by Gershwin himself as well as on a recording of the Hollywood Bowl Gershwin memorial concert in the summer of 1937. Abbie Mitchell, who played Clara and introduced "Summertime," had starred opposite Todd Duncan in *Cavalleria Rusticana*. The villainous Crown was played by baritone Warren Coleman, who had studied at the New England Conservatory of Music and whose concert career had included an appearance at the Worcester Music Festival. The only cast principals without formal music training were Georgette Harvey, who played Maria (she had introduced the role of Maria in the stage play) and vaudevillian John W. Bubbles (his real name was John William Sublett), a favorite of Gershwin's, who would play Sportin' Life. Bubbles was half of the song and dance team of Buck and Bubbles. His partner, Ford L. Buck (real name Ford Lee Washington), took the minor role of Mingo.

The off-stage talent showed Gershwin's predilection for Russians. Mamoulian was from Tbilisi, Georgia. Smallens was a Jewish immigrant from St. Petersburg who in late 1934 had conducted the American premiere of Stravinsky's opera *Mavra*. The set designer for *Mavra*, Sergei Soudeikine, became the set designer for *Porgy and Bess*. Looking for a musical coach for the singers, Gershwin went to a reception for Igor Stravinsky and introduced himself to Alexander Steinert, who had worked with the Russian Opera Company and who was himself a pianist, conductor, and composer. (He had won the coveted American Prix de Rome for composition in 1927.) Gershwin, who was still seeing his Kiev-born psychiatrist Dr. Zilboorg and studying composition with the Kharkov-born Joseph Schillinger, often spoke of his own Russianness. One of the finest arias in *Porgy*, "The Buzzard Song," was, he told Duncan, patterned after Mussorgsky's "Song of the Flea." At a restaurant one night after a day of rehearsals, when Mamoulian began whistling something by Rimsky-Korsakov, Gershwin was at first insulted that anyone could listen to his music all day and then whistle something by someone else—until the answer came to him. "I know why you hummed that Russian music—it's because *my* parents came from Russia."[6]

This team of singers, directors, and coaches, handpicked by Gershwin, was probably the greatest collection of talent ever assembled for any Broadway production. The level of musicianship was so high that rehearsals of the complex score went smoothly. John Bubbles posed the only big problem, as he could not read music and was not in the habit of performing anything twice in the same way. Gershwin indulged him, at one point stepping in to keep Smallens from firing him. It was Steinert who figured out that Bubbles could memorize the rhythms of his songs and recitatives by tap-dancing them.

During the rehearsals, which began on August 26, Gershwin usually stayed at the rear of the theater, out of the way, nervously cracking peanuts as he watched everyone at work. Sometimes when someone was getting a rhythm or a note wrong, he would hurry down the aisle and intervene. But usually he was just a presence, sitting in one of the back seats. He had taken a liking to Duncan's wife, Gladys, and there were times when Duncan saw the two of them standing together, chatting and laughing. This irked the singer who, knowing George's reputation as an operator, took him aside at one point to inform him that they were going to have to settle things with their fists if the composer had any intentions toward his wife. Gershwin's reaction was, as Duncan later recalled, one of surprise—and diplomacy. "Todd, you do have a most beautiful wife and she is lovely to talk with. But I know that you are happily married and love her so much. I would never take advantage of either of you."[7] Actually, by this time Gershwin and Duncan had formed a strong bond. There was a joke between them about the one being Jewish and the other black, the question being which was which. Gershwin wanted Duncan to see the Charleston locale, and they traveled there together. Because Heyward was away at his North Carolina residence at the time, they had to find lodgings. Duncan knew he would not be permitted to stay at a white hotel and found alternate quarters with a black family in town. Gershwin asked if he could stay there too, but the family refused. Such things just were not done. As for prejudice on Gershwin's part, he "didn't have any of that in him," Duncan said.[8] Anne Brown concurred, recalling how "Mamoulian, Smallens, even the two stage managers—they would often go out together but they never invited Todd and me. They never invited any members of the cast. But George, he would come to my house, come to our parties, and always the first thing he did was to sit down at the piano and begin to play. And that he would do for the whole evening!"[9]

Gershwin could be upset by wrong notes (at one point, he became so distressed he left the theater and went home), but he was pleased when an innovative interpretation produced interesting variations on what he had written. He gave Bubbles and others in the cast latitude in interpreting and even adding to his music. Ruby Elzy's impromptu vocal flourishes in "My Man's Gone Now" delighted him. In fact, everything about the *Porgy* experience delighted him—the cast, the crew, and, above all, the music. Duncan recalled one memorable moment, when they were rehearsing the "Oh, Dr. Jesus" prayer from act II, scene III:

One day we were in the midst of hard work in Serena's Prayer Scene, he walked in and immediately disappeared into the back of the dark theater where he quietly took his seat. The director, Rouben Mamoulian, was working like mad with the actors, setting the entrances, positions, the music, and action. This is a very quiet scene, one of profound religious fervor. We singers were very tired, tired enough fortunately to set up the exact atmosphere required for the prayer. It must have been our tenth consecutive trial when I sang the following words about my Bess, "I think that maybe she gonna sleep now, a whole week gone and now she ain't no better." Serena, the pious old lady of Catfish Row, came over to me in order to offer a prayer for the sick woman, and so the prayer began. Miss Elzy [Serena] went down on her knees as if her own mother had been ill for weeks; she felt the need of prayer. Two seconds of silence intervened that seemed like hours, and presently there rose the most glorious tones and wails with accompanying amens and hallelujahs for our sick Bess that I ever hope to experience. This particular scene should have normally moved into the scene of the Street Cries, but it did not. It stopped there. The piano accompaniment ceased, every actor (and there were sixty-five of them) had come out of his rest position, sitting at the edge of his seat and R.M. was standing before us quietly moving his inevitable cigar from one side of his mouth to the other, his face lighted to sheer delight in realization, and then, George Gershwin, like a ghost from the dark rows of the Guild Theater appeared before the footlights. He simply could not stand it. He knew then that he had put down on paper accurately and truthfully something from the depth of soul of a South Carolina Negro woman who feels the need of help and carries her troubles to her God.[10]

Toward the end of rehearsals, the Theatre Guild's publicity department began to worry that audiences would think that *Porgy* the opera was actually a revival of *Porgy* the play. To prevent such a misconception Heyward came up with the title *Porgy and Bess*. He liked the idea of a new pair of operatic lovers who would take their place beside *Tristan und Isolde* and *Pelléas et Mélisande*. This satisfied the guild, but they had another concern: that the word "opera" would scare off customers. In 1935, Broadway theatergoers were already in short supply. Only about half as many musicals opened in the 1935–36 season as in the last pre-Depression year of 1928–29. But Gershwin would not budge on this point. He insisted that *Porgy and Bess* be correctly labeled as an opera. He did, however, allow the guild to mitigate the scary word by preceding it with "folk." From then on, it would be called a folk opera, although no one could say for certain just what a folk opera was.

For Gershwin, there would be one more day of euphoria before his professional troubles, defrayed during the two years he had taken off to write *Porgy and Bess*, and continuous since the early 1930s, began again in earnest. On September 2, 1935,[11] a performance was given in Carnegie Hall with only friends and family in the audience. The performance was without sets or costumes, but it was the first time the entire orchestra accompanied the chorus and all the soloists in the complete work. In Ira's words: "Until then only George knew what it would sound like. I couldn't believe my ears. That wonderful orchestra and the full chorus on the stage. I never realized it would be like that. It was one of the great thrills of my life."[12] Anne Brown remembered it this way: "When the echoes of the last chords of *Porgy and Bess* had disappeared into the nearly empty hall, we were—all of us—in tears. It had been so moving. Todd Duncan turned to me and said, 'Do you realize, Anne, that we are making history?' George Gershwin stood on the stage as if in a trance for a few minutes. Then, seeming to awaken, he said, 'This music is so wonderful, so beautiful that I can hardly believe that I have written it myself.'"[13] It was to be the one time he would hear the work performed in its entirety. Before the day was over, director Mamoulian was already warning him that cuts were going to have to be made, "harsh cuts."[14]

SIXTEEN

The Critics Have Their Say

He had now come into his full musical prime as a great composer, a master. Photos from this period show a physical maturity as well: still trim, but with a receding hairline that gave him a professorial look. A kindly, forgiving smile had replaced the one that had been by turns brash and quizzical. A mantle of musical gravitas had settled upon him, one he would never doff.

Yet his coltish personal behavior had not changed at all. Although Kay was still his lover, friend, and musical sounding board, he continued to gad about town with the likes of Kay Halle and Kitty Carlisle. There was also an ongoing relationship with Julia Van Norman (the writer/musician who had moved with her husband and children from Minneapolis to New York in the late 1920s to be near him), although whatever fire there had been in their relationship had dwindled, so that it was now conducted mainly by mail and phone, she writing most of the letters and making most of the calls. At one point, when she put it to him directly and asked if he loved her he said, simply, no. But her devotion never wavered. She seemed to be the only person who reacted to his complaints about physical illness—the stomach problems and now the headaches—with genuine concern.

Another woman in his life was Nebraska-born composer Ann Ronell. Born Ann Rosenblatt, she had been a Radcliffe student working for the school's music magazine when, on a 1926 trip to New York, she phoned the Gershwin family residence at 103rd Street to ask if she might come over to interview George. Ira picked up the phone and said no, but George had grabbed an extension and told her to come right over. During their ensuing chat, he suggested, as he had with so many others, a name change. Thus, from then on she was Ann Ronell. He found her work as a rehearsal pianist and introduced her to his music publisher, Max Dreyfus. Gershwin and Ronell may or may not have had a physical relationship, but it was an enduring friendship. In 1932, she dedicated her song "Willow Weep for Me" to him. Nor were she, Kay Halle, Kitty Carlisle, and Julia Van Norman the only competition Kay Swift had for his romantic attentions. An English actress, Elizabeth Allen, was also a favorite at this time.

There is no evidence that Kay pressured him directly about marriage, although it was clear she had divorced Jimmy along with the Warburg fortune to make such a thing possible. A mutual friend, Emil Mosbacher, later said, "George had such great admiration for her, and they both talked to me about marriage—separately, mind you—and I had one answer to both of them. I said that I wasn't going to open my mouth. I wasn't that crazy. From George I'd get it every day. He was nuts about her."[1]

It was not very far from his penthouse to her apartment, and he often walked there, although it bothered him to have to cross through a German neighborhood. "You *would* have to get an apartment way over here," he said. "This little Jewish boy has a hard time walking through the German section!"[2] He said this only half-jokingly; he was acutely aware of anti-Semitism, both foreign and domestic. In the fall of 1934, two hours before his 6:00 P.M. Sunday radio broadcasts were heard in New York over radio station WABC, New Yorkers could hear Father Coughlin fulminating against the Jews on WOR.

Kay had found a good job. In early 1935, she became a staff songwriter at Radio City Music Hall. Her new lyricist was Al Stillman. Stillman had been born Alfred Silverman, but Gershwin had renamed him too. Before becoming a song lyricist, he had attended New York University, published poetry in *The New Yorker*, and, in addition to his other accomplishments, was an award-winning speed typist. He was also an avid tennis player, and sometimes, while he and Kay were in their fifth-floor cubicle writing a number for the Rockettes, Gershwin would show up and steal him for a while to play a set on the Radio City roof (to be joined, on one occasion, by Bill Tilden).[3] Thus, Kay, on her own for the first time in her life at the age of thirty-eight, had become a well-paid professional songwriter. She worked at Radio City for the next year and a half, writing music to order for kick dancers, comedians, and magicians—one of her and Stillman's numbers was called "Sawing a Woman in Half"—averaging about a song a week.

After *Porgy and Bess*'s Carnegie Hall tryout, she traveled with George to Boston, where the opera was to have its first performance for a paying audience. Tensions about the show were building. Mamoulian was not alone in thinking it was too long. Warren Munsell, the Theatre Guild's production manager, told George that the opening scene—where the overture segues into the Jasbo Brown dancehall piano music—would have to be cut, as it required a set that was not otherwise used in the opera and, thus, too expensive. Gershwin had not previously allowed the Theatre Guild to have any say about his music. That was the side of him that Kay was championing. The other side, however—the Broadway veteran who was used to preopening changes and fixes—gave in without a struggle.

Opening night was on September 30, 1935, at Boston's venerable turn-of-the-century Colonial Theatre. That performance was done as a charity event, with the New England Hospital for Women and Children as beneficiaries. At the conclusion, the packed house gave the cast and creators a fifteen-minute standing ovation. During the applause, Gershwin gradually drifted to stage center and then stepped forward. Heyward stood behind him. Ira remained offstage, not being one for the limelight. After the audience's thunderous applause came almost universally enthusiastic notices. Ann Ames, in the *Boston American*, called Gershwin a genius and said that *Porgy and Bess* was the first American opera. Similar encomiums appeared in the *Boston Transcript*. Only *Variety* expressed doubts, but not about the production or music. Their concern was about the ability of an opera to

Critics Have Their Say

draw crowds. They need not have worried, at least not for the one-week Boston run. All tickets quickly sold out.

Behind the scenes, however, a struggle was going on. Mamoulian was insisting on more cuts. In fact, he wanted to cut a full forty-five minutes from the show. As written, it took a little over three hours to perform. With two intermissions, the audience would be in the theater for nearly four hours. Mamoulian thought this way too long. He later wrote that George completely agreed that the cuts needed to be made. Not having worked previously with Gershwin, he did not realize that accommodation and deference were a significant part of the composer's makeup. Mamoulian told the story of how, shortly after the New York opening, George gave him as a birthday present manuscript pages of the cut *Porgy* music wrapped in a ribbon. From anyone else such a gift would have appeared suspiciously sarcastic. From Gershwin, it was genuine, just as was his phone call to Alexander Glazunov to thank him for his brutal honesty. The two sides of his musical personality—Broadway and Carnegie Hall—may have met triumphantly in *Porgy and Bess*, but the two sides of his human personality—self confidence and deference—had also met, and with less beneficial consequences. Very late on the night of September 30, after the triumphant Boston opening, George, Kay, Mamoulian, and Steinert took a walk on Boston Common to discuss the proposed cuts. As Todd Duncan later recalled, "All night long they fussed and walked in the Commons in front of that theater, and fought all night. That's what they said. And they almost weren't speaking the next day."[4] Kay was adamantly opposed to the cuts. She saw them as the evisceration of a work she dearly loved: one she had watched take shape and whose shape was a unified architecture. She could play the entire 559–page piano/vocal score from memory. Thus, when George caved in to Mamoulian that night, she was devastated. Later, there were reports of an uncharacteristic—and loud—argument between her and George at the hotel. But the cuts were made. In addition to the opening piano music, out came much of the act I crap game music, "The Buzzard Song," the six simultaneous prayers, the "Oh, Where's My Bess" trio, and nearly forty pages of the final act. Later that week as George and Kay were sitting together in the back of the Colonial Theatre, he comforted her, saying, "someday, Kay, you'll sit in that same seat and you'll hear what I wrote, I promise you."[5]

The New York opening came on October 10 at the 1,300–seat Alvin Theatre on West Fifty-second Street. The theater had been named for producers Alex Aarons and Vinton Freedley, for whom George and Ira had written so many hit shows in the 1920s as well as the 1933 flop *Pardon My English*. Aarons and Freedley had fallen on hard times in the early 1930s and the theater had passed from their hands in 1932 (eventually, in 1983, it would be renamed the Neil Simon Theatre). George, Kay, Ira, and Leonore sat together in the last row of the orchestra section. During the intermission, George and Kay went outside to the alley for a breath of fresh, autumn air. There they were approached by Libby Holman, who had introduced Kay's song "Can't We Be Friends" in 1929, and who now told them over and over again in tears how great *Porgy and Bess* was. Encouraged, they went back into the theater only to watch in trepidation as John Bubbles missed the cue for his act III, scene II entrance. The orchestra played his music again but still no Sportin' Life. Kay dug her fingers into George's sleeve. When Bubbles finally took the stage, he was wearing a costume no one had seen before: an emerald green jumpsuit he had purchased just that day. The problem was that its zipper had stuck. He had to sing "There's a Boat Dat's Leavin' Soon for New York" with his back to the audience. Otherwise, the show went flawlessly. After a huge ovation, the authors and cast went to one of the biggest opening night parties in Broadway history. The party was Kay's doing. She had secured the financing from CBS founder and president, William Paley, as well as from Averell Harriman, an advisor to FDR. She had obtained the venue from publisher Condé Nast—the party took place at his thirty-room Park Avenue penthouse. She made the guest list of four hundred, got the invitations designed and printed, and arranged for the entertainment, which included Enric Madriguera's Latin band and twelve members of Paul Whiteman's orchestra—although most of the entertaining, inevitably, was provided by Gershwin, who accompanied the singers in another performance of *Porgy and Bess*.

By the time the festivities were over, it was seven in the morning and the *Times* was out with reviews by its drama *and* music critics. The former,

111

Brooks Atkinson, began his evaluation encouragingly. "Mr. Gershwin's music," he wrote, "gives a personal voice to Porgy's loneliness." He then questioned the need for recitative, called "I Got Plenty o' Nuttin'" a "lazy darky solo," and referred readers who wanted to know more about the show to the *Times's* music critic, Olin Downes. "Mr. Downes," Atkinson wrote, "soothsayer of the diatonic scale, is now beetling his brow in the adjoining cubicle. There is an authoritative ring to his typewriter clatter tonight."[6] Downes may have been beetling his brow because he had never much liked Gershwin's music and, as a friend and champion of Finnish composer Jean Sibelius, was perhaps nettled that the *Porgy* premiere had kept him from going to Carnegie Hall that night to hear Otto Klemperer conduct the Sibelius *Fifth.* He wrote that Gershwin had "turned with the score of *Porgy and Bess* to the more pretentious ways of the musical theatre" and that it did not "utilize all the resources of the operatic composer or pierce very often to the depths of the simple and pathetic drama."[7] Reviewers from other periodicals took a similar tack. Samuel Chotzinoff of the *New York Post,* long one of George's great admirers, called the opera a hybrid and wondered "why Mr. Gershwin continued to impose the recitative on matter that did not require it."[8] Paul Rosenfeld, who had several years earlier written that Gershwin was "a gifted composer of the lower, unpretentious order" and that "there was a question whether his vision permits him an association with the artists,"[9] called the new work "an aggrandized musical show" and said that Gershwin "incompletely felt the drama of the two protagonists."[10]

The knockout blows came from two other critics, each a composer. One was Virgil Thomson, whose *Four Saints in Three Acts* had been a *succès d'estime* but not the kind of triumph that allowed him to support himself by writing music. He had been disheartened when no one would publish the score (it would be published twelve years later) and annoyed that his only financial gain from it was a $300 commission by the League of Composers for a new choral piece. Thus, he was finding it necessary to make a living as a music critic, and in his review of *Porgy and Bess,* which appeared in the November-December issue of the League of Composers quarterly *Modern Music,* he wrote the following: "One can see, through *Porgy,* that Gershwin has not and never did have any power of sustained musical development. . . . The material is straight from the melting pot. At best it is a piquant but highly unsavory stirring-up together of Israel, Africa and the Gaelic Isles. . . . His lack of understanding of all the major problems of form, of continuity, and of serious or direct musical expression is not surprising in view of the impurity of his musical sources and his frank acceptance of the same. . . . It is clear, by now, that Gershwin hasn't learned the business of being a serious composer, which one has always gathered to be the business he wanted to learn. . . . His efforts at recitative are as ineffective as anything I've heard. . . . I do not like fake folklore, nor fidgety accompaniments, nor bittersweet harmony, nor six-part choruses, nor plum-pudding orchestration."[11] Not that his review of *Porgy and Bess* was entirely negative. In it, he also said that he liked "being able to listen to a work for three hours and to be fascinated at every moment," and that the continuing freshness of Gershwin's music was "the hall-mark of *les grand natures.*" Moreover, Gershwin had, Thomson concluded, "presented his astonished and somewhat perturbed public with a real live baby, all warm and dripping and friendly." And to a fellow member of the League of Composers, George Antheil, he confided, "Gershwin is the greatest of American composers."[12] Antheil, who had caused an uproar in 1924 with a piece, *Ballet Mécanique,* that featured airplane propellers in its instrumentation, wrote an admiring letter to George after the *Porgy* premiere and received an appreciative reply: "It was very kind of you to write me telling me that you liked my opera," Gershwin wrote to him on April 13, 1936. "I also appreciate your antagonism toward the snobberies of our high-hat confreres."[13] In 1938, a year after George's death, Antheil would recall how much Gershwin had wanted the admiration and understanding of his fellow American composers, and how they all wrote about him with "a condescension that was as ill-mannered as it was ignorant. Only one of them—Virgil Thomson—ever really recognized the true worth of Gershwin, but he restricted his praise to the sheerly oral; his writings on Gershwin, on the contrary, were often as condescending as the others."[14]

The other composer who took a critical swing at *Porgy* was Duke Ellington. Ellington had long respected Gershwin's work but he was taken aback by the effrontery of white people trying to portray the lives of blacks. He told interviewer Edward Morrow that *Porgy and Bess* did "not use the

Negro musical idiom" and that "it was not the music of Catfish Row or any other kind of Negroes." "Gershwin," he continued, "surely didn't discriminate: he borrowed from everyone from Liszt to Dickie Wells' kazoo band. . . . I do not believe that people honestly like, much less understand, things like *Porgy and Bess*. . . . He missed beautiful chances to really do something . . . when he tried to build up the characterizations he failed. What happened when the girl selling strawberries came on the stage? Did he get the rhythm, the speech, and the swing of the street-vendor? No sir, he did not; he went dramatic! Gershwin had the girl stop cold, take her stance, and sing an aria in the Italian, would-be Negro manner."[15]

Morrow went on to add comments of his own, often wrongly attributed to Ellington: "The times are here to debunk such tripe as Gershwin's lamp-black Negroisms, and the melodramatic trash of the script of *Porgy*. The Negro artists are becoming socially-conscious and class-conscious, and more courageous. Broadway will find it harder to keep them on the chain-gang of the hot-cha merchants. The Ellingtons and the [Langston] Hughes' [sic] will take their themes from their blood. There will be fewer generalized gin-guzzling, homicidal maniacs, and more understanding of rotten socio-economic conditions which give rise to neurotic escapists, compensating for overwrought nerves."[16]

Even Oscar Levant had reservations. On the night of the New York premiere, when the show was half over, he turned to the person sitting next to him and said, "It's a right step in the wrong direction."[17]

As for Kay, she stayed at the opening night party until it ended and then, four hours later, was on her way to the Curtis Institute in Philadelphia, where she delivered the first lecture on *Porgy and Bess*, playing musical examples at the piano.

SEVENTEEN

Limbo

While George was encountering these difficulties with *Porgy and Bess,* Ira was finding solid success collaborating with others. His show *Life Begins at 8:40,* written with Harold Arlen and Yip Harburg, had done very well in the 1934–35 season. In the late summer of 1935, as the final touches were being put on the opera, he turned to another collaborator, Vernon Duke. Born Vladimir Dukelsky in Belarus and trained at the Kiev Conservatory, Duke had started out as a gifted pianist and composer of concert music (he was a good friend of Prokofiev and had written a ballet for Diaghilev). He left Russia during its postrevolution civil war and went to Constantinople, where he first heard American show music and where he found George's then-current hit "Swanee" so irresistible that it permanently bifurcated his career. When he got to America, he continued his symphonic work as Dukelsky, but Gershwin welcomed him to the fold and gave him the moniker Vernon Duke, which would be attached to such great songs as "April in Paris," "I Like the Likes of You," and "Autumn in New York." In these songs, he showed both his musical erudition and a total command of the American musical vernacular. In the fall of 1935, he and Ira began work on the score of *Ziegfeld Follies of 1936* (Ziegfeld was dead but his name was still selling shows), which would be as successful as *Life Begins at 8:40*. The *Follies* spawned one big hit, "I Can't Get Started," but it contained a wealth of fine material. In it, Ira wrote skits for the first time, collaborating with the renowned comedy writer David Freedman to create some of the show's best scenes.

Meanwhile, George was doing all he could to keep *Porgy and Bess* alive. On October 14, four days after the New York opening, he supervised the first commercial recording of its music. Conductor Smallens was brought in from the stage production, as was the chorus, but the featured singers were not Duncan and Brown. Instead, two big stars of the Metropolitan Opera Company were hired: Helen Jepson and Lawrence Tibbett. Jepson recorded "Summertime" and "My Man's Gone Now." Tibbett sang "It Ain't Necessarily So," "The Buzzard Song," "Oh, Bess, Oh Where's My Bess," and "I Got Plenty o' Nuttin.'" Together they did "Bess, You Is My Woman Now," and portions of act I, scene I ("Summertime," the crap game music, and "A Woman Is a Sometime Thing"). Oddly enough, the record label wrongly gave Heyward credit for the lyric to "It Ain't Necessarily So." Also, Gershwin's old friend Nathaniel Shilkret was brought in to handle conducting chores for "My Man's Gone Now." Shilkret had been at the helm of the very successful first recording of *An American in Paris*, made in early 1929.

During *Porgy and Bess*'s rehearsals, Duncan and Brown had watched in awe as Jepson and Tibbett came in day after day to watch them work. The handsome, broad-shouldered Tibbett had recently sung the lead in the Met's production of Louis Gruenberg's operatic version of *The Emperor Jones*—appearing in blackface. Jepson was a blonde beauty who had come to the Met via a career in radio. Duncan and Brown were hoping that these two stars were there as talent scouts to appraise them. In fact, they were learning the music so they could be the first to record it. When Brown complained about this to Gershwin, he replied, "I would prefer that you and Todd would sing these parts but I don't have much to say about it. This is business."[1] It may have been business but this first recording sold poorly. "Poor Lawrence Tibbett!" Brown recalled. "He never got the feel of the dialect or the inflection in the voice needed to sing an effective Porgy, he simply never got it."[2]

It was left to the swing bands to popularize the songs. A month after the opening, Edward Matthews, who was playing Jake in the show, recorded "I Got Plenty o' Nuttin'" and "It Ain't Necessarily So" with Leo Reisman and His Orchestra. Those songs and "Summertime" quickly became hits, as versions by Billie Holiday, Guy Lombardo, Bob Crosby, and others reached the public. This helped popularize the music and keep it alive, but the breadth and intricacy of the score were to remain all but unknown. In 1940, Duncan and Brown made their first recordings, which were true to Gershwin's original conception but, again, these were songs, not scenes. Sales were good but the record company, Decca, paid them a minimal one-time fee and no royalties.

A week after overseeing the Jepson-Tibbett recording session, Gershwin further promoted the show by writing an article for the October 20 edition of the *New York Times*. As had been the case in an article he wrote in October 1926 for a periodical called *Singing*, this one was about definitions. In 1926, the subject had been the definition of the word "jazz," which, he wrote, had "been used for so many things that it has ceased to have any definite meaning." Now, having billed *Porgy and Bess* as a "folk opera," he found himself having to define that term, which proved all but impossible. He wrote: "I have been asked frequently why it is called a folk opera. The explanation is a simple one. *Porgy and Bess* is a folk tale. Its people naturally would sing folk music. When I first began work on the music I decided against the use of original folk material because I wanted the music to be all of one piece. Therefore I wrote my own spirituals and folksongs. But they are still folk music—and therefore, being in operatic form, *Porgy and Bess* becomes a folk opera."[3] This tortured paragraph did little to clear things up.

Meanwhile, theatergoers were steering clear. Gershwin told Duncan that Broadway people were avoiding the show because they thought it was opera, and operagoers were not going because they thought it was Broadway.[4] In the 1935–36 season, an opera buff could choose between Met offerings of *Aida*, *Carmen*, and *Die Walküre*, while those who preferred Broadway could go to Rodgers and Hart's *Jumbo* at the Hippodrome ("The

Most Beautiful Girl in the World," "My Romance," "Little Girl Blue") and Cole Porter's *Jubilee* at the Imperial ("Begin the Beguine," "Just One of Those Things"). There was no need to spend one's Depression era dollars on what had been deemed a pretentious hodgepodge.

George tried to keep the production alive by cutting costs. He was willing to reduce the size of the orchestra but the musicians union forbade it. The only alternative was to lower ticket prices. The best seats had been going for $4.40 when the show opened in October. In November, they were down to $3.30. By early January, one could attend a Saturday matinee for a dollar and get a glimpse of the composer—he was at nearly every performance—standing at the rear of the theater. After the curtain, he would go back stage and profusely thank the performers.

The 1922 failure of *Blue Monday* had so affected him that it brought on a permanent digestive disorder—and *that* opera was a juvenile effort dashed off in less than a week. It was only to be expected that the floundering of this work, two years in the making and created in his maturity, would affect him profoundly. Yet, he did not appear to be despondent. At one point, he did vent to Harold Arlen, saying, "What do they want me to do? What are they criticizing me for?"[5] But for the most part people saw the same Gershwin as usual. He was always so gregarious that it was hard to know if he was keeping anything to himself. But *Porgy and Bess*'s poor reception made him miserable—a misery made all the worse by his continuing inability to come to a decision about Kay. And concern about his relationship with Kay fed a longstanding fear that he was incapable of falling convincingly in love and, thus, destined never to have a home and family of his own.

In the fall of 1935, these quandaries were understood by Dr. Zilboorg, whom he was still seeing, and who, in response, recommended that he get away for a while—that *they* get away. Dr. Zilboorg suggested they take a vacation together. They might go to Mexico. George was receptive to the idea. His trips to France in the 1920s had resulted in *An American in Paris*, and his 1932 holiday in Cuba had inspired the *Cuban Overture*. Perhaps a visit to Mexico would provide not only a needed rest and change of scene, but also a chance to meet Mexican composers and painters he greatly admired, especially the renowned muralist Diego Rivera. Dr. Zilboorg invited two others to come along, each a patient of his and both friends of Gershwin. One was Edward Warburg—James's cousin who had commissioned Kay to write the score for *Alma Mater*. The other was Marshall Field III of the Chicago department store family. They may have all known each other, but Dr. Zilboorg was the only one privy to everyone else's secrets.

The four men traveled by ship, which gave the doctor time to hold regular psychoanalytic sessions with his patients and then openly discuss—usually at breakfast—what they had confided in him. He was fluent in Spanish, which gave him another leg up on his companions. They arrived in Mexico City in late November, checking into the San Angel Inn. Vernon Duke had told Gershwin of a woman, Estrella Elizaga, through whom he could meet Mexican composers and artists. Elizaga was elegant, musical (she was a pianist and a composer), and rich—she had financed Duke's ballets. She threw the party Gershwin had hoped for, inviting a salon-full of great artists: composer Carlos Chávez; sculptor Isamu Noguchi; and painters David Siqueiros, Miguel Covarrubias, and Diego Rivera.

At this party, Dr. Zilboorg used his knowledge of Gershwin's insecurities to his advantage. He dominated the gathering, speaking Spanish to the assembled guests while George sat left out, quietly waiting to be asked to play the piano. Because some of the guests present were pro-Marxist, Zilboorg, given his own first-hand experience with Bolshevism, was carrying a loaded gun. It was a volatile mix of people. Siqueiros (from whom Gershwin would commission a painting of himself playing to a packed concert hall) had been a captain in the Mexican revolutionary army. Chávez, as a teenage noncombatant, had had a close encounter with a stray bullet during the revolution. Noguchi (who had sculpted a bronze bust of Gershwin in 1929) had been a lover of Frida Kahlo, Rivera's wife. As for Rivera, no one could have been less like Gershwin. He was slovenly and obese, with a history of perfidy (he had caused a completed mural by a rival, Jean Charlot, to be destroyed to make way for his own fresco), and a violent temper (at a gathering in Paris, he had screamed at and pulled the hair of an art critic). Gershwin was hoping that Rivera would do his portrait. When that did not happen, he sketched Rivera instead.

In addition to Mexico City, Gershwin visited Cuernavaca, Taxco, and Mazatlán. He enjoyed the sights but got nothing lasting out of the trip. Interviewed upon his return to New York on December 17, he did not say much about art or music, but seemed to have developed some political views, telling reporters, "I am going to interest myself in politics, and it is true that in Mexico I talked a great deal with Diego Rivera and with his radical friends, who discussed at length their doctrines and intentions."[6] It was a moment of naïveté, one that might have gotten him into trouble with congressional red-baiters in the late forties had he lived that long. In fact, Senator Joseph McCarthy included Gershwin's name on a list of those whose Americanism was in question.[7] This was probably due to the financial contributions he had made to Siqueiros's Experimental Workshop, which painted portraits of the Communist Party's 1936 presidential and vice-presidential candidates. But George's actual political activities were limited to efforts to transport Jewish children from Germany to Palestine and support for Roosevelt and the New Deal. He had found nothing in Mexico to inspire him or dispel his sour mood. On the voyage home from Mexico on the S.S. *Santa Paula*, he had sent a telegram to singer Rudy Vallee saying he was on the Pacific Ocean off the coast of Guatemala doing "plenty o nuttin."[8]

Porgy and Bess closed on January 26, 1936. The Gershwin brothers and Heyward lost the money they had invested in it. On the other hand, royalties were coming in from the songs. George alone earned more than $10,000 in royalties in the two-and-a-half month period between the premiere and the end of the year. For the Theatre Guild, however, it had been a bust, and they tried to recoup their losses with a five-city tour in locations where the musicians union could not prevent a smaller, less costly orchestra. The tour began in Philadelphia on January 27, 1936. George went there a few days prior, on January 21, to stir up interest by giving a concert where he played his piano concerto and Smallens conducted an orchestral suite fashioned by Gershwin from *Porgy and Bess*. This suite was no collection of song hits. It contained much of the music that had been removed in Boston (and would be missing from the touring production). In it, one could hear the opening piano music, the fugue, the hurricane music, and much of what had been excised from act III. Gershwin himself would conduct his suite several times in the coming year, but after his death, the manuscript was forgotten until Ira's secretary found it in a closet in 1958.

At that point, Ira renamed it *Catfish Row* (to distinguish it from Robert Russell Bennett's popular *A Symphonic Picture of Porgy and Bess*).

On January 30, 1936, he returned to New York for the premiere of Ira's *Ziegfeld Follies of 1936*, but the next day he was back with the tour. It visited Pittsburgh and then Chicago. The next stop was Washington D.C., but before the cast traveled there, it held a meeting in Chicago to discuss what to do about the segregation policy in effect at Washington's National Theatre. In much of the nation's capitol, blacks and whites could attend events together—baseball at Griffith Stadium, for instance. But the National Theatre held to a whites-only policy. At the meeting, Duncan and Brown both said they would refuse to perform for a segregated audience. Abbie Mitchell agreed with them. Edward Matthews and others did not.[9] Duncan then wrote letters to Eleanor Roosevelt and fellow Howard University professor (and future Nobel Peace Prize winner) Ralph Bunch. The latter got in touch with the management of the National Theatre and urged them to change their policy. The theater's manager, S. E. Cochran, who had been severely criticized several years earlier for letting African Americans attend performances of *The Green Pastures* (albeit in a separate, roped-off section), warily agreed to allow blacks to come to Wednesday and Saturday matinees. When Brown and Duncan said this was not good enough, Cochran agreed to allow black attendance at every performance, but only in second balcony seats. There is no evidence that Gershwin was aware of these goings on, although it is hard to believe he was not. Only when he heard that Brown had said she would end her career there and then if their demands were not met did he enter the picture. "Did you really say that?" he asked her. "Yes," she told him. "I won't sing, not even your opera. I won't sing in the National Theater." "All right, Annie," he replied. "We'll see what we can do."[10] It is not known what he did, if anything. But what Duncan did is not in doubt. He refused to compromise, even when the musicians union threatened to fine him $10,000 and suspend him for a year. In the end, Cochran gave in. For the week of *Porgy and Bess*'s run, this theater on Pennsylvania Avenue—a few blocks from the White House—was desegregated. After that, the old rules returned, to remain in effect for another twenty years.

The tour was not a financial success. It ended with a final performance in Washington on March 21, 1936. At that moment, it seemed that Gershwin's grand achievement was headed for the obscurity that awaited so many other new operas. That being the case, he drifted into lassitude. Never before had he ended one project without having another in mind. But during the first half of 1936 there would be nothing except a half-hearted attempt to write a few songs with Kay's lyricist, Al Stillman. Only one of their collaborations, "King of Swing," was performed—by John Bubbles at Radio City Music Hall—but it went nowhere and the others were not even published.

Aside from the *Porgy and Bess* tour, he had spent some time in early 1936 making public appearances. In January, he attended a concert and reception in his honor at the Plaza Hotel, sponsored by the American-Palestine Musical Association. The same month, he attended a Metropolitan Opera performance of *La Juive* in support of the American Jewish Physicians Committee. *La Juive* was an 1835 opera by Jewish composer Jacques Halévy about anti-Semitism. It had recently been banned by the Nazis. In February, he was accompanist for Arkansas-born soprano Mary Lewis at a birthday ball for President Roosevelt at the Central Park Casino. He also appeared that month as a guest conductor of the National Symphony Orchestra, invited by its founder and permanent conductor, Hans Kindler, to conduct the *Porgy and Bess* suite. On March 1, he conducted the suite again, this time with the St. Louis Symphony at their annual pension fund concert.

Meanwhile, there was desultory talk about a new Broadway venture, this time a musical comedy. On February 26, the *New York Times* announced that Carleton P. Hoagland was hoping to get him and Ira to write the songs for a play about horse racing by Damon Runyon and Irving Caesar to be called *Saratoga Chips* and to star Ethel Merman. Nothing came of the idea. A few weeks later, silent era film star Harold Lloyd spoke to the *Times* of having discussed a possible project with the Gershwin brothers and George S. Kaufman. He said, somewhat perturbed, that he did not know what they had in mind and neither did they. In April, there was a pleasant occasion: two Gershwin paintings were shown at an exhibition at the Grand Central Palace sponsored by the Society of Independent Artists. Otherwise, it was an aimless time for a man who had never been aimless before. He spoke to friends about composing a symphony, maybe taking a couple of years off to do it. The trouble was he had just taken a couple of years off to write an opera. He had the financial wherewithal to do it. Royalties were coming in and his concert fee was $2,000. But he now had to contend with doubts about his place in the world of popular songwriting. Cole Porter and the Rodgers and Hart team were enjoying solid Broadway successes. In Hollywood, Jerome Kern and Irving Berlin were topping themselves with scores for the movies. Spending two years on a symphony would be tantamount to renouncing that world—the world that he knew best and that had always welcomed him most warmly. And yet, as Anne Brown observed, "He was afraid not to be the person he was supposed to be."[11]

EIGHTEEN

Hollywood Beckons

On February 17, 1936, a few days before Ira left with Leonore and *Follies* set and costume designer Vincente Minnelli for a Caribbean holiday, George heard from a Hollywood agent. This was Sam Howard of the Phil Berg-Bert Allenberg Agency, asking if he and Ira would be interested in coming to California to write songs for a yet to be determined Hollywood studio. Gershwin told Howard they would be interested if they could get $100,000 plus a percentage of the film's profits. On their one previous visit to Hollywood, in 1930, they had spent a few weeks writing the *Delicious* score for Fox Film Corporation and gotten $100,000. Now George wanted an equal amount *plus* a percentage of the profits. Or, at least, that was his opening gambit. When Howard was unable to come up with anything, George and Ira, the latter back from vacation, allowed another agent, Arthur Lyons, a month to come up with a suitable deal. Lyons quickly came back with proposals from RKO Pictures involving Fred Astaire.

RKO had been saved from bankruptcy by the Fred Astaire and Ginger Rogers movies. Most recently, the two had done *Top Hat* with great songs by Irving Berlin including "Top Hat, White Tie and Tails," "Isn't This a Lovely Day," and "Cheek to Cheek." In February 1936, as the Gershwins were beginning their Hollywood negotiations, Fred and Ginger's new film, *Follow the Fleet*, was released, with another superb score by Berlin, this one featuring "Let's Face the Music and Dance." Astaire and Rogers were currently working on *Swing Time*, whose songs by Jerome Kern and Dorothy Fields would include "The Way You Look Tonight," "Pick Yourself Up," and "A Fine Romance." Kern's fee, after protracted negotiations, was $50,000 plus a percentage of the gross up to an additional $37,500 (he got the additional). Berlin's deal on *Top Hat* was $100,000 plus a percentage of the gross that brought him another $285,000.[1]

On May 14, Lyons telegrammed the Gershwins to say that RKO was offering the brothers $60,000 with no percentage. They passed on this, and Lyons's month expired without a deal. At that point, George and Ira turned to another agent, Alex S. Kempner, who let them in on the truth: Hollywood was dubious about George's ability to write hits because he was reputedly interested only in highbrow material. At that point, Lyons got back into the act, using psychology to get the Gershwins to come to terms. In a June 10 telegram telling them that RKO boss Pandro Berman was offering $60,000 for twenty weeks' work, he added: "Both Fred Astaire and Ginger Rogers delighted with possibility of your doing this. . . . After you talk with Berman you will be convinced that this is the right setup for you and that this is the type of picture you have been looking for."

Astaire and Rogers each had been associated with Gershwin for a long time. Fred and his sister Adele were a teenage vaudeville act when they first met George, then a teenage song plugger at Remick's. The three of them had daydreamed about someday working together on Broadway—a dream that came true in 1924 when *Lady, Be Good!* made them—and Ira— celebrities along the Great White Way. In 1926, the Astaires gave George a signed photo with an inscription by Adele that said, "To George—whom I admire more than anyone in the world" and an accompanying addendum by Fred that read, "Adele said it for me."[2] That year Fred and Adele recorded several Gershwin songs with the composer at the piano. In "The Half of It, Dearie Blues," Fred exclaims during his tap dance, "How's that, George?" and George laughingly calls back, "That's great, Freddie, do it again!"[3]

In 1930, nineteen-year old Ginger Rogers became a Broadway star when she was cast in *Girl Crazy*. During rehearsals for that show, George asked Astaire for help with the dance routines, and that is where Fred first met Ginger. George and Fred both courted Ginger at the time, although nothing serious developed between her and either man. In 1932 Adele retired to marry Britain's Lord Cavendish (and move to an Irish castle), leaving Fred without a partner. He moved to Hollywood where he managed to get a minor role in the 1933 RKO film *Flying Down to Rio*. Paired with Ginger, they stole the show with their first movie dance, "The Carioca." By their next movie together, *The Gay Divorcee*, they were the biggest song and dance act in motion pictures. Thus, an offer to write for them was tempting to George, not only because these were old friends, but because it was the best way for him to reestablish himself in the songwriting pantheon. The Astaire-Rogers movies had featured scores not only by Berlin and Kern but also by Vincent Youmans and Cole Porter, and all were doing their best work.

Still, George wavered. When another agent, Archie Selwyn, wired that Hollywood was "afraid you will only do highbrow songs so wire me on this score so I can reassure them," he held onto that telegram for ten days before responding to it. Finally, he wired back: "Rumors about highbrow music ridiculous stop am out to write hits." He and Ira signed for sixteen-weeks at $55,000 with an option for a second sixteen-week contract at $70,000. Also, independent film producer Samuel Goldwyn was expressing an interest in their services. It added up to steady work, probably for a year, and if George Gershwin was not getting as much money as Kern and Berlin (he and Ira were each earning less than a tenth of what the studio was paying Irving Berlin), he would be back among the songwriters and show people he loved and would be able to demonstrate that the pop songwriter in him was far from dead.

It also gave him a chance to make a final decision about Kay. Through the spring of 1936, they had remained a couple. But ten years had passed since they had first become enamored of one another and each now wanted something more. There were still moments that seemed like the old days, the late twenties, when they popped up around town like a couple of sprites, full of fun. In March, they attended a performance of *Die Meistersinger* and, after the final curtain, played an old game: seeing how fast they could get out of the theater. Racing up the aisle side by side and in step, they darted past everyone else and zoomed out of the lobby with so much momentum they found themselves sprawled in the snow, their expensive theater clothes soaked, both of them laughing, as were passersby who recognized Gershwin. In the taxi, he turned to her and said, "Always leave them laughing when you say goodbye."[4]

Which is what he was about to do. Nonconfrontational as always, he broke up with her by pretending to leave the door open for a future reconciliation. He had worked it all out beforehand to make it seem like a game. They would not communicate with each other the entire time he was in California. During that period, they would be free to see others. If the trial separation did not work, then they would get back together. Nothing was said about what getting back together again might mean. But Gershwin expected the separation to take hold. Hollywood was replete with beautiful, talented young women—some of them Jewish—and he was young, rich, and famous. Certainly, he was bound to meet *the* woman out there. As for Kay, she was unhappy about the split and uneasy about him being so far away—she continued to have forebodings about him. But she was not one to sit around feeling sorry for herself. She was busy creating a new life and, as much as he, always looked forward to the next adventure.

Before leaving, George had just a few more commitments to keep. On May 14, 1936, the *Times* announced that in early July he would appear in back-to-back all-Gershwin Lewisohn Stadium concerts. It had been a great source of pride to him that his prior appearances there had broken attendance records. Now he eagerly looked forward to these events, not least because they would allow him to introduce the music of his opera to thousands who had not yet heard it. He was not going to present the orchestral suite; instead, he reassembled the original team, including Todd Duncan, Anne Brown, Ruby Elzy, the Eva Jessye Choir, and conductor Smallens. In addition to the *Porgy and Bess* excerpts, the audience would hear *An American in Paris*, *Rhapsody in Blue*, and *Concerto in F* with Gershwin as piano soloist. On July 9, the first of the two concerts took place. But only 7,000 people showed up. This was mostly due to the weather. It was the hottest day in the history of New York. A temperature of 115 degrees had been recorded in Times Square as the heat, reflected from the sidewalks,

Hollywood Beckons

blasted the faces of pedestrians. Also, the concert was broadcast live on radio, further reducing the incentive to attend. But Gershwin was still disappointed by the low turnout. The *Times* wrote, "It was George Gershwin night at the Lewisohn Stadium, and there were empty seats in the amphitheatre last night. That is news."[5] The thermometer high for the next day was 100 degrees and that night's concert was subjected to a lightning storm. Only 4,500 braved the elements to attend what would be Gershwin's final public performance in his hometown. Two weeks later, he played at the Ravinia Festival with the Chicago Symphony Orchestra. Then it was time to pack.

Just before leaving for Hollywood, he and Ira began working together for the first time in a year. The song was "Let's Call the Whole Thing Off," whose lyric would seem to have been based on George and Kay but in fact came from Ira and Leonore's different ways of pronouncing words. As Ira explained in his 1959 book *Lyrics on Several Occasions*, "my wife still 'eyethers' and 'tomahtoes' me, while I 'either' and 'tomato' her." The main melody showed that George really was "out to write hits." But in the introductory eighteen-bar verse ("Things have come to a pretty pass") he created a kind of colloquial recitative. The music flowed in a conversational style but was harmonically as ingenious, subtle, and affecting as his work in *Porgy and Bess*. Shortly thereafter, while at a party at Vincente Minnelli's, he and Ira improvised the kernel of what turned out to be another fine song, "By Strauss." Its main strain was a catchy waltz complete with the occasional Strauss-style luftpause, but it too was given an introductory verse ("Away with the music of Broadway!") in this *recitativo* style. In the verse, Ira humorously named some of the great songwriters of the day: Berlin, Kern, Porter, building up to Gershwin himself. The brothers would complete the song in California and send it to Minnelli for use in his Broadway revue *The Show Is On*. It was hardly noticed there. Nor did it attract much attention when Minnelli revived it in 1951 for the movie *An American in Paris*. But it, like "Let's Call the Whole Thing Off," was a masterpiece.

On August 10, 1936, George, Ira, and Leonore went to the Newark Airport. They were seen off by Kay, William Daly, and Mabel Schirmer. Ira and Leonore took one taxi, George and Kay another. George made sure that Mabel sat between Kay and himself to avoid any last minute emoting.

At the airport, Kay watched as the Gershwins walked up the steps to the Trans World Airline aircraft—a plane that was a bit small for Ira's comfort. The brothers turned to face their friends while a news photographer took their picture. "We said goodbye," Kay recalled, "and he walked up the ramp. And I knew for sure I'd never see him again. I don't know why, but I knew that was all, that was it."[6]

Hollywood Beckons

NINETEEN

Pleasure Island

When they got to Los Angeles, the sky was cloudless and the temperature in the low eighties. They checked into a suite at the ornate Beverly Wilshire Hotel, the three of them living under the same roof again, and while Leonore went looking for a house to rent, George and Ira had a piano delivered and got to work. George's first composition in California was "Hi-Ho," which, besides being more than three times the length of the usual thirty-two–bar tune, had a complex piano accompaniment, sudden key changes, and a melody that surged with lighthearted grandeur. One musician exclaimed, "It's a miniature piano sonata!"[1]

In Hollywood, however, it was not as it had been with *Porgy and Bess*. This time the producers and cast had chosen Gershwin, not the other way around, and they had veto power over his and Ira's songs. The brothers were lucky that the stars in this case were Astaire and Rogers, who were friends and admirers. They were also lucky to be dealing with the only benign studio chief in town, Pandro S. Berman of RKO. Berman, Astaire, and Rogers were favorably disposed to "Hi-Ho," as was the director, Mark

Sandrich, who had previously directed the team in *The Gay Divorcee, Top Hat,* and *Follow the Fleet.* But the song was rejected because it would have been too expensive to produce. The Gershwins, having no script to work from, had imagined their own scene, one that had Astaire dancing around Paris, seeing posters of Ginger Rogers everywhere and falling in love with her. As this scene would have cost $44,000 to shoot,[2] RKO, with its limited financial resources, refused to do it. "Hi-Ho" was therefore put away, not to be published for thirty years.

Leonore found a suitable house on palm tree–lined North Roxbury Drive in the heart of Beverly Hills, which they rented for $800 a month. It was a lovely, Spanish-style stucco home, with gardens, a fifty-foot swimming pool with cabana, a tennis court, and a history. Built in 1928, it had been the home of singer, film star, and composer Russ Columbo who, in 1934 at age twenty-six, died violently when a friend accidentally (or maybe not) set off an antique dueling pistol a few feet from his face. The shooting occurred at the friend's home in West Hollywood, so there were, presumably, no ghosts to worry about on North Roxbury Drive. The palm trees, gardens, backyard pool, and clement weather provided a setting as removed as could be from the brick facades, humidity, and electrical storms of New York City. The social life proved to be, in George's word, gemütlich, because so many of their New York songwriter friends were living nearby: Irving Berlin, Jerome Kern, Harry Warren, Harold Arlen, Yip Harburg, and Sigmund Romberg.

Like George and Ira, Oscar Levant was living on Roxbury Drive, although he was in an apartment, not a house, and on the less fashionable South Roxbury. He had come to Los Angeles in 1935 to work in films as a songwriter and had written two hits: "Lady, Play Your Mandolin" and "Blame It on My Youth." At the time of the Gershwins' arrival, Levant had just completed an assignment for Twentieth Century Fox, writing the opera sequence in *Charlie Chan at the Opera.* Also, his orchestral piece *Nocturne* had recently been published. He wrote this and other symphonic works under the tutelage of Arnold Schoenberg. The latter, born in Vienna in 1874 to Jewish parents (he became a Lutheran in 1898 and returned to Judaism in 1933) was a refugee from Nazi Berlin, lately arrived in the United States. As the inventor of the twelve-tone system for musical composition, he had a huge reputation among musicians, but very little public recognition and not much money. His professorship at University of California, Los Angeles brought in just $5,000 a year. So, he took in students. Levant became one of them.

Gershwin had helped pay for Schoenberg's passage to America in 1933, and the two had met in New York, where Schoenberg discovered that Gershwin greatly admired his work. In Los Angeles, Levant brought them together again. Once a week Schoenberg, who lived in Brentwood near UCLA, would arrive at the Gershwin "plantation" (as Ira called it) to play tennis, partake of the open buffet, and join the other guests, mostly musicians and writers, in witty, erudite conversation. He had a good time at the Gershwin home. Years later, when his children watched home movies taken of him there, they were amazed to see their father smiling. His was usually a sour, if Olympian attitude, as when, after Levant expressed a preference for the second of his four string quartets, he responded, "I am above comparisons."[3] Gershwin was happy to have made this, his first ongoing friendship with a world-renowned "serious" composer, and he financed the recording of all four Schoenberg quartets.

In the meantime, nothing much was happening with the Astaire-Rogers film. Eight weeks into the Gershwins' sixteen-week contract, the script, whose title had been changed from *Stepping Toes* to *Watch Your Step*, was still not ready. It was being worked on by Allan Scott and Ernest Pagano, who were basing their plot on P. J. Wolfson's suggestion regarding an adaptation of a Lee Loeb–Harold Buchman story. All those people were apparently needed to come up with the customary series of misunderstandings among the usual cast of characters. There being little reason to show up at the studio, George and Ira worked at home. With no script to guide them, they created numbers that would fit into any Astaire-Rogers movie. A September 13 letter from William Daly offered encouragement. Tell Astaire, Daly advised, "he'll really get some tunes now."[4] He was correct. During their first week in the new house, George and Ira wrote the memorable "They All Laughed." Then came "They Can't Take That Away From Me." Upon completing it, George rushed to Harold Arlen's house, entered without knocking, and played the piece for Arlen and his wife Anya. The Arlens recognized the song's greatness right away, and the three of them sang it, with Anya—a former model whose visage was on Breck shampoo containers—improvising a countermelody that delighted Gershwin and her husband.

As work on the film finally got underway at the studio, George began showing up, hoping to lend a hand in any way he could. Astaire was portraying a ballet dancer, and the finale called for ballet music, which Gershwin was to provide. He also made himself available to write whatever other incidental music was required. One day as he was sitting alone at a sound stage piano, Hermes Pan walked into the room. Pan was Astaire's co-choreographer. Together he and Astaire created all of the stunning Fred and Ginger dances, working these routines out by dancing with one another, Pan doing Ginger's steps. Because he looked so much like Astaire, people who saw them at work said it looked like Fred dancing with himself. Pan had never met the composer before and apparently had not seen a photo either because he did not recognize him. Thinking he was dealing with a rehearsal pianist, he handed him a sheaf of manuscript pages from the *Shall We Dance* score and asked to hear the songs. Gershwin readily assented. Pan later recalled what happened next:

I said, "Gee, that's like a march—can you play it a little slower?" He said, "Oh, sure." But it got worse. I said, "Well, that's like a funeral march." He tried it different ways, but nothing worked for me. "You know something?" I said. "Gershwin or no Gershwin, I think this stinks." After trying it a few more times, I finally said, "Well, excuse me, but there's a meeting I have to go to. I'll see you later." After I'd been in the meeting for about five minutes the rehearsal pianist came in. Everybody stood up and said, "Mr. Gershwin!" Oh, I practically went through the floor. Finally, after everybody had gone, I said, "Mr. Gershwin, as you know, I'm embarrassed and very sorry I said what I did." And he said, "You know something? You might just be right."[5]

Gershwin's bemused response notwithstanding, the incident with Pan was the beginning of a series of increasingly unpalatable events during work on the picture. George *was* offended by what the filmmakers were doing to "They Can't Take That Away From Me." Although Astaire sang it well and the musical arrangement was fine, Fred and Ginger did not dance to it. It just came and went with nothing like the elaborate showcasing that had been given to Kern's "The Way You Look Tonight" in *Swing Time* or Berlin's "Cheek to Cheek" in *Top Hat*. Although it was not in Gershwin's nature to complain, he was greatly disappointed. This song was special to him, as was shown by his reaction when he later heard Astaire's studio recording of it, as arranged and conducted by fellow songwriter Johnny Green. Green remembered: "I put the recordings on and when George heard "They Can't Take That Away From Me," he broke down, reached his hand out to me, and came close to tears. He kept saying 'Thank you.'"[6]

Gershwin did not confront anyone about what was being done—or not done—with his music, but he found a way to get in a dig. Upon being asked for background music to be played as Astaire and Rogers walked their mismatched dogs aboard ship, he headed to a soundstage piano and instantly devised an ingratiating tune that was referred to on studio cue sheets as "Walking the Dog." Then he orchestrated it himself, scoring it for two pianos and a small ensemble in an intentionally non-Hollywood style. As RKO had two orchestrators on hand, this constituted an act of defiance. Just a year earlier, he had been writing every sung and played note for powerful dramatic scenes—Crown appearing, as from the dead, in the middle of a hurricane while residents of Catfish Row cowered before him and God. Now here he was sneaking in an orchestration of a three-minute ditty that would accompany a flirtatious couple as they walked their respective pooches. "Walking the Dog" was heard on the film's soundtrack but for many years, the score was considered lost. Then, in 1960, a solo piano version was recreated from memory by Hal Borne, who had been the film's rehearsal pianist, and Ira published it with the more dignified title, *Promenade*. Nearly thirty years after that, George's orchestrated version turned up in a Warner Bros. warehouse in Secaucus, New Jersey, whence this little orchestral work, his last, was taken up and played by orchestras in its original form.

The ballet was not so easily accomplished. Sandrich wanted another *An American in Paris*. The trouble was that it had taken the composer the better part of a year to compose that piece. Now he was given a week to come up with something similar. A conductor-arranger working on the film, George's old friend and associate Nat Shilkret, recalled: "George arrived and played the ballet he had written. We listened—then silence. Either it sounded different from what they expected, or they could not connect the music with their flimsy idea of the story."[7] The composition Gershwin provided has never been identified, although Shilkret remembered it sounding like Cuban or Mexican music. He also recalled that there was little enthusiasm for the other songs Gershwin had written. Remembering a meeting with Gershwin, Sandrich, and Astaire, he wrote: "We were seated on the floor of the studio. Astaire started and said, 'George, I do not like the song you wrote for the last part of the ballet. In fact, it stinks.' (I do not remember the exact word, but it was an emphatic expression.) Sandrich, the director, backed him up. I was hoping that George would take offense, but, instead, he quietly said, 'I like the song, but you don't have to accept it.'"[8]

For the first time in their long association, Astaire was criticizing Gershwin's work. Being a lot higher in the pecking order than Gershwin, both in billing and salary, his opinion was what counted. And at this point he decided to write the ballet music himself. At his behest, the studio hired the Jimmy Dorsey Orchestra, whose arranger, Fud Livingston, was brought in to orchestrate Astaire's tune. According to Shilkret, Livingston was a fine arranger but, upon finding Astaire's sketch incomprehensible, began drinking. Shilkret, in turn, was unable to make heads or tails out of Livingston's arrangement. Moreover, he was angry that Astaire had tried to "compose for Gershwin."[9] Finally, Shilkret and orchestrator Robert Russell Bennett (also a longtime Gershwin friend and associate) and Gershwin stayed up all night writing the ballet. It consisted of some new music by Gershwin, followed by arrangements by Shilkret and Bennett of several songs from the movie, including a few bars of the otherwise unused "Wake Up, Brother, and Dance."

George's first negative comments about life in Los Angeles were made about a month after his arrival. In a letter to Mabel Schirmer, he wrote, "There's nothing like the phony glamour in Hollywood to bring out the need for one's real friends." He then became more direct. "Have You seen Kay? I haven't written to her nor have I heard from her. I should like to know if you ever see her?"[10] On his birthday, in late September, he waited in vain for a call from her while she, in New York, was waiting for a call from him.[11] But each was sticking, however uncomfortably, to the agreed upon

Pleasure Island

moratorium. Kay was now earning her living writing radio scripts, her stint as house songwriter for Radio City having ended. Socially, she was involved with radio writer Edward Byron, whom she had met when he worked on scripts for Gershwin's program. Byron was a fun-loving, hard-drinking fellow who provided companionship, but he could not replace George. She kept tabs on Gershwin through their mutual friends Mabel and Emily, and via Gershwin's valet Paul, who had gotten his position with George on her recommendation. George continued to think about her. In October, he asked about her in a letter to Mabel, writing, "I think about her a great deal and wonder if she is all right."[12] But he too was having an affair.

She was Simone Simon, a twenty-six year old actress who had been discovered by French director Marc Allégret and to whom, like Allégret's later discovery, Brigitte Bardot, the word "kittenish" was invariably applied. Simon had been successful in French cinema but was finding the going tough in Hollywood, where Twentieth Century Fox head Darryl F. Zanuck repeatedly assigned her to B movies such as *Girls Dormitory*. Her connection with Gershwin might have actually been a publicity ploy on her part to jump-start her career. A year later, when she was sued by her secretary, it came out that she had given all her boyfriends, including Gershwin, gold-plated keys to her home. The others were not named. Gershwin, by then deceased, was.

In early December 1936, he wrote Mabel, "Have not yet found a steady girl out here—you may be interested to know. The girls are surprisingly selfish, stupid [and] career conscious." Leonore had gone back east and George, referring to her, wrote Mabel, "She wrote saying she called you. She also made some mention about wanting to go see Kay with you and your making some remark about Kay considering the whole thing a closed book. That sounds very much as though you have some items of great interest to me."[13]

In the midst of this uneasiness, something truly depressing happened. Late in the evening on December 3, William Daly returned to his Fifth Avenue residence after working the evening in his office and he suddenly died of a heart attack. He was forty-nine. George and Ira did not go to the funeral, which was held two days later in Boston. It is not known if they contacted Daly's widow, Elizabeth (a novelist, destined to die suddenly a few months later at forty-eight) or their young daughter Emily. They did not talk about Daly's demise with friends or mention it in letters. But they probably had him in mind when, shortly after his passing, they put into their song "Shall We Dance" such unusual phrases as "Life is short; we're growing older" and "shall we give in to despair?" They had done something similar in the song "So What?" written after their father's death. Otherwise, then and now, they hid their feelings from view. But the effect of the loss was profound, especially on George. Daly was someone he had known for twenty years, someone he learned from, looked up to, counted on, and called his best friend. Now he was gone. It was another closed book.

With their work on *Shall We Dance* finished, George and Ira learned that RKO had exercised their option to hire them for another picture, this one also with Astaire. They were in for an extended stay in Hollywood—not just Hollywood, but Hollywood intrigue. Astaire, it turned out, although pleased to be working with the Gershwins again, was anxious to make a film without Rogers. He was wary of being dependent on a partner, having had the bottom drop out on him when his sister retired. Now, his name was more attached to Ginger's than it had ever been to Adele's, and Ginger could pull the plug on him too. So, in this next film, it was decided that he would work with someone else.

The trouble came when the studio picked Joan Fontaine as his co-star, inasmuch as she could not dance *or* sing. That sort of Hollywood logic was also applied to the screenplay. RKO had taken the story of *A Damsel in Distress* from a P. G. Wodehouse novel and assigned the scriptwriting job to a staff writer who proceeded to turn it into a detective story that bore no resemblance to Wodehouse's idea. They then hired Wodehouse to rewrite the script. The Gershwins had sailed through script problems many times before in their Broadway days. But now there was the additional difficulty of a nonsinger/nondancer playing the female lead, which did not augur well for their new compositions. Very likely the new songs would suffer a fate at least as bad as what had befallen "They Can't Take That Away From Me." It was at about this time that George, interviewed by the *Los Angeles Evening News*, said that he would not bother writing incidental music for his next movies but would, instead, leave that job to the "hacks."[14]

Pleasure Island

His tone was strangely vituperative. In publicly attaching the word "hack" to Hollywood's orchestrators, he was apparently applying it to the two he had worked with on *Shall We Dance*—esteemed friends Nat Shilkret and Robert Russell Bennett. People took this uncharacteristic moodiness as a sign of anger at the way the studio was treating him and his music. Evidence that this was so came when he took the first chance he could to get out of Hollywood by accepting a series of concert dates for the period after he finished *Shall We Dance* and before he began work on *A Damsel in Distress*. On December 15, he appeared with the Seattle Symphony playing *Rhapsody in Blue* and conducting his suite from *Porgy and Bess*. More concerts would follow in January, but first he returned to Los Angeles for the Christmas holidays where he, Ira, and Leonore were joined by Rose and Frankie and by Frankie's husband, Leopold Godowsky, Jr. As 1937 began, all the Gershwins except younger brother Arthur were again under one roof. During these days, George told his sister, somewhat dejectedly: "I don't think I've scratched the surface. I'm out here to make enough money with movies so that I don't have to think of money anymore. Because I just want to work on American music: symphonies, chamber music, opera. That is what I really want to do."[15]

As January loomed, he wrote to Mabel, who was recently divorced, to wish her a happy new year. His letter did not directly mention the end of his relationship with Kay or the death of William Daly, but those two earthquakes were certainly on his mind. "Dear Mabel—I am welcoming 1937. How about you? Perhaps, dear Mabel, this is our year. A year that will see both of us finding that elusive something that seems to bring happiness to the lucky. The pendulum swings back, so I've heard, and it's due to swing us back to a more satisfying state. 1936 was a year of important changes to me. They are too obvious to you to mention here. So, sweet Mabel, lift your glass with me [and] drink a toast to two nice people who will, in a happy state, go places this year."[16]

TWENTY

Final Concert, Final Affair

In early January 1937, George and Ira went to a ranch outside Carmel to meet with RKO Pictures' production chief Pandro Berman and director George Stevens to discuss the new Astaire film, but this was only a brief stop on the way to the Bay Area, where George was to appear with Pierre Monteux and the San Francisco Symphony. Two months would pass before he and Ira got to work on the new songs. In the meantime, there would be five concerts.

Present at the San Francisco and Berkeley performances were Ira, Rose, Leonore, Jerome Kern, Kern's wife Eva, and their daughter Betty. George then went alone to Detroit (literally alone; he was the only passenger on the DC 3, the public being air-shy at the time due to several recent crashes). All of these concerts were well received and when he returned to Los Angeles, he put his energy into preparations for the next two and biggest events, with the Los Angeles Philharmonic Orchestra downtown at the Philharmonic Auditorium. His plan was to use this venue, as he had tried to do at Lewisohn Stadium, to introduce *Porgy and Bess* to a new audience. As had been the case at Lewisohn the previous July, he eschewed the orchestral suite. Instead, Duncan would sing and Smallens would conduct. The hope was that the *Porgy* music would stir up demand for a new production and/or a movie version. Gershwin wrote Heyward on January 26 to tell him about this, saying the studios were "keen" about a filmed version, if "slightly afraid on account of the color question." He also sounded Heyward out about doing another opera, telling him to "put your mind to it, old boy, and I know you can evolve something interesting."[1]

He had other projects in mind as well. He met with Native American playwright Lynn Riggs to discuss collaborating on an opera to be called *The Lights of Lamy*, about the tribulations of Mexican Americans in New

Mexico. He had been asked by Chicago's Ravinia Festival to return in the summer of 1937 with a new orchestral composition and was thinking about what he might write. At that moment, he was favoring "a bright overture."[2] Also, he was composing a string quartet. It was taking shape in his mind, away from the piano, away even from manuscript paper. He told the impresario who was producing the upcoming Los Angeles concerts, Merle Armitage, that it was "going through my head all the time and as soon as I have finished scoring the next picture, I'm going to rent a little cabin in Coldwater Canyon, away from Hollywood, and get the thing down on paper. It's about to drive me crazy, it's so damned full of new ideas!"[3] And there was talk of a new Broadway musical with writers George S. Kaufman and Moss Hart. To be called *Curtain Going Up*, it was to have Hart, Kaufman, and the Gershwin brothers playing onstage roles. That George entertained such an idea indicates that, despite his talk about devoting himself to opera, chamber, and symphonic pieces, his love for Broadway musicals and show business was undiminished. It is also indicative of how hard it was for him to say no, especially to old friends like Kaufman and Hart. Not that the idea of his going on stage as an actor was completely unprecedented. On his World War I draft card, he had listed his occupation as "actor-composer." And as recently as May 1936, he and Kaufman had appeared at New York's Vanderbilt Theatre in a one-performance show called *Spring Tonic,* which featured skits by Kaufman and others, and music— nothing new—by Gershwin and others. On that night, for tickets ranging in price from $2 to $4, the audience could watch sketches performed by

Gershwin, Kaufman, Ben Hecht, and striptease artist Gypsy Rose Lee. The idea of treading the boards before an audience did not, needless to say, appeal to Ira, who quickly nixed the project or, at least, his part in it.

These plans brought a renewed optimism. Also salutary was the fact that he, along with Brazilian composer Heitor Villa-Lobos, had been elected to honorary membership in the Academy of Santa Cecilia, Rome. George was informed of this in a letter dated February 9, 1937, from composer Alfredo Casella who addressed him as "Dear Master" and asked for a new piece for September's Venice Fifth International Music Festival. In his reply, Gershwin thanked the academy for the honor and expressed regret that, due to current commitments, he would be unable to provide the requested composition. Casella wrote back to extend an invitation to the following year's festival in September 1938. The Italians had a history of looking with favor on Gershwin's music. On a visit to the United States in March 1932, Ottorino Respighi had expressed his admiration. Then, at the 1932 Venice International Music Festival, when conductor Fritz Reiner and pianist Harry Kaufman played the *Concerto in F*, the audience would not leave until the third movement was repeated—a fact that gave Gershwin no end of pleasure. He loved telling people that the only other time such a thing had happened was at the 1875 Boston premiere of Tchaikovsky's *First Piano Concerto*.

Thus, he went into the Los Angeles Philharmonic concerts armed with signs of approbation from the classical community. All seats were quickly sold, and he was happier than he had been in months. He was particularly pleased that the music of *Porgy and Bess* would be introduced to the West Coast. When Armitage refused to pay Todd Duncan's travel expenses to Los Angeles, George provided the necessary $500 from his own $2,000 fee. Then, when Armitage refused to pay for an extra rehearsal, George docked himself for that expense too. He was determined that the audience hear Duncan sing the *Porgy* songs, believing that this would stir up enthusiasm for a West Coast production of the opera. On February 9, the day before the first concert, he wrote Mabel of his anticipation, saying, "they've seen nothing like the excitement for a concert in years."[4]

Dr. Zilboorg had given him a Leica camera and some lessons in photography. Gershwin, in turn, instructed Paul Mueller. So it was that during rehearsals for the February 10 concert, Mueller was taking photographs as Gershwin rehearsed the orchestra. These photos show the composer, baton in hand, with alternately severe and ethereal expressions as he worked with the Los Angeles Philharmonic. While Mueller was taking the pictures, Gershwin lost his balance and nearly fell off the podium. Mueller caught him and kept him from landing on the floor. Gershwin promptly recovered, thanked his assistant, assured him that he was fine, and resumed the rehearsal.

The first concert went well. On the second night, however, Oscar Levant noticed something going wrong as George played the concerto. His fingers stumbled over an easy passage in the first movement and again while he was playing the four simple octaves that conclude the second. Backstage, Levant kidded him about these goofs only to have George turn on him with unexpected belligerence, calling him a son of a bitch. Then he revealed to Levant that a couple of other odd moments had taken place. At one point, he had smelled a burning odor. At another, he had had a sudden dizzying headache.

He had always been the epitome of good health. In Beverly Hills, he eagerly accepted what Sam Behrman called "the cult of the body" by hiring a trainer and staking out a six-mile daily walk for himself, one that took him into the Santa Monica Mountains. He extolled this new exercise plan in a letter dated January 9, 1937, to Emily, saying, "my masseur suggested a hike in the hills. I acquiesced [and] have become a victim of its vigorous charm. For the past week, every day, hot or cold, we walked back in the hills [and] really, Em, I feel as if I have discovered something wonderful. It is refreshing [and] invigorating. Better than golf, because it eliminates the aggravation that comes with that pastime."[5]

After the concerts, there was a grand party in Gershwin's honor, and the strange physical episodes were temporarily forgotten. His agent, Arthur Lyons, rented a banquet room at the Trocadero Ballroom on Sunset Boulevard and invited 250 people for a fete that was nearly as big as the one Kay had organized after *Porgy and Bess*'s New York premiere. Like the earlier party, this one had two dance bands. The guests included Cole Porter, Otto Klemperer, Frank Capra, Jimmy Stewart, Fred Astaire, and Ginger Rogers. Fred and Ginger, upon an attention-getting *ta-da* from the musicians, stood up and addressed George with some affectionate remarks, then took to the dance floor with a routine they had created in his honor. Never before had they danced together in a public setting. George, as Rogers later remembered, "was dumbfounded and pleased that Fred and I would dance for him."[6] She and Gershwin had lately resumed their romance, although it was no more serious than the last time. There were a few dinner dates at beach restaurants, he driving her up the coast in his new maroon Cord convertible. She had recently separated from her second husband, actor Lew Ayres, and was moving rapidly through a string of beaus, including Jimmy Stewart, Howard Hughes, Cary Grant, and Alfred Vanderbilt in addition to Gershwin.

The February 10 and 11 concerts were reviewed in the February 27 edition of the *Musical Courier* by critic Richard Drake Saunders, who thus became the final reviewer of George's last public performance. Saunders had two points to make. One was that "Gershwin has a certain individual flair and an occasional work of his on a program is all very well, but an entire evening is too much. It is like a meal of chocolate éclairs." The other was that a concert such as this was worthwhile because it made "a certain class of people conscious of such a thing as symphonic ensemble. It was obvious that a large number had never been in the auditorium before. Anyway, they saw some movie stars."[7] The *Porgy and Bess* music came and went all but unnoticed.

Dr. Zilboorg later claimed that George had called him in New York for advice after the February incidents and that he told the composer the problem was most likely organic rather than psychological. There is some reason to question this because Zilboorg and his wife both went out of their way after Gershwin's death to deny that the doctor had played any role in a misdiagnosis. What is known is that in late February, Gershwin sought an explanation from medical doctors, who were unable to find anything wrong with him. This was a relief to him and to his family and friends, who used this conclusion—or lack of one—as their basis for believing the symptoms to be products of neurosis and depression. George's only previous neuroses—if they qualify as such—were his obsessive womanizing and the eagerness with which he discussed his stomach troubles. Nor was he ever one for despair—quite the opposite. But the people around him had

Final Concert, Final Affair

good reason to believe he was depressed. Five years had passed without a successful show or concert work, capped by the dismal reception given *Porgy and Bess*. In addition, there was the insensitive treatment he had received at the hands of his Hollywood overseers, his failure to find anyone to replace Kay in his life, and Daly's death. Thus, the people close to him decided that he was acting out. Irving Berlin said, "there is nothing wrong with Gershwin that a hit song wouldn't cure."[8]

In early March, George and Ira began work on the new film, *A Damsel in Distress*. Their first song was "Nice Work if You Can Get It," whose title came from a magazine cartoon that showed one woman telling another that a third lady's daughter had become a prostitute. To this the second replied, "It's nice work if you can get it." Ira immediately saw that the "nice work" could, instead, be love. George's introductory verse employed more of his by-now perfected colloquial recitative, while both verse and refrain had sounds that were alternatingly strange and playful—sometimes both. Just about everything he had written since beginning work on *Porgy and Bess* had been a masterpiece, and this was another. Next came "A Foggy Day," which the brothers wrote late at night, after George came home from a party. Composer Alec Wilder, in discussing this one, referred to its "heartbreak quality" and to the "truly chilling" musical moment at the end, on the word "suddenly."[9] These two songs became the best-known of a score which, written in March and April, also included "Things Are Looking Up," "I Can't Be Bothered Now," and two madrigal-style songs set by George for four-part chorus with piano accompaniment, one entitled "The Jolly Tar and the Milk Maid" and the other "Sing of Spring." All of these pieces were extraordinary. In a May 12 letter to Isaac Goldberg, George said that he and Ira had written the latter two numbers "so the audience will get a chance to hear some singing besides the crooning of the stars." Earlier in the same letter, he had taken another dig at Astaire, this time in reference to *Shall We Dance*, saying that that film had thrown "one or two songs away without any kind of a plug. This is mainly due to the structure of the story which does not include any other singers than Fred and Ginger and the amount of singing one can stand of these two is quite limited."[10] Gershwin had never before had anything negative to say about either Astaire or Rogers, and it is significant that these comments were made in May, when his pain and edginess were worsening significantly. Yet, his musical gift was all the time growing stronger. The songs for *A Damsel in Distress* were beautiful, gentle, and deeply felt.

Ira, too, was at the height of his powers. Whenever George wrote a fine piece, Ira matched it with a perfect, memorable lyric. In "It Ain't Necessarily So," "Let's Call the Whole Thing Off," "They Can't Take That Away From Me," and "A Foggy Day," he caught the wit and feeling of the music and always avoided, as did George, overstatements and mawkishness. Their intimacy as collaborators, which playwright Morrie Ryskind described as "telepathic," was matched by their closeness as brothers and friends. At one point, they were observed sitting at a piano, making each other laugh so hard they ended up falling backward off the bench. Their love for one another showed even in their arguments. When the Pulitzer Prize was awarded in 1932 to Ira but not to George for *Of Thee I Sing* (there being no Pulitzer for music at the time), they got into a yelling match, with Ira insisting that he would *not* accept the prize unless George got it too, while George demanded that Ira accept it, no ifs, ands, or buts.[11] In the end, Ira did take the award, but he hung it in his bathroom, slightly askew.[12]

Not that all of their disputes were of the Alphonse and Gaston[13] variety. Publisher Bennett Cerf recalled a dinner party where George showed off a gold cigarette case that had been engraved with the signatures of a number of celebrities. He passed it around the room, taking pleasure in every ooh and aah. After the case had made the rounds, Ira managed to pop George's balloon and simultaneously poke fun at himself by taking from his pocket a crumpled pack of Camels and saying "Anybody want a cigarette?"[14] And sometimes there was real nastiness. Cerf recalled another occasion, this time when he and the brothers were playing golf and George out of the blue asked Ira if he knew why "The Man I Love" was not selling well. Ira said "No. Why?" and George replied that it was because "the lyrics stink." Ira shrugged the insult off, saying, "All right. The lyrics stink. Come on and play golf."[15] But he was human and the comment had to have rankled. Nor could he—or Leonore—completely ignore the fact that the financial split between them as partners was not 50–50 or even 60–40 but generally 70–30. Still, it was obvious that Ira took great pleasure in his brother's achievements—more pleasure, it seemed, than he took in his own work.

Final Concert, Final Affair

Rouben Mamoulian described the time the brothers first played the score of *Porgy* for him: "Ira sang—he threw his head back with abandon, his eyes closed, and sang like a nightingale. . . . It was touching to see how he, while singing, would become so overwhelmed with admiration for his brother that he would look from him to me with half-open eyes and pantomime with a soft gesture of his hand, as if saying, 'He did it. Isn't he wonderful?'"[16]

In home movies made during these months in Hollywood, they can be seen clowning around by the pool. George runs across the patio, sneaks up on Frankie, drapes his arms around her neck, and kisses her on the cheek. Then he becomes a waiter, a towel folded over his arm, and takes an order from a guest, while Ira fits upside-down bowls atop the heads of Harold Arlen's wife, Anya, and Henry Botkin and then switches the bowls from one head to the other as if playing a shell game.

But, happy as these moments were, and as great as the collaboration had become, the relationship was in trouble. George was anxious to return to New York while Ira, having found the indolent weather of Los Angeles to his taste, had decided to remain in California. He and Leonore were already looking for a home to buy.[17] So far as is known, no formal breakup of the partnership was discussed. But it was clear that if the brothers were separated by a continent they would no longer be able to work together as the mood struck them. To collaborate on a film score, George would have to pull up stakes again and leave New York for Hollywood, which, given his current feelings about the studios, was an unlikely prospect. Were they to work together on a Broadway show, sedentary Ira would have to travel cross-country and set up temporary residence in New York. Should George compose another opera, Ira would be ancillary to the project. Certainly, there would be no role for him in the string quartets and symphonic works his brother was planning. Nor was he as attached as George was to the rest of the family in New York. He was distant from their mother, on whom George doted, and standoffish to his other siblings, especially Arthur. At that moment, Rose, George, Ira, and Leonore were living under the same roof. But the household was run by Lee, not Rose, and she was enjoying this new primacy. Life in Beverly Hills allowed her to captain the Gershwin salon, uncontested by mother Rose or sister Emily or potential sister-in-law Kay. With Rose set to return to New York and

Kay out of the picture, Lee was, as long as George remained in California, the de facto doyenne of the family.

True to his word, George took no part in writing the background orchestral music for *A Damsel in Distress*, leaving that task to Russell Bennett, with the result that his work on this film was a happier experience than had been the case with *Shall We Dance*. It also helped that the director this time was George Stevens. RKO head Berman had decided that Sandrich and Stevens would take turns directing Astaire's movies, and now it was Stevens's turn. Although Stevens gave short shrift to some songs ("Nice Work if You Can Get It" and "Sing of Spring" were never quite heard; they were interrupted by spoken dialogue), he proved masterful in staging "A Foggy Day."

It was during the composition of this second Astaire score that George, at a mid-March dinner party given by Edward G. Robinson in honor of Igor Stravinsky, found himself sitting beside someone who was, he became convinced, the woman he had been looking for. She was actress Paulette Goddard who, upon being introduced to Gershwin, immediately distinguished herself from every other beautiful woman he had met by saying, "Why don't you compose music people will hiss to?"[18] Along with the naughty irreverence, there was an impish smile, luminous green eyes, dark brown hair, and a waiflike shape that made her the sort of woman George had always favored. Moreover, she was Jewish *and* his mother liked her.

Goddard enjoyed making a mystery of herself. Definitive biographical information was hard to come by. Sometimes her birth name was given as Marion Levy, sometimes it was Pauline Marion Levy. Sometimes her parents were Joe and Alta Levy, sometimes Joe and Alta Goddard. Her year of birth was 1910 or 1911 or 1915, although the latter was unlikely because it would have made her twelve at the time of her first marriage in 1927. That first husband—the first of three or, possibly, four, was Edward or Edwin or Edgar James of North Carolina, who was reputedly much older than she, although no one knows how old, and whose wealth probably came from his connection with the Southern States Lumber Company of Asheville, North Carolina. What is uncontestable is that their divorce in 1929 provided her with $100,000 in cash, which meant that she would never be poor again. At the time Gershwin met her, one of the biggest guessing games in Hollywood was whether, after four years as Charlie Chaplin's live-in lover, she had married him. If they did marry, the ceremony took place in a Singapore church or perhaps at sea off the coast of Malaysia. She took great pleasure in kidding reporters who tried to pin her down about this, and it was never exactly confirmed, but never quite denied. Chaplin, who had the same elusive bent when it came to biographical details, was equally vague.

When Gershwin met Goddard in March 1937, Chaplin had recently released a masterpiece, *Modern Times*, his first film in five years, costarring Goddard. It had met with mixed reviews and poor box office earnings, at least in the United States. He and Gershwin were at similar points in their careers in that their art had matured ahead of their audiences. He was also like Gershwin in his womanizing, although Chaplin was more controlling. He needed to exert complete dominion over everything that mattered to him. In 1918, he built his own film studio and ran it like a fiefdom. His films were distributed by United Artists, which he had cofounded in 1919. When it came to women, there had been a series of relationships with girls he had met as teenagers and over whom he exerted Svengali-style power. This need of his to dominate only fueled Goddard's rebelliousness, which meant that she was open to a romance with Gershwin. A large part of her enjoyment of the affair with George came from the stealth with which it was conducted. Chaplin had his suspicions and hired a private detective, but, according to Mueller, George and Paulette worked out a ruse that had Paulette driving to a prearranged location where Paul would be waiting. She would leave her car, get into Paul's, and hunker down in the back seat while he took her to Gershwin's place in Beverly Hills.[19] It has never been explained how this simple stratagem could possibly have fooled any self-respecting private detective. In any event, Gershwin was not much for secrecy. Walter Winchell's nationally read newspaper celebrity gossip column mentioned the Gershwin-Goddard romance. And the couple was seen together in Palm Springs.

Shortly after meeting Paulette, George began talking about marrying her. Alexander Steinert, who had been the musical coach for *Porgy and Bess*, tried to set him straight in this regard, saying that she, an actress, was not about to leave filmmaker Chaplin, who could do so much more for her career than could composer Gershwin. For the first time in his life, George had gotten himself a rival who was bigger than he was in the popular culture and who had him at a disadvantage when it came to celebrity. "In our century," wrote Alistair Cooke, "more people have come out everywhere to catch a glimpse of Charles Chaplin than did so for any other human in history."[20] Chaplin was no James Warburg. Nor was Paulette a Kay Swift; this fling of hers with Gershwin was just that and nothing more. Perhaps he should have been forewarned rather than charmed by her wisecrack about writing music people could "hiss to"; music was not an important part of her life. His friends tried to get him to see the reality of the situation. As Steinert was trying to make him understand that Goddard would never leave a movie legend to take up with a composer, Harold Arlen was taking a different tack, telling him he was not the marrying kind and that when push came to shove he would never give up the freedom that allowed him to go endlessly from party to party, piano to piano, woman to woman.[21] George bridled at this and cut the discussion with Arlen short. He was, he believed, ready to marry—and ready to marry Paulette.

Although he had come to understand that his status in the movie industry was not equal to the status of the actors and directors, what he had not yet realized, but was about to discover, was that this lesser prestige also diminished his worth as an eligible man. Just as quickly as she had taken up with him, Paulette dropped him. She was one of several actresses under consideration for the role of Scarlett O'Hara in the upcoming production of *Gone With the Wind*, and this was certainly an inopportune time for her to sever her ties to a film giant like Chaplin.

TWENTY-ONE

Last Songs

It was at this point that Gershwin began displaying an almost irrational irritability. Harold Arlen remembered an occasion when he and George were at a party with several other songwriters and each was having a turn at the piano. As Arlen stepped forward to demonstrate his latest wares, George said to him, "No you don't. I'm not going to follow you." This shocked Arlen. "Since we were always together in one bunch trying to help one another, there was little show of jealousy. When he acted that way, I felt uneasy. I knew something was wrong with him, and I thought it was Hollywooditis."[1]

In his May 12 letter to Isaac Goldberg, George said that he and Ira had completed their work on *A Damsel in Distress* and were to report immediately, despite fatigue, to Samuel Goldwyn. A week later, on May 19, he wrote Mabel: "Ira and I have had to literally drag ourselves to work the last few days as we have just finished the second Astaire score and have to start right in on *The Goldwyn Follies*. Even the Gershwins can't take that kind of routine."[2] He was dissembling here. The fatigue was his, not

Ira's. He *had* always been able to handle that much work and more. In the spring of 1930, he had performed the *Rhapsody in Blue* live on stage at the Roxy Theater more than thirty times in a single week in conjunction with the premiere of the film *The King of Jazz*. In January 1934, there had been the month-long, twelve-thousand-mile, twenty-eight–city tour with the Leo Reisman Orchestra followed immediately by the twice-a-week radio program. Somehow, throughout that period, he had found the time and energy to work on *Porgy and Bess*. He could not have been unaware that the fatigue he felt now in May 1937 was not normal for him. Nevertheless, it did not occur to him to insist on a few days' rest before going to work for Goldwyn. He had never dodged any assignment.

"The Great Goldwyn," as George mockingly called him, had begun life
in the meanest of circumstances. Born in Warsaw in 1879 to a large family that lived on the verge of starvation, he set out at sixteen alone and on foot for America, walking five hundred miles to Hamburg where he worked as a glove maker long enough to earn his fare to London. Then came a 120–mile walk to Birmingham, where he worked as a blacksmith's apprentice to pay for a voyage in steerage class to Halifax, Nova Scotia. That was followed by another walk—this one a mid-winter trek to the United States, whose border he crossed illegally somewhere in Maine. Then came years as a glove salesman in New York until April 1913, when he stepped into a nickelodeon on Thirty-fourth Street and saw his first movie—and his future.

He was a trim, bald, brutish-looking man who found it all but impossible to show empathy for other human beings except when he was watching tearjerker movies. Most of his personal relationships and all of his business partnerships had ended in hatred and mistrust. He refused to provide court-ordered alimony to his first wife or child support to their daughter. He battled his motion picture associates until they would no longer have anything to do with him. When his connections to Paramount Pictures and Metro-Goldwyn-Mayer ended, he went on to head the independent Samuel Goldwyn Studio, renting space at the site of the old Pickford-Fairbanks lot on Santa Monica Boulevard in West Hollywood. He could not act, direct, or write. All he could do was hire. And sometimes he was not good at that. In the early 1930s, he pinned his hopes on a Russian-born actress, Anna Sten, even though she could not speak a word of English. His greatest film, *The Best Years of Our Lives*, which brought him a long-coveted first Oscar in 1946, came from an idea suggested by his second wife, Frances, after she read an article in *Time* about returning World War II soldiers. He had at first dismissed her suggestion. It took her months to talk him into it.[3]

It was to this man that George, suffering now from fatigue and headaches, reported on May 12, 1937. Goldwyn had hired him and Ira as well as writers Lillian Hellman and Ben Hecht and choreographer George Balanchine to make himself the Hollywood equivalent of Broadway's Ziegfeld. As had been the case with *Shall We Dance*, George was expected to write a ballet, this time with Balanchine's choreography. There was so much talent involved in the project that when Goldwyn, sitting in a room with Hellman, Balanchine, and the Gershwins, mused, "It sure is wonderful to have a genius" each of them thought he or she had been singled out and turned toward the producer. He had been referring to Balanchine.[4]

Once again, George found himself working with some longstanding friends. The orchestrator was Edward Powell, a fellow Schillinger student. The conductor was Alfred Newman, whom he had first met in 1916 and who had conducted his music for the 1920 and 1921 editions of the *George White Scandals* and for *Funny Face* in 1927. The film's stars, however, were people he did not know and of a lesser magnitude than Fred Astaire. The new George and Ira songs were to be sung by Ella Logan, Kenny Baker, and Charlie McCarthy—the latter a wooden dummy who shot sarcastic remarks back to his ventriloquist, Edgar Bergen. The ballet was to be danced by German-born ballerina Vera Zorina, to whom Goldwyn was attracted, although she did not return the favor. She later married Balanchine.

The first Gershwin songs for the new film were as good as the ones just written for Astaire. "I Was Doing All Right," "Just Another Rhumba," and "I Love to Rhyme" were fun, gentle, breezy, and adventurous. George was able to write this music despite the now nearly constant, pounding headaches. He had purchased a strange device, a vibrating metal helmet advertised by its manufacturer, the Crosley Radio Corporation, as a hair restorer. At first, he used it for that purpose and wrote jokingly to Mabel about how ridiculous he looked with it on his head. But soon he was sitting under it in the hope that it would lessen the severity of the pain behind his eyes. Some of the headaches were, according to his friend, writer Anita Loos, "of alarming intensity." At one point, while sitting with others by his swimming pool, he had, according to Loos, "a sudden excruciating headache that made him scream in agony."[5]

It had always been in his nature to talk about himself, especially about his health. His stomach hurt. He had not had a bowel movement in days. But now, threatened by something truly serious, he kept silent. This was his way when faced with mortality—most recently the death of Bill Daly. He could not have been unconcerned about, much less unaware of, his physical decline. Yet no one heard him speak of it. Instead, just as he was attempting to get past the Goldwyn assignment, he tried to push himself past the illness. Although the headaches and fatigue were all too real, he may have been reassured by the fact that his family and friends viewed them as manifestations of emotional distress. If everyone believed that to be so, perhaps they were right. Yet, it was hard to be comforted by the way they, especially Ira and Leonore, acted upon these views. Gershwin biographer Lawrence D. Stewart, who worked as Ira's secretary in the 1950s, concluded that Lee and Ira viewed George's illness "as some sort of cop-out—trying to get out of the Goldwyn commitment."[6] To Leonore the problem was not only not physical, it was not even psychosomatic; she was convinced that George was intentionally putting on an act. To her the headaches were the attention-getting ploy of a frustrated showoff, and she was not about to indulge him. She became strict with him, as if he were a child, showing distaste when, as now sometimes happened, he fumbled at the table with his knife and fork. It was her expectation that she and Ira would soon be living far from him. He would return to New York and they would stay on in Los Angeles. It is not clear why this choice had been made but, given that the brothers had never lived more than a few feet away from one another, it was an imminent upheaval—one that, added to the breakup with Kay, the death of Daly, and the years of failed projects, might explain why Ira and Leonore were so ready to believe that George's illness was emotional. Emotions must have been running high on all sides. In retrospect, neither brother seems to have had anything to gain from a geographical divide. Leonore was the only obvious beneficiary, as it would allow her to establish a separate West Coast Gershwin suzerainty.

Last Songs

153

While George remained under her roof, he was under her power. As he grew weaker, she grew stronger. Ira, not knowing what to do, stepped back. And Rose, despite George's illness, decided it was time to return to New York. She traveled by ship through the Panama Canal, making a vacation of it. As she was leaving, cousin Henry Botkin was arriving, taking up residence with the Gershwins. George had had his painting materials shipped to him from the East Coast, and he and Botkin discussed one another's art work. George had recently completed two new oil portraits: one of Jerome Kern, the other of Arnold Schoenberg. He was proud of his progress as a painter, and Botkin was, as always, encouraging. During these talks, George told his cousin what he had been telling everyone all year: that he was wasting his time working on movies, that he wanted to write symphonic works and opera. On May 21, he and Botkin went to look at property that Ira was thinking of buying. Los Angeles, he told his cousin, was a good place for Ira but not for him. He needed to be in New York.[7]

During this period, Kay was in an impossible situation. She knew George was ill but had no way of knowing if it was serious. The ban on communications still in effect, she had to get her information from Mabel, Emily, and Lou in New York or from Paul in Los Angeles. The New York friends were getting their facts from Leonore. Paul had firsthand knowledge but he lived at North Roxbury, whose telephone was controlled by Leonore.

George had never stopped corresponding with Julia Van Norman, although his ardor for her had cooled as it became increasingly apparent that she was mentally unstable. "Dear George," she had written him in August 1933, "Yes, I needed to love you, but still I feel that I may possibly need more than that. Since my mother died no creature has really loved me but my white Persian cat, whom a kindly neighbor poisoned."[8] Yet there was a weird prescience in the letters she wrote to him in California, in which she expressed anxiety about his health even before there was any reason for such concern. By mid-April, she was writing, somewhat hysterically, that she feared she would never see him again.

In the midst of all this, the brothers continued their work on the Goldwyn movie. Next up was a ballad whose main strain had been written in 1931 during work on *Of Thee I Sing*. George had always referred to it as his "Brahmsian" tune, and as he returned to it, he became convinced that it was a beauty. Ira was not so sure. They argued about it, Ira claiming it was nothing more than a pop song and not up to their theater song standards. George replied, "What's wrong with a pop song?" In the middle of this dispute, George placed a midnight phone call to lyricist Yip Harburg, who arrived at the Gershwin house to arbitrate. He listened to George play the piece and, in judging it, seemed to take both sides, finding that it "did not have the blaze of the Gershwin hallmark but it was a brave sweep of melody."[9] He did, however, correctly assess Ira's difficulty. This melody needed a straightforward love lyric, which was just what Ira most hated to write. Moreover, the tune was very spare; Ira would have just eighty-five notes to work with. Finally, Ira said, "I'll write it, but the song will be Goldwyn not Gershwin."[10] Eventually, he grew to love this music, but he never much liked the words he wrote for it or the title he gave it, "Love Walked In." It was their last completed collaboration.

Immediately after finishing "Love Walked In," George began work on a fifth song for the picture, an as-yet untitled melody. At this point, he could work only when his head stopped pounding. During those interludes, which were becoming increasingly rare, he labored over the new tune, beginning it with three pick-up notes, each supported by its own distinctive chord. Then there spun forth a gorgeous melody that had the unaffected grandeur of his best work. Oscar Levant came by while he was writing it and recognized its worth, although he felt it could be improved. He suggested that George give the long phrases more breathing space by adding a couple of bars here and there. George spent the next two days trying to do that before deciding the music was fine as it was. When Ira listened to it, he thought ahead to a lyric and made his own suggestion. He wanted a couple of dotted notes. George agreed to this suggestion, and those notes would later be the *ands* in "The radio and / the telephone and / the movies that we know." It was the final moment of their collaboration and the last piece that George would write.

At this point, Goldwyn summoned the composer to the studio to play the score-in-progress. He ostensibly wanted to hear what he was getting for his money. Actually, he—a famously tin-eared man—was showing dominance over a hireling. A year earlier, when producer David O. Selznick had made the same request of Jerome Kern, the latter's response had been, "I don't play samples."[11] But Gershwin complied. He went to the studio, sat at the piano for Goldwyn and several of his subordinates, and the songs they heard, which included "Love Walked In," and what Ira would later entitle "Love Is Here to Stay," were summarily dismissed—although Goldwyn did like the middle eight bars of the gently up-tempo "I Was Doing All Right." That evening, Gershwin returned home with Goldwyn's demand that he "write hits like Irving Berlin" ringing in his ears.

The headaches were so bad now that he was spending hours in his upstairs room with the blinds closed, sitting on the floor, holding his head. He also began having problems chewing his food. Leonore, in disgust, found herself having to cut it up for him. She and Ira concluded at this point that he needed another medical checkup. However, rather than take him to a doctor or a hospital, they invited a team of physicians to the house. Their reason for having the examination conducted at home has never been given, although it was probably a desire to avoid publicity. On June 9, the doctors, led by Dr. Gabriel Segall, had a look. Under the circumstances, there was little they could do in the way of tests, but they were able to satisfy themselves and everyone else that nothing was seriously wrong. The next day George wrote his mother, affecting cheerfulness: "Dear Mom—Your writing is certainly improving and if you don't watch out some Hollywood studio will sign you up—I think I've got something there because the only thing the Gershwin family lacks is a book writer and it would be simply wonderful if the posters read—Book by Rose Gershwin—Lyrics by Ira Gershwin—Music by George Gershwin—and we've got to get Arthur in somewhere, so let's say Entire Production Staged by Arthur Gershwin. . . . I have had quite enough of Hollywood . . . of late I haven't been feeling particularly well. Yesterday I put myself in the hands of a Dr. Segall and he is going to try to find out the reason for the slight dizziness I get every once in a while." He then told her he would soon be having lunch with Paulette, whom Rose liked, and that "Leonore has been extremely active working for a few charity and labor causes out here. In fact, tomorrow she is having a large tea party to try to collect some money to help Martin Mooney, the laborer in prison."[12]

A few days later George became too ill to go to work. When Ira phoned the studio with this news, Goldwyn, who had known about George's affair with Paulette Goddard and believed his inability to work to be due to late night carousing, ordered him off the payroll. George had never before failed to live up to a contract and felt not anger but guilt. He offered to let Goldwyn use *An American in Paris* free of charge in place of the ballet he would now be unable to write. Goldwyn was pleased with this present although he eventually decided that a ballet based on *An American in Paris* would be too intellectual for movie audiences.

On June 12, George finally got to go on his vacation. He traveled with Arthur Lyons to Coronado, an island in San Diego Bay. His time on the beach there under the sun seemed to help. But a few days later, back in Los Angeles, the headaches returned and, with them, moments of alarming behavior. Now when Paul chauffeured him from place to place, George made him call out the names of all the streets they passed, and if Paul skipped one, he had to go back and pass it again so it could be identified in proper order. This was harmless enough, if strange, but one evening, George reached over and opened the driver's door and tried to push Paul out of the car. Mueller managed to shut the door, gain control over the swerving vehicle, and pull over to the side of the road. When he asked his employer why he had done such a thing, Gershwin, sweating, put his hands to his brow and said, "I don't know."[13]

There were times when these symptoms vanished, leaving George something like himself again. It was during one of those periods that Levant brought Aaron Copland to see him. Copland wanted to join the American Society of Composers, Authors, and Publishers so he could write for Hollywood, and he asked George to sign his application. Gershwin did so and then complimented him on his children's opera, *The Second Hurricane*, which had recently been broadcast on the radio. In fact, Gershwin had been one of the sponsors of the first performance of that piece.[14] Copland found George's luxurious residence impressive, musing later that "it was hard for me to realize that you could get all that for writing songs and lyrics."[15]

Because there were such periods when the symptoms disappeared, people were all the more willing to believe that George's illness was emotional in nature. During those intervals, he and Ira would again discuss work. But then the headaches, fatigue, and irrational behavior returned. Finally, Ira and Leonore took him to Cedars of Lebanon, where for three days he was examined by one specialist after another. All of them except one concluded that the illness was emotional. The exception was Dr. Eugene Ziskind, a neurologist who, in finding the patient highly sensitive to light, suspected a swelling of the retina due to an increase of pressure in the brain. In short, he had deduced a brain tumor, and it was his recommendation that Gershwin undergo a spinal tap to rule that possibility in or out. Gershwin refused to allow the procedure, having heard that it might increase the severity of his headaches. Instead, he was released from the hospital on June 26 with a diagnosis that read, "Most likely hysteria."[16]

This opinion convinced Leonore all the more that her reaction was the appropriate one. She told George's friends not to indulge his "artistic temper tantrums."[17] What he needed, she decided, was a good psychiatrist. The most prominent practitioner in the area was Dr. Ernest Simmel, who was engaged to observe George's behavior and come to some conclusions. His diagnosis was the same as Dr. Ziskind's—that the symptoms were organic in origin, not emotional. Still, no action was recommended or taken. But the family knew that something critical was happening. Ira phoned his mother in New York and told her to hurry back to California. She demurred. As she told her sister Kate, "What good would I do if I went? I probably would even be in the way."[18]

In the meantime, George was receiving increasingly frantic letters from Julia. On April 15, he had written to her, jokingly, "You remember me, don't you? Composer, about 5 ft. 10½ in. weight 155, eyes brown, hair black." On April 19, her reply was serious and strangely prescient: "Sometimes I think that perhaps I will never see you again but I know that isn't so." Then on June 14, she wrote to say, "When I tune in on your spirit lately there seems to be quite a lot of static. Something is proving troublesome. I'm afraid." On June 30, after returning from the hospital, he sent her a telegram: "Thanks for letter home from hospital feeling somewhat better don't worry expect to be well in a week or so warm regards to you and yours." The next day she wrote back: "I dreamt you sent me a letter and I simply could not decipher it. It looked as if your co-ordination had gone haywire."[19]

By this time, that was so. George was unable to eat without assistance. When he went to his room he could not make it there unescorted. Once there he would sit on the floor with the blinds drawn, holding his head. He slept for long intervals, sometimes due to the sedatives he was taking to control the pain. Levant remembered going to the drugstore to fill a prescription for "one-fourth or one-half a grain of Phenobarbital, an inadequate anodyne for anyone in exquisite pain."[20]

A few days later, George felt better and gamely went to lunch with Ira and Leonore at the Brown Derby restaurant on Vine Street in Hollywood. But upon leaving the building, he became dizzy and fell to the sidewalk. "Leave him there," Lee said to her husband as George lay sprawled on the pavement. "All he wants is attention."[21] It is not known if Ira eventually helped him up or if George was able to rise on his own or if a Good Samaritan came by. Given Ira's inability to disobey any of Leonore's commands, it was probably one of the latter two. A few days after the Brown Derby incident, Lee ordered George from the table when he fumbled his utensils and spilled his water. As always, Ira obeyed her orders without question. As he was helping his brother upstairs to his room, George turned to stare at him. Ira later told a friend, "I'll never forget that look as long as I live."[22] It can only be imagined what the look conveyed, although it had to have been "Why aren't you protecting me from her?" or "Am I dying?" or both.

Toward the beginning of July, Lillian Hellman was a guest at a gathering at the Gershwin home. In her book, *An Unfinished Woman*, she remembered that "what we all thought was a mildly sick, overanxious man came downstairs for dinner in a dressing gown and, as usual, went immediately to the piano. I was talking to somebody, only half listening to the piano, when I turned my head; his fingers had moved to the wrong notes for a passage of *An American in Paris*. Startled, I went over to the piano, but by the time I reached it, George had stopped playing and was staring at his hands as if he had never seen them before."[23] Shortly after that, on July 3, George's old friend Sam Behrman stopped by for a visit, accompanied by Levant and writer Sonya Levien. Behrman had phoned ahead before coming and was told by Ira that George had not been well for a few weeks and that the problem seemed to be a nervous disorder. Levant told Behrman that the prevailing opinion was that George's condition had been brought on by his disappointment over the failure of *Shall We Dance* to do very well at the box office. But when Behrman arrived at the North Roxbury residence, the man he saw was suffering from a lot more than melancholy. "George came downstairs accompanied by a male nurse," Behrman recalled. "I stared at him. It was not the George we all knew. He was very pale. The light had gone from his eyes. He seemed old. He greeted me mirthlessly. His handshake was limp, the spring had gone out of his walk. He came to a sofa near where I was sitting and lay down on it. He tried to adjust his head against the pillows. The nurse hovered over him. I asked him if he felt pain. 'Behind my eyes,' he said, and repeated it: 'Behind my eyes.' I knelt beside him on the sofa and put my hand under his head. I asked him if he felt like playing the piano. He shook his head. It was the first such refusal I'd ever heard from him. 'I had to live for this,' he said, 'that Sam Goldwyn should say to me: 'Why don't you write hits like Irving Berlin?'"[24] Then George asked to be taken back to his room. After his departure, Behrman asked Leonore how long he had been this way. "For several weeks," she replied. "He seems worse tonight. Maybe it's seeing you—reminds him of the past."[25]

Upon learning that Harold Arlen and Yip Harburg were leaving for New York to write a Broadway show and that Harburg's nearby house would be unoccupied, Leonore arranged for George to be moved there.[26] He was taken to the new location on Sunday, July 4, and attended there by Mueller and a nurse, Paul Levy, who worked for George's psychiatrist, Dr. Simmel. When Leonore sent George a gift, a box of chocolates, he angrily crushed the pieces in his hands and rubbed the glutinous mass over his face and body.[27]

Frankie and Mabel, who were traveling in Europe, received a wire from Leonore advising them that there was no need to come to Los Angeles, that George's condition was not serious. However, Emily and Lou Paley, as well as their cousin George Pallay, flew in from New York and took residence with Ira and Leonore. Cousin Henry Botkin was still in Los Angeles but had left the Gershwin residence and was living on Franklin Avenue in Hollywood. They, Ira, and Oscar Levant went to see George every day. At one point Levant, trying to cheer him up, sat at the piano and played some of Gershwin's favorite passages from *Porgy and Bess*. George was especially fond of Crown's dramatic leitmotif. As Levant played and sang it, George went over to Oscar's lady friend and future wife, June Gale. She later recalled the moment: "Oscar stayed at the piano and George came over, put his arm around me, and looked deeply into my eyes. It was a beseeching look, an expression that touched me as little else ever has. I felt so uncomfortable. Oscar was very jealous about me so I never told him about it, even after George died. But I have been haunted by that look on his face all my life."[28]

Levant was so phobic about the subject of death that he could not bear to hear words such as "funeral" or even "insurance." Nevertheless, he stuck around. Others, such as Arlen, Harburg, and Behrman, left town. "All my friends are leaving me," Gershwin said sadly to Harold and Anya Arlen when they came to say goodbye. But Emily and Lou Paley were arriving, and Kay would have come too but for her lack of status as a family member and her poor relationship with Leonore. She was the one person who could have made sure that George's interests came first. Ira had taken on that role early in his brother's life, but Kay was the only one who could and would have done so at the end. In deciding not to marry her or even communicate with her, George had set things up so that she would not be allowed to take charge at this horrifying moment. However, now that he was in the Harburg house, they began speaking again by phone. Nothing is known of these conversations except that she told an interviewer nearly fifty years later that George said, "I'm coming back for both of us" and that he was "very brave about it."[29]

On the evening of July 9, a Friday, he woke from a deep sleep and was helped to the bathroom by Levy and Mueller, where he began to tremble uncontrollably. He was brought back to bed, and doctors were called. They arrived at the house, saw swelling in his eyes, and had him admitted to Cedars of Lebanon. By this time, he was in a coma. The doctors were all but certain now that it was a brain tumor—a diagnosis made official the next day after a spinal tap. An immediate operation was necessary and it was decided to send for the best neurosurgeon in the country. This was Dr. Walter E. Dandy of Johns Hopkins in Baltimore. Dr. Dandy, however, had gone fishing with the governor of Maryland and was on a yacht on Chesapeake Bay. When the White House was informed of the situation, a

Coast Guard cutter was dispatched to pick Dr. Dandy up, and then a police escort took him to the Cumberland airport, where Gershwin's friend Emil Mosbacher had chartered an airplane to take him to Los Angeles. By then, however, the situation had deteriorated so much there was no time to wait for Dr. Dandy's arrival. Another vacationing surgeon, Dr. Howard C. Naffziger, was flown in from Lake Tahoe, Nevada. Surgery began after midnight, the morning of July 11. George Pallay stationed himself outside the operating room and brought information to Ira, Leonore, Emily, Lou, Levant, and Alexander Steinert, who sat in a waiting room several floors below. At first, the reports were good. A benign cyst had been found and removed. Then, however, the doctors found the real problem: an inoperable malignant glioblastoma. At 7:00 A.M., George was returned to his room. But by then everyone had gone home. Pallay, having learned the truth from the doctors, had informed Leonore, but she chose not to tell Ira or the others. They all left the hospital at 6:15 A.M., and no one was at George's side—not a relative, friend, or even a doctor or a nurse—when he died later that morning on Sunday, July 11, 1937. He was thirty-eight years old.

By this time, Kay had made reservations to fly to Los Angeles but when the Gershwin party arrived back at North Roxbury on Sunday morning, Emily, who had also been told by Leonore that George would be okay, immediately telegrammed her with the news. Kay's telegram in reply reads, "Dear Emily thanks a million for the good news stop my best love to you two and Lee and Ira stop cancelled plane passage and will hope for report of further good progress from you joyfully Kay."[30] That evening, as word of George's death was about to make headlines in the early morning papers, it was not Emily but her sister Leonore who phoned Kay with the news.

Upon hearing that George was gone, Kay's stunned response was, "Oh, no."

Leonore, with a strange note of triumph in her voice, replied, "Oh, yes."[31]

TWENTY-TWO

Epilogue

The day following George's death, a Monday, Ira was in court presenting papers prepared by his law firm to gain control over his brother's estate. George had died intestate, and this was an attempt to preempt Rose, who was ready with papers of her own, filed on July 16 in New York. The issue would be decided by determining whether George, at the end, was a resident of California or New York. New York's jurisdiction won out and the estate was awarded to Rose. Her lawyer was also successful in petitioning the judge to spare her the strain of personally appearing in court, given her grief.

Ira was under orders from his wife to keep his own grief in check, which he managed to do for the next several hectic weeks. After the court appearance came the air trip to New York (George's body was sent by train), and then, on Thursday, July 15, the funeral. So many showed up at Temple Emanu-El on Fifth Avenue—more than 3,500—that traffic came to a halt as a crowd gathered outside in the rain. None of George's music was played during the service, it being, apparently, considered unequal to the occasion. Beethoven, Bach, Schumann, and Handel were heard instead. The consensus of the moment was that Gershwin's music was, like the man himself, of his time. In its July 19, 1937, obituary, *Time* magazine said: "If songs like 'Somebody Loves Me,' 'I Got Rhythm,' 'Embraceable You,' 'Let's Call the Whole Thing Off' were ephemeral, Gershwin at least had the satisfaction of hearing a nation sing them."[1] He was buried alongside his father. Several years later, his mother would have a mausoleum built for the Gershwin family, and George and Morris were moved from the ground to marble crypts.

On August 9, 1937, a month after his death, there was a memorial concert at Lewisohn Stadium. It was a little more than a year since his final appearance there, when he was disappointed when only a few thousand showed up. The attendance this time topped 20,000—a new stadium record. The *New York Times* reported: "Aside from the regular seating accommodations, every extra inch of space had been utilized for the expected overflow, but the crowd was more than authorities had counted on. Standees lined both extension walls of the shell and occupied every point of vantage. The aisles of the stands were filled. Hundreds stood by at the stadium fences on Convent Avenue, 136th and 138th Streets."[2] Among the participants was Harry Kaufman, who had played the *Concerto in F* to such acclaim in Venice, and who now played it again, with Alexander Smallens conducting. Todd Duncan, Anne Brown, Ruby Elzy, and the Eva Jessye Choir were there to sing selections from *Porgy and Bess*.

Another memorial concert a month later at the Hollywood Bowl in Los Angeles drew more than 22,000 people, causing Highland Avenue to become so clogged with traffic that the performers needed a police escort to reach the stage. This time, the performers included Al Jolson, who sang "Swanee"; Otto Klemperer conducting his own orchestral arrangement of the *Second Prelude;* Todd Duncan, Anne Brown, and Ruby Elzy with selections from *Porgy and Bess;* Fred Astaire singing "They Can't Take That Away From Me"; and Oscar Levant, who overcame five years of stage fright to play the *Concerto in F.*

When Ira and Leonore returned to Beverly Hills, Lee was adamant that there be no emotional displays. Ira was able to comply, at least for a while. He went back to work for Goldwyn and finished the score for *The Goldwyn*

Follies with Vernon Duke, who was brought in at Ira's suggestion. George had not written the verses for several of his final songs and that now had to be done. Years later, Duke would recall in his autobiography, *Passport to Paris*, that he wrote the music for the verse to "Love Is Here to Stay." Ira remembered it differently, saying that he wrote both the words ("The more I read the papers") *and* the music—that he sang the melody to Duke, who notated it. When Michael Feinstein asked Ira about this discrepancy, the latter, by that time past eighty, replied, "It's so undistinguished, isn't it obvious that I wrote it?"[3] Actually, this verse is not at all undistinguished. It is in the same quiet, ruminative, and through-composed style that characterized so many of George's last verses, and it was a worthy introduction to the refrain. If Ira did compose it, it offers proof, if any is needed, that a great lyricist is necessarily a fine musician. George had not had a chance to completely notate the refrain ("It's very clear our love is here to stay"), but Levant remembered it and wrote it down. It was all but ignored in *The Goldwyn Follies* and did not become a standard until Gene Kelly and Leslie Caron performed it in Vincente Minnelli's 1951 film *An American in Paris*—a movie that proved Goldwyn wrong not only about the song but about the suitability of Gershwin's tone poem as an on-screen ballet. *The Goldwyn Follies* did showcase "Love Walked In," and it went on to become a huge Irving Berlin–style popular hit.

In mid-August, Goldwyn fired Ira. He had contracted for two Gershwins and now that one was dead, he was under no legal obligation to pay the other for the remainder of the sixteen-week term. Ira was not happy about this, but it freed him to go back to his home on North Roxbury Drive and drift into despair. One day that summer, Fred Astaire called on him, and as they were reminiscing, Astaire suddenly burst into tears. Ira, in response, began to sob.[4] The floodgates had opened, and they would never really close. He would live another forty-six years, and throughout that time, his own career would always be less important to him than his role as caretaker of his brother's artifacts and reputation. This is not to say that he completely retired from songwriting. Some months after George's death, Jerome Kern coaxed him into collaborating on a few songs, one that Ira entitled "Once There Were Two of Us." A little later, in 1939, when Arlen and Harburg were writing the score for the *Wizard of Oz*, Harburg

Epilogue

had doubts about an expansive melody that Arlen had written for Judy Garland and, just as George had sought Harburg's opinion when he and Ira disagreed over "Love Walked In," Harburg now asked for Ira's opinion about "Over the Rainbow." Ira listened to Arlen play the music and correctly diagnosed the problem: the composer was making it too flowery, adding too much piano ornamentation. Played more simply, it worked. Ira then provided the concluding words: "If happy little bluebirds fly beyond the rainbow why, oh why can't I?"[5]

In 1941, he returned to Broadway, writing the lyrics to Kurt Weill's music for the hit show *Lady in the Dark*. In 1944, there was another team-up with Kern, this one producing the beautiful "Long Ago and Far Away," which, to Ira's chagrin, earned more royalties than any song he had written with his brother. In 1954, he and Arlen wrote the songs for Judy Garland's film *A Star is Born*, including one of the greatest of all torch songs, "The Man That Got Away." In 1959, Ira published one of the best books ever about songwriting, *Lyrics on Several Occasions*. He and Leonore had, in 1940, bought the house next door to the one they had been renting when George died, and they lived there until the end. Through these years, they remained married and unhappily dependent on one another. Rose died in 1948, and her will, which included George's estate, left Ira less than it did Frances and Arthur, but the three siblings worked out a satisfactory arrangement.

Predictably, Lee's power in the family became absolute. When Lou Paley died in 1952, Lee did not bestow any largesse on her widowed sister Emily—George's favorite. Not that Emily asked for help. She enrolled in a typing school at the age of 55 and found employment as a receptionist at *Woman's Wear Daily* magazine, where she eventually became personal assistant to the editor. Lee could be more generous when rivalry was not an issue. When John Bubbles—the original Sportin' Life—fell on hard times and became ill, she regularly sent him checks.[6] She also worked hard to keep up the Gershwin salon, making a homey and welcoming refuge for all the old friends as well as a growing circle of Hollywood people that included Humphrey Bogart, Lauren Bacall, and William Holden. She became especially close to Samuel and Frances Goldwyn and did what she could to help them deal with their rebellious son, Sam, Jr.

As Ira grew older, he became not less but more obsessed with George. When he was in his eighties, Michael Feinstein, who had become something of a surrogate son to him, heard him talking to George in his sleep. These were, according to Feinstein, "lengthy conversations" that were "often filled with anger, centering around Ira's desire not to stay here on earth and George's insistence that he stay."[7] Just before Ira's death in 1983, he revealed to Feinstein in a hushed voice something he had never told anyone else. Shortly after George's passing, he had looked into his brother's workroom upstairs at 1019 North Roxbury and seen him "sitting on the sofa, smiling and nodding to me. It terrified me. I wasn't drinking. I wasn't drunk. But I saw him."[8]

After Ira died, Lee devoted much of her time to establishing what became known as the Ira and Leonore Gershwin Trusts. Ira and other members of the family had donated many of George's manuscripts and papers to the Library of Congress, and Lee now spent a lot of money buying rare Gershwin items to add to that collection. She also established a fund to subsidize performances and recordings of obscure Gershwin songs and shows. She did these things on the proviso that Ira's name be as prominent as George's. Thus, *Porgy and Bess* became *The Gershwins' Porgy and Bess*, while the name of DuBose Heyward, who had died at 55 in 1940, was left off title pages, posters, and CD covers. This was something Ira would never have sanctioned. Lee also managed to get Frankie to give up her claim to a crypt in the Gershwin mausoleum so that she could take the remaining spot beside Ira, George, Morris, Rose, and Arthur. Seven years after Ira's death, when Leonore was slipping into senility and nearing her own end, she said aloud and out of the blue, "You know, George was really the one. George was the one I truly loved."[9] She died in 1991, was cremated, and placed in an urn. Thus, it was Frankie who, upon passing on in 1999, got the contested vault.

In the late 1930s, Kay traveled to California to help Ira sort through George's unpublished manuscripts. They went though all of George's notebooks (including one George and Kay had used in common, he writing front to back, she back to front), numbering the melodies, giving some of them tentative titles, and flagging many for possible publication. Kay's remarkable musical memory allowed her to fill in sections and harmonies that George had not gotten around to writing down. By this time, she had a job as director of light music for the upcoming 1939 New York World's Fair. Her task there was to book the musicians who would provide free entertainment as people strolled from one exhibit to another. It was also her responsibility to supply the fair's theme song. She might have given herself that plum assignment but instead worked with Ira to create George's first posthumously published composition, "Dawn of a New Day." In 1945, she and Ira worked together again, this time to create enough new Gershwin songs to make a movie score. They were hoping—in vain, it turned out—that their work for the film *The Shocking Miss Pilgrim* would add at least one more George and Ira classic to the literature.

At the world's fair, Kay, always fascinated by horses and riding, found herself drifting over to the rodeo events. It was at an attraction called the American Jubilee that she got to know a championship bulldogger named Faye Hubbard. The John Wayne–size Hubbard's job was to leap from his horse, grab a steer, and throw it onto its side. Kay astonished her friends by bringing this man, nine years her junior, into her life. In June 1939, she and Mary (formerly Mary Reinhardt and soon to become Mary Lasker) gave a "Midsummer's Night Party" at Mary's East Fifty-second Street penthouse, and the attendees included Wendell Willkie, Margaret Sanger, David Sarnoff, and Hubbard.[10] Kay then amazed her friends all the more by marrying the fellow and moving with him to a ranch near Bend, Oregon, in the eastern foothills of the Cascade Mountains. They lived a hardscrabble life for several years, raising and selling horses, until Kay wrote a witty novel about her experiences as an urbanite turned rancher. Entitled *Who Could Ask for Anything More?*, it was published in 1943 by Simon and Schuster and sold well enough to attract the attention of Hollywood. When RKO bought the film rights, she and Faye sold their Oregon spread and moved to California. Kay was again surrounded by show folk and was in her element, but Faye was out of his. Also, he was drinking too much. In June 1946, they divorced.

A year later Kay married again, this time a man twelve years her junior, Hunter Galloway (born Hunter Galloway Kaufman). He had been a signal corpsman during the war, and they met when each was volunteering in a Southern California veterans' hospital. Although he had worked a bit in the theater and broadcasting, he never really had a profession and was always, in Kay's words, "betwixt and between."[11] Like her, he was from New York City, and they moved back there in 1948, where they lived a less than luxurious existence. During their more than twenty years together, they worked tirelessly to reinvigorate her career but successes were few and far between. In 1950, RKO finally released the movie version of her book—a forgettable picture called *Never a Dull Moment* starring Fred MacMurray and Irene Dunne. For it, Kay wrote the words and music for nine songs but only three were used and just one, "Once You Find Your Guy," was published. In 1952 came her second complete Broadway score: a one-character drama called *Paris '90* starring Cornelia Otis Skinner. It received good reviews and went on to play in Paris, London, and Dublin. But the music, despite its quality, never achieved popularity, and this show proved to be her last for Broadway. In 1953, there was a song cycle called *Reaching for the Brass Ring*, with one song for each of her grandchildren (she had seven at the time). The music was orchestrated by Robert Russell Bennett, and the piece was played by several symphony orchestras, including the Cleveland Orchestra and the Philadelphia Symphony. Later, as subsequent grandchildren were born, Kay added to the suite. Other projects, such as a television sitcom about baseball, fell through. Paying jobs consisted mostly of assignments for special occasions. In 1960, she wrote a show, *One Little Girl*, that marked the fiftieth anniversary of the Camp Fire Girls. This music was released on an LP and it shows that, in her sixties, she had not lost her musical gift. In 1962, Century 21 paid her to write the music for their pavilion at the Seattle World's Fair, and she provided an elaborate twenty-minute composition, made up of vocal and instrumental pieces, orchestrations again by Bennett. Two years later, Clairol and Borden hired her for similar work in connection with their exhibits at the New York World's Fair of 1964. In 1968, she divorced Galloway after it turned out that he had all but bankrupted her by bidding nearly half a million dollars at an art auction—money they did not have. She was also concerned about a sizable bill from a local jewelry store. Hunter had apparently bought an expensive bracelet to impress Miss Venezuela. In early 1969, he took his own life.

Epilogue

In 1976, the Houston Grand Opera mounted the first-ever complete-score full-scale production of *Porgy and Bess*. The producer, Sherwin Goldman, consulted with Kay, who asked him for a favor. If the touring company came to Boston, would he make sure it played at the Colonial Theatre? Goldman understood the reason for this request and got Kay the seat she wanted: at the back of the theater, where she had sat with George that evening, forty-one years earlier, and where he had told her, "Someday, Kay, you'll sit in that same seat and you'll hear what I wrote, I promise you."[12]

It had been a long strange road for *Porgy and Bess* before it reached that moment. The first production after George's death was one by Merle Armitage in Los Angeles in 1938. Once again, Rouben Mamoulian directed and the leads were sung by Todd Duncan and Anne Brown. This was essentially the same as the 1935 New York show and, thus, lacked a lot of Gershwin's music. It did, however, appear to be headed for solid success—that is, until a torrential downpour and subsequent flooding made it impossible for people to attend performances in San Francisco or for the troupe to travel on to its next engagements.

It was not until 1942 that a financially successful production was mounted. This was producer Cheryl Crawford's adaptation, brought to Broadway with an orchestra half the size of the one called for by Gershwin and without any recitatives. In this incarnation, it became a *Show Boat*–style musical and, as such, won the kudos of critics who had shunned it in 1935. Virgil Thomson, in the *New York Herald Tribune*, said the show could now be considered lovable despite its "numberless faults" because it was without "the embarrassments due to Gershwin's incredibly amateurish way of writing recitative." Gershwin "didn't know much about musical aesthetics and he couldn't orchestrate for shucks," Thomson continued, "but his strength was as the strength of ten because his musical heart was really pure." All in all, "one is inclined to be more than proud of our little Georgie."[13]

In subsequent years, critics would find fewer and fewer faults, but in 1942, a glaring one *was* identified and corrected. Heyward's characters frequently referred to themselves and each other with the word "nigger." Although the author had been striving for authenticity and not disparagement, by the early forties the word was offensive in any context. Even in the 1935 production there had been grumbling about it among the cast. In

June 1942, when Etta Moten replaced Anne Brown as Bess she refused to have anything to do with the word, and Ira Gershwin—by that time the last surviving author of the work—quickly agreed to edit it from the script.

Porgy and Bess was now contending not only with music and drama critics but also with the civil rights movement. In 1943, it managed to gain some standing as a symbol of human rights when the Danish Royal Opera mounted the first European production in Copenhagen. The German occupiers of Denmark were less than pleased with this musical by a Jew about blacks but the show went on for a time, thanks to the Danish police who formed a protective cordon around the opera house. As it turned out, the Danes could not protect the building from the Luftwaffe; when the Germans threatened to bomb the building, *Porgy and Bess* was forced to close. However, the Danish underground took to interrupting German victory announcements on the radio with a recording of "It Ain't Necessarily So." It is not difficult to imagine how pleased George Gershwin would have been about that.

In the 1950s, political activists in the African American community greeted new productions warily and sometimes with outright hostility. Yet, a 1952 production, mounted by Blevins Davis and Robert Breen, was used to counter Soviet propaganda about the continued enslavement of America's black population. In their production, which featured William Warfield as Porgy, Leontyne Price as Bess, Cab Calloway as Sportin' Life, and Maya Angelou as Maria, much of the music that had previously been cut was restored. The State Department sponsored successful tours in Latin America, the Middle East, Europe (including the first performance of an American opera at La Scala in Milan), as well as the Soviet Union. It was during this tour that Duke Ellington reversed his initial negative response to the piece and wired the producers and cast: "Your *Porgy and Bess* the superbest, singing the gonest, acting the craziest, Gershwin the greatest."[14]

But the going was still tough. After Samuel Goldwyn purchased the film rights in the late 1950s, he found it all but impossible to get anyone to appear in his movie version. The role of Porgy was turned down first by Harry Belafonte and then by Sidney Poitier. Only after a freelance agent announced that Poitier had accepted the role, and after Poitier's agent told him his hand had been forced, did the actor agree to appear. "I had a considerable aversion to *Porgy and Bess*," he said later, "because of its inherent racial attitudes."[15] Then, during filming, the expensive sets were destroyed by a nighttime fire that many believed to be the work of black arsonists. The film was completed, but it was untrue to Gershwin's intentions (recitatives were removed, Gershwin's orchestrations were thrown out) and less than a success. It proved to be Goldwyn's final movie.

In 1976 came the first recording of the complete work, all cuts restored, by Lorin Maazel and the Cleveland Orchestra, with Willard White as Porgy and Leona Mitchell as Bess. This was followed by the Houston Grand Opera production, with inspired performances by all, particularly Donnie Ray Albert as Porgy and Clamma Dale as Bess. This was the production that Kay saw in Boston's Colonial Theatre. When it reached Washington, D.C., Todd Duncan was asked to come on stage and accept a standing ovation for his achievements as a singer, teacher, and civil rights pioneer. Over a long career, he had appeared in more than 2,000 recitals in 56 countries, had been the first African American to sing with the New York City Opera (this was in 1945, ten years before Marian Anderson became the first black singer hired by the Metropolitan Opera Company), appeared on Broadway in the 1940 Vernon Duke show *Cabin in the Sky* and in Kurt Weill's 1949 musical *Lost in the Stars*, and was venerated as a teacher by several generations of students. In 1985, on the occasion of the fiftieth anniversary of the Gershwin opera, he and Anne Brown were reunited in New York to celebrate the Metropolitan Opera Company's first ever production of *Porgy and Bess*. In the intervening years, she had performed in the 1937 Broadway revue *Pins and Needles*, the 1939 dramatized version of DuBose Heyward's novel *Mamba's Daughters*, sung as soprano soloist in a 1941 performance of Beethoven's *Ninth Symphony* with Leopold Stokowski and the NBC Symphony Orchestra, and appeared in recitals throughout the United States and Europe. Tired of racial incidents in the United States (she was denied use of a concert hall in her home town of Baltimore), Brown eventually settled in Norway, where, as of this writing, she still lives.

At the time of the first Met production of Gershwin's opera, Duncan gave an interview in which he summed the work up: "The communication, the strength, the drama, the passion that come in the grand operas is in *Porgy and Bess*, and the main ingredient that is in *Porgy and Bess* is the same ingredient that's in *Tosca*, the same ingredient that's in *Siegfried*, and that means performance, passion, communication, sheer heaven, excitement, theater."[16]

Kay, like Brown and Duncan, would live to see a consensus form about Gershwin: that he had, with many of his works but especially with this one, made the world a more interesting and a more loving place. Duncan died at age 95 in 1998 at home, while one of his students waited in the anteroom for a voice lesson. Kay died in 1993, also at 95. Toward the end, suffering from Alzheimer's disease, she was placed in a nursing care facility. One day when she returned to her room after a walk, she looked at the two nameplates on her door, hers above and her roommate's below, and exclaimed, "Look! Top billing!"[17]

George Gershwin lived his life with purpose and gusto, but with melancholy as well, for he was unable to make a home for himself—no familial home and no home in music. The contrast between his élan and these struggles, ending in the horror of his final days, gives a dramatic arc to his biography and gives it the shape of a story.

This book has emphasized that story and, in doing so, has been less concerned than other biographies with the details of his workaday life in the theater. Such particulars are available in longer accounts, some of them very good, and the best—by Edward Jablonski, William Hyland, and Howard Pollack—are essential reading for anyone who wants to know more about the man.

Gershwin's musical dilemma was not, as is so often stated, about whether to choose between jazz or classical, songs or concert works. He had no need to split his musical personality. He wrote in the Gershwin idiom, which was as personal and original a musical voice as Chopin's. The conflict, rather, was about whether he would make full use of his powers, becoming, in Anne Brown's words, "the person he was supposed to be."[1] On Broadway, he spent a lot of his time composing works he knew to be forgettable—ephemeral numbers for quickly forgotten shows. Composer Meredith Willson mused, "I know, I know—of course 'he did all right,' but he might have left the world some four hundred–odd symphonies like Papa Haydn instead of a handful of beautiful melodies."[2] There was the sense—and Gershwin felt it—that he was not doing right by his gift, it being a profound talent that thrived best on ambitious undertakings. He seems to have understood from the beginning that this conflict would have to eventually resolve itself in a work such as *Porgy and Bess*. But he knew too that when that resolution came, it would be up to professional music critics to validate it. As it turned out, they were not up to the job.

The other problem was his desire for family. All four Gershwin siblings longed for a home. Their parents had done well enough in providing for their material needs, but there was little love from their mother, Rose, and no direction from their father, Morris. Ira made a home for himself when—in something of a Faustian bargain—he married Leonore Strunsky. George made a home of sorts—an illusory one—through his longtime relationship with Kay Swift. He loved her but could not comprehend—until the last minutes of his life—how much he really needed her.

Some things about him we do not know. For instance, there is a man who calls himself Alan Gershwin (born Albert Schneider) and who claims to be the composer's illegitimate son, born to a chorus girl named Margaret Manners in 1926 and raised by an aunt, Fannie Schneider. Alan Gershwin has never submitted to blood or DNA testing to prove this assertion. Two facts do favor his contention. One is his remarkable resemblance to George Gershwin. The other is that Paul Mueller, in his old age, signed an affidavit attesting to the validity of Alan's claim. But it is doubtful if we will ever know the truth about this.

Another unanswered question is whether George and Ira really were about to split up. Some evidence argues yes. "I think there is no doubt that George and Ira had come to a parting of the ways," concluded Lawrence D. Stewart, Ira's secretary.[3] Certainly, George wanted to concentrate on symphonic works and opera, and when he discussed ideas for new operas, he did so with writers Heyward and Riggs, not with Ira. Most telling is Ira's decision to remain in California, made in the full knowledge of George's determination to go home to New York. This must have had something to do with a need on his part—or Leonore's—to be away from George. Yet, there is evidence that they were not breaking up. In the spring of 1937, the brothers were talking to Kaufman and Hart about doing a new Broadway show. And, had Paulette Goddard said yes to George, he was prepared to remain in Los Angeles.[4]

Some things we can know for sure. In the end, George was grievously mistreated by Leonore while Ira stood by, immobile and transfixed. Prior biographers have tiptoed around this fact, partly to avoid hurting Ira, who was universally loved, and, after his death, to curry favor with Leonore or evade her wrath. Just when it was that the Iago side of her character

AUTHOR'S NOTE

came to the fore is not clear. There is no evidence that she was a thorn in George's side prior to his final days or that she ever stirred up dissension between the brothers or interfered with their work. Stewart, having long pondered the mystery of Leonore, wrote that her heart was "all there and functioning, but somewhat askew."[5]

Finally, we can know for certain that Kay Swift was the one who best loved and understood George, and that, had he allowed her to be with him in California, she would not have abandoned him.

It is quite a story, George Gershwin's life. In my effort to tell it truthfully and accurately, I have been helped by many people. My first thanks go to the librarians: Jennifer B. Lee of the Rare Book and Manuscript Library at Columbia University, Melissa Brown of Yale University's Oral History American Music collection, Ray White and Mark Herwitz of the Library of Congress, Richard Workman of the Harry Ransom Center at The University of Texas at Austin, and Brian Feeney at the Charleston County Public Library.

People at the Ira and Leonore Gershwin Trusts in San Francisco have been continuously helpful. I want to thank Michael and Jean Strunsky for taking the time to share their recollections with me, and Michael Owen, archivist, for cheerfully answering my questions and providing photographs. I have dedicated this book to the trusts' late executive director, Mark Trent Goldberg, who was a notable expert on the Gershwins and the American musical theater, as well as a gracious man who, like George Gershwin, died much too young.

Thanks to Vivian Perlis for granting access to transcripts of her interviews with Kay Swift, Frances Gershwin Godowsky, and Kate Wolpin. Thanks to Berthe Schuchat for allowing me to quote from her interview of Todd Duncan and for her friendship and support.

Encouragement, research help, proofreading, and friendship also came from Joseph Spampinato and Richard Lewis, each a Gershwin expert. The late William Hyland, who, after a distinguished career in government, wrote a number of excellent books about the American musical theater, including biographies of George Gershwin and Richard Rodgers, was kind enough to read an early draft of this book and offer his enthusiasm, valuable suggestions, and a box full of his own research materials. I

AUTHOR'S NOTE

am also indebted to two other notable authors, Philip Furia and Stephen Banfield, who each took the time read this book in manuscript and offer approval and advice. Thanks, too, to Katharine Weber for answering my questions about her grandmother, Kay Swift, and telling me about the cache of Swift's correspondence in Columbia University's Mary Lasker collection. Robert Kimball, Joan Peyser, Donald Swan, Kevin Cole, John Loomis of Washington, D.C.'s National Theatre, and American Society of Composers, Authors, and Publishers's Jim Steinblatt and Michael Kerker were all generous in allowing me to interview them.

Thanks also to Raechelle Manis for her assistance in researching the Jablonski/Stewart papers at the Harry Ransom Humanities Research Center at the University of Texas at Austin; Ann and Chris Teras for friendship (and free room and board) while I was looking through Gershwin materials at the Library of Congress; Joan Alexander for friendship and encouragement as well as a thorough proofreading of the manuscript; my sister, Rona Arato, for heartening words during discouraging times; my wife, Peg, and our children, Jacob, Jesse, and Rose, for lively discussions, valuable insights, and proofreading; and Laurie Matheson, senior acquisitions editor at University of Illinois Press, for understanding where I was going with this book and for believing that I actually got there.

NOTES

Chapter 1. From Street Kid to Wunderkind

1. Isaac Goldberg, *George Gershwin: A Study in American Music* (New York: Frederick Ungar Publishing Co., 1958), 56.
2. Ibid., 61.
3. Howard Pollack, *George Gershwin: His Life and Work* (Berkeley: University of California Press, 2006), 32.
4. Goldberg, *George Gershwin*, 121.
5. William G. Hyland, *George Gershwin* (Westport, Conn.: Praeger, 2003), 158.
6. Edward Jablonski, *Gershwin* (New York: Doubleday, 1987), 53.
7. David Ewen, *George Gershwin: His Journey to Greatness* (Englewood Cliffs, N.J.: Prentice-Hall, Inc., 1970), 75.
8. "Tales of Tin Pan Alley," *Edison Musical Magazine,* October 20, 1920, 9.

Chapter 2. Falling in Love With Kay

1. Isaac Goldberg, "In Memoriam: George Gershwin," *B'Nai B'rith Magazine,* August-September 1937, 2.
2. Alexander Woollcott, *Long, Long Ago* (New York: Viking Press, 1943), 100.
3. Pollack, *George Gershwin: His Life and Work,* 100.
4. Kay Swift, interview by Vivian Perlis, May 1, 1975. Oral History American Music, Yale University.
5. Woollcott, *Long, Long Ago,* 100.
6. Robert Payne, *Gershwin* (New York: Pyramid, 1960), 74.
7. James Warburg, *The Long Road Home* (New York: Doubleday & Company, 1964), 44.
8. Kay Swift, interview, May 1, 1975.
9. Jablonski, *Gershwin,* 121.

Chapter 3. A Piano Concerto

1. Gregory R. Suriano, ed., *Gershwin in His Time* (New York: Random House, 1998), 47.
2. Except for the trombones and tuba.
3. Pollack, *George Gershwin: His Life and Work,* 52.
4. Olin Downes, "Music," *New York Times,* December 4, 1925.
5. Hyland, *George Gershwin,* 95.

6. Charles Schwartz, *Gershwin: His Life and Music* (Indianapolis: The Bobbs-Merrill Company, Inc., 1973), 190.

7. James P. Warburg, in his autobiography, *The Long Road Home*, says the year of purchase was 1925, but Ron Chernow, in *The Warburgs* (see chap. 11, n. 3), 69, and Vicki Ohl in her biography of Kay Swift, *Fine and Dandy* (see chap. 10, n. 12), put it in 1924.

8. Kay Swift, February 1966 speech, box 15, the Kay Swift Papers in the Irving S. Gilmore Music Library of Yale University.

Chapter 4. Ira Takes a Wife

1. Ira Gershwin, letter to Benjamin Botkin, August 18, 1966, box 64, Library of Congress Gershwin Collection.

2. Robert Kimball and Alfred Simon, *The Gershwins* (New York: Atheneum, 1973), 136.

3. Michael Feinstein, *Nice Work If You Can Get It* (New York: Hyperion, 1995), 103.

4. Michael Strunsky and Jean Strunsky, in-person interview by the author, March 11, 2005.

5. Ibid.

6. Feinstein, *Nice Work If You Can Get It*, 114.

7. Ibid., 101.

Chapter 5. Porgy

1. Olin Downes, "Music," *New York Times*, January 2, 1926.

2. Pollack, *George Gershwin: His Life and Work*, 399–400.

3. Ibid., 401.

4. Warburg, *The Long Road Home*, 69.

5. Kay Swift, letter to Mary Lasker, December 30, [1948], Mary Lasker Papers, Rare Book and Manuscript Library, Columbia University.

6. Frances Gershwin Godowsky, interview by Vivian Perlis, June 3, 1983. Oral History American Music, Yale University.

7. Ibid.

8. Kay Swift, letter to Mary Lasker, August 2, [1942], Mary Lasker Papers, Rare Book and Manuscript Library, Columbia University.

9. In a 1972 interview, George's valet, Paul Mueller, told Gershwin biographers Edward Jablonski and Lawrence D. Stewart that "George hated her" (Harry Ransom Humanities Research Center, The University of Texas at Austin).

10. Michael and Jean Strunsky, interview, March 11, 2005.

11. Kimball and Simon, *The Gershwins*, 138.

Chapter 6. Paris

1. Pollack, *George Gershwin: His Life and Work*, 120.

2. This encounter with Braggiotti and Fray may have actually occurred two

years earlier, when Gershwin spent a week in Paris, staying with Mabel and Robert Schirmer. Braggiotti remembered that after his and Fray's meeting with Gershwin; the latter got them a job playing in the orchestra in the 1928 London production of *Funny Face*. However, other information indicates that they were duo pianists in the orchestra of the 1926 London production of *Lady, Be Good!*

3. Mario Braggiotti, interview by Al Simon, Oral History American Music, Yale University.

4. Pollack, *George Gershwin: His Life and Work*, 138.

5. Ibid., 139.

6. Ibid., 142.

7. Ibid., 143.

8. Jablonski, *Gershwin*, 167.

9. Rosamond Walling Tirana, speech entitled "George Gershwin, American Composer," January 6, 1950, Library of Congress Gershwin Collection.

Chapter 7. "That Long Drip of Human Tears"

1. Hyland, *George Gershwin*, 127.

2. Schwartz, *Gershwin: His Life and Music*, 170.

3. Olin Downes, "Music," *New York Times*, December 14, 1928.

4. Goldberg, *George Gershwin*, 239.

5. Jablonski, *Gershwin*, 178–79.

6. C. B. Pyper, "Gershwin Says Vulgarity Has Place in Good Music," *Toronto Evening Telegram*, January 19, 1934.

7. Jablonski, *Gershwin*, 22.

8. Joseph Horowitz, "An Upstart Named Gershwin Gets His Start," *New York Times*, October 2, 2005.

9. Pyper, "Gershwin Says Vulgarity Has Place in Good Music."

10. Burton Lane, interview by Al Simon, September 28, 1972. Oral History American Music, Yale University.

11. Pollack, *George Gershwin: His Life and Work*, 495.

12. Jablonski, *Gershwin*, 232.

13. Ibid.

14. Pollack, *George Gershwin: His Life and Work*, 139.

15. Duke Ellington, *Music Is My Mistress* (New York: Da Capo Press, Inc., 1973), 106.

16. Pollack, *George Gershwin: His Life and Work*, 164.

17. Philip Furia, *Ira Gershwin: The Art of the Lyricist* (New York: Oxford University Press, 1996), 119.

18. Jablonski, *Gershwin*, xiv.

19. Walter Simmons, *Voices in the Wilderness* (Lanham, Md.: The Scarecrow Press, 2006), 35.

20. Goldberg, *George Gershwin*, 40.

21. Kay Swift, interview, May 1, 1975.

Chapter 8. The Losing Streak Begins

1. The Reminiscences of Joseph Meyer (1958), p. 5, in the Oral History Collection of Columbia University.
2. Kate Wolpin, interview by Vivian Perlis, January 30, 1986. Oral History American Music, Yale University.
3. Merle Armitage, ed., *George Gershwin* (New York: Da Capo Press edition, 1995), 114.
4. Written by Heyward in 1928 and quoted by Dorothy Heyward in her Foreword to DuBose Heyward, *Porgy* (New York: Bantam Books, 1957), page unnumbered.
5. Kate Wolpin, interview, January 30, 1986.
6. Walter Rimler, *A Gershwin Companion* (Ann Arbor, Mich.: Popular Culture Ink, 1991), 296.
7. Edward Jablonski and Lawrence D. Stewart, *The Gershwin Years* (Garden City, N.Y.: Doubleday & Company, Inc., 1958), 170.
8. "Music of Modernists is Heard in Saratoga," *New York Times*, May 1, 1932.
9. Oscar Levant, *A Smattering of Ignorance* (New York: Doubleday & Company, Inc.), 165.
10. Howard Taubman, "17,000 Hear Gershwin Program," *New York Times*, August 17, 1932.
11. Kay Swift, interview, May 1, 1975.
12. Jablonski, *Gershwin*, 236.
13. Robert Wyatt and John Andrew Johnson, eds., *The George Gershwin Reader* (New York: Oxford University Press, 2004), 174.
14. Ibid., 176.
15. Allan Lincoln Langley, "Gershwin, Daly and Langley," *New York Times*, January 22, 1933.
16. Jablonski, *Gershwin*, xii.
17. Kimball and Simon, *The Gershwins*, 138.
18. Brooks Atkinson, "Jack Pearl as Germanic Commissioner of Police in 'Pardon My English,'" *New York Times*, January 21, 1933.
19. Ibid.
20. Jablonski, *Gershwin*, 240.
21. Ibid., 106.
22. Henry Taylor Parker, "Juliet and Alice Now Woo Boston," *New York Times*, October 22, 1933.

Chapter 9. "Something Big"

1. DuBose Heyward, *Mamba's Daughters* (Columbia: University of South Carolina Press, 1995), 302.
2. Wyatt and Johnson, eds., *The George Gershwin Reader*, 202.
3. Ibid., 203.

4. Ibid.

5. Jablonski and Stewart, *The Gershwin Years*, 181.

6. James M. Hutchisson, *DuBose Heyward* (Jackson: University of Mississippi Press, 2000), 142.

7. Pollack, *George Gershwin: His Life and Work*, 558.

8. Furia, *Ira Gershwin*, 99.

9. "To Present 'Porgy' as a Musical Show," *New York Times*, November 3, 1933.

10. Dorothy Heyward, letter to Mrs. E. C. Plimpton, March 2, 1931, University of South Carolina Libraries, South Carolina Libraries Manuscripts Division.

11. Mark C. Carnes, *Invisible Giants—Fifty Americans Who Shaped the Nation but Missed the History Books* (New York: Oxford University Press, 2002), 150.

12. Hutchisson, *DuBose Heyward*, 145.

13. Ibid., 144.

14. Steven C. Smith, *A Heart at Fire's Center: The Life and Music of Bernard Herrmann* (Berkeley: University of California Press, 2002), 41.

Chapter 10. "Don't Make It Too Good, George!"

1. Ellington, *Music Is My Mistress*, 104.

2. Wyatt and Johnson, eds., *The George Gershwin Reader*, 230.

3. Ibid., 224.

4. Paul Mueller, diary, box 68, Library of Congress Gershwin Collection.

5. Joan Peyser, *The Memory of All That: The Life of George Gershwin* (New York: Simon & Schuster, 1993), 217.

6. The Reminiscences of Mitchell William Miller (1959), p. 11, in the Oral History Collection of Columbia University.

7. Ira and Leonore Gershwin Trusts, WJZ radio script, April 6, 1934.

8. Hutchisson, *DuBose Heyward*, 145.

9. John Lahr, "Come Rain or Come Shine," *New Yorker*, September 19, 2005.

10. Arthur Spaeth, "Kay Swift Here Talks 'Porgy' and Gershwin," *Cleveland News*, October 28, 1959, 22.

11. Kay Swift, letter to Mary Lasker, April 26, 1942, Mary Lasker Papers, Rare Book and Manuscript Library, Columbia University.

12. Vicki Ohl, *Fine and Dandy: The Life and Work of Kay Swift* (New Haven, Conn.: Yale University Press, 2004), 180.

13. Wyatt and Johnson, eds. *The George Gershwin Reader*, 228.

14. Barry Singer, "On Hearing Her Sing, Gershwin Made 'Porgy' 'Porgy and Bess,'" *New York Times*, March 29, 1998, sec. AR, 39.

15. Ibid.

16. Wyatt and Johnson, eds., *The George Gershwin Reader*, 229.

17. Ibid., 231.

18. Ira and Leonore Gershwin Trusts, WJZ radio script, May 18, 1934.

Chapter 11. Kay, Jimmy, and FDR

1. Warburg, *The Long Road Home*, 107.
2. The Reminiscences of James Paul Warburg (1952), pp. 497–98, in the Oral History Collection of Columbia University.
3. Ron Chernow, *The Warburgs* (New York, Vintage Books, 1993), 395.
4. Ohl, *Fine and Dandy*, 117.
5. Ibid., 334.
6. Hyland, *George Gershwin*, 222.
7. Ohl, *Fine and Dandy*, 89.
8. Warburg, *The Long Road Home*, 159.
9. Ohl, *Fine and Dandy*, 89.

Chapter 12. The Heart of American Music

1. Jablonski, *Gershwin*, 275.
2. Jablonski and Stewart, *The Gershwin Years*, 207.
3. Jablonski, *Gershwin*, 275.
4. Schwartz, *Gershwin: His Life and Music*, 261.
5. Edward Jablonski, *Gershwin Remembered* (Portland, Ore.: Amadeus Press, 1992), 99.
6. Ibid., 100.
7. Pollack, *George Gershwin: His Life and Work*, 203.
8. Armitage, ed., *George Gershwin*, 39.
9. Wyatt and Johnson, eds., *The George Gershwin Reader*, 235–36.
10. Armitage, ed., *George Gershwin*, 40.
11. Sophie W. Burkhim, "George Gershwin, Composer of Extraordinary Ability, Visits Resort for a Winter Vacation," *Palm Beach News*, February 12, 1930.

Chapter 13. Kay's Divorce

1. Ira and Leonore Gershwin Trusts, CBS radio script, December 23, 1934.
2. Mary Lasker, "Notes for an Autobiography," undated, Mary Lasker Papers, Rare Book and Manuscript Library, Columbia University.
3. Ohl, *Fine and Dandy*, 266.
4. Katharine Weber, e-mail to the author, June 6, 2005.
5. Kimball and Simon, *The Gershwins*, xiii.
6. Ibid.
7. Ibid., 198.
8. Lasker, "Notes for an Autobiography."

Chapter 14. Todd Duncan

1. Hutchisson, *DuBose Heyward*, 144.
2. Paul Robeson, Jr., *The Undiscovered Paul Robeson* (New York: John Wiley & Sons, Inc., 2001), 215.
3. "News of the Stage," *New York Times*, October 17, 1934, 27.

4. Wyatt and Johnson, eds., *The George Gershwin Reader*, 229.

5. Kimball and Simon, *The Gershwins*, 179.

6. Wyatt and Johnson, eds., *The George Gershwin Reader*, 221.

7. Kay Swift, interview, May 1, 1975.

8. Kimball and Simon, *The Gershwins*, 179.

9. Ibid., 180.

10. Wyatt and Johnson, eds., *The George Gershwin Reader*, 222.

11. Todd Duncan, interview by Berthe Schuchat, "A Sound Portrait of Porgy & Bess," radio station WAMU-FM, September 29, 1976.

12. Wyatt and Johnson, eds., *The George Gershwin Reader*, 222.

13. Jablonski, *Gershwin*, 269.

14. Hollis Alpert, *The Life and Times of Porgy and Bess* (New York: Alfred A. Knopf, 1990), 91.

15. Ibid., 291.

16. Wyatt and Johnson, eds., *The George Gershwin Reader*, 222.

17. Kimball and Simon, *The Gershwins*, 181.

18. Ibid., 223.

185

Chapter 15. Casting, Rehearsals, and an Omen

1. Wyatt and Johnson, eds., *The George Gershwin Reader*, 230.

2. Virgil Thomson, *Virgil Thomson* (New York: E. P. Dutton, Inc., 1985), 239–40.

3. Ibid., 242.

4. Anthony Tommasini, *Virgil Thomson: Composer on the Aisle* (New York: W. W. Norton & Company Ltd.,1997), 208.

5. Pollack, *George Gershwin: His Life and Work*, 150.

6. Ewen, *George Gershwin: His Journey to Greatness*, 228.

7. Wyatt and Johnson, eds., *The George Gershwin Reader*, 226.

8. Todd Duncan, interview, September 29, 1976.

9. Wyatt and Johnson, eds., *The George Gershwin Reader*, 235.

10. Armitage, ed., *George Gershwin*, 59–60.

11. Wyatt and Johnson, eds., *The George Gershwin Reader*, 320.

12. Alpert, *The Life and Times of Porgy and Bess*, 110.

13. Wyatt and Johnson, eds., *The George Gershwin Reader*, 232.

14. Alpert, *The Life and Times of Porgy and Bess*, 110.

Chapter 16. The Critics Have Their Say

1. Kimball and Simon, *The Gershwins*, 151.

2. Pollack, *George Gershwin: His Life and Work*,11.

3. Donald Swan (nephew of Al Stillman), interview by the author, June 30, 2005.

4. Todd Duncan, interview, September 29, 1976.

5. Ohl, *Fine and Dandy*, 211.

6. Brooks Atkinson, "Dramatic Values of Community Legend Gloriously

Transposed in New Form with Fine Regard for Its Verities," *New York Times*, October 11, 1935.

7. Olin Downes, "Exotic Richness of Negro Music and Color of Charleston, S.C. Admirably Conveyed in Score of Catfish Row Tragedy," *New York Times*, October 11, 1935.

8. Hutchisson, *DuBose Heyward*, 159–60.

9. Paul Rosenfeld, *An Hour With American Music* (Philadelphia: J. B. Lippincott Company, 1929), 138–39.

10. Jablonski, *Gershwin*, 289.

11. When Thomson reprinted this review in a book of his writings, he changed "plum-pudding orchestration" to "gefilte fish orchestration." Virgil Thomson, "George Gershwin," *Modern Music* (November–December, 1935), 13–19.

12. Armitage, ed. *George Gershwin*, 116.

13. George Antheil to George Gershwin, April 13, 1936, George Antheil Papers, Rare Book and Manuscript Library, Columbia University.

14. Armitage, ed., *George Gershwin*, 115.

15. Mark Tucker, ed., *The Duke Ellington Reader* (New York: Oxford University Press, 1993), 116.

16. Ibid., 117.

17. Sam Kashner and Nancy Schoenberger, *A Talent For Genius: The Life and Times of Oscar Levant* (Los Angeles: Silman-James Press), 157.

Chapter 17. Limbo

1. Wyatt and Johnson, eds., *The George Gershwin Reader*, 234.

2. Ibid.

3. George Gershwin, "Rhapsody in Catfish Row," *New York Times*, October 20, 1935.

4. Todd Duncan, interview, September 29, 1976.

5. Kimball and Simon, *The Gershwins*, 167.

6. "Gershwin Goes Political After Chats With Rivera," *New York Post*, December 17, 1935.

7. Schwartz, *Gershwin: His Life and Music*, 314.

8. George Gershwin, telegram to Rudy Valee, Joseph Spampinato Collection, December 6, 1935.

9. Anne Brown, interview in the *Washington Star*, March 1936.

10. Wyatt and Johnson, eds., *The George Gershwin Reader*, 234.

11. Ibid., 236.

Chapter 18. Hollywood Beckons

1. Bob Thomas, *Astaire* (New York: St. Martin's Press, 1984), 153.

2. Pollack, *George Gershwin: His Life and Work*, 333.

3. Rimler, *A Gershwin Companion*, 114.

4. Ohl, *Fine and Dandy*, 120. It is likely that Gershwin, in making this playful re-

mark, was referring to the 1903 George M. Cohan song, "Always Leave Them Laughing When You Say Goodbye."

5. Howard Taubman, "Gershwin Draws 7,000 to Stadium," *New York Times*, July 10, 1936.

6. Kimball and Simon, *The Gershwins*, 200.

Chapter 19. Pleasure Island

1. Jablonski, *Gershwin*, 299.

2. Jablonski and Stewart, *The Gershwin Years*, 235.

3. Kashner and Schoenberger, *A Talent for Genius*, 153.

4. William Daly, letter to George Gershwin, September 13, 1936, Ira and Leonore Gershwin Trusts.

5. Peyser, *The Memory of All That*, 290–91.

6. Kimball and Simon, *The Gershwins*, 226.

7. Nathaniel Shilkret, *Sixty Years in the Music Business* (Metuchen, N.J.: Scarecrow Press, 2005), 172.

8. Ibid., 173.

9. Ibid.

10. Jablonski, *Gershwin*, 301.

11. Kay Swift to Mary Lasker, September 28, 1949, Mary Lasker Papers, Rare Book and Manuscript Library, Columbia University.

12. Jablonski, *Gershwin*, 303.

13. Ibid., 305.

14. Ibid., 311.

15. Ean Wood, *George Gershwin: His Life & Music* (London: Sanctuary Publishing Limited, 1996), 232.

16. Jablonski, *Gershwin*, 305.

Chapter 20. Final Concert, Final Affair

1. Hutchisson, *DuBose Heyward*, 176.

2. Jablonski, *Gershwin*, 301.

3. Ibid., 310.

4. Ibid.

5. Ibid., 308.

6. Ginger Rogers, *Ginger: My Story* (New York: HarperCollins, 1991), 182.

7. Jablonski, *Gershwin*, 278–79.

8. Peyser, *The Memory of All That*, 263.

9. Alec Wilder, *American Popular Song* (New York: Oxford University Press, 1972), 158.

10. Pollack, *George Gershwin: His Life and Work*, 675.

11. Mark Goldberg and Michael Strunsky, interview by the author, March 11, 2005.

12. George was awarded a posthumous Pulitzer Prize in 1998, his centennial year.

13. Alphonse and Gaston were the title characters in an American comic strip by Frederick Burr Opper. They could never get around to doing anything because of their excessive politeness toward each other ("After you, Alphonse." "No, you first, my dear Gaston!").

14. The Reminiscences of Bennett Alfred Cerf (1968), p. 600, in the Oral History Collection of Columbia University.

15. Ibid.

16. Armitage, ed., *George Gershwin*, 109.

17. Henry Botkin, handwritten notes, "Financial and Legal" box, Library of Congress Gershwin Collection.

18. Schwartz, *Gershwin: His Life and Music*, 307.

19. Jablonski, *Gershwin*, 317.

20. Alistair Cook, *Six Men* (New York: Alfred A. Knopf, 1978), 12.

21. Joe Morella and Edward Z. Epstein, *Paulette* (New York: St. Martin's Press, 1985), 57.

Chapter 21. Last Songs

1. Morella and Epstein, *Paulette*, 58.

2. Jablonski, *Gershwin*, 314.

3. A. Scott Berg, *Goldwyn* (New York: Alfred A. Knopf, 1989), 393.

4. Ibid., 300.

5. Peyser, *The Memory of All That*, 286.

6. Lawrence D. Stewart to Edith and Edward Jablonski, March 26, 1972, Harry Ransom Humanities Research Center, The University of Texas at Austin.

7. Henry Botkin, handwritten notes, "Financial and Legal" box, Library of Congress Gershwin Collection.

8. Julia Van Norman, letter to George Gershwin, August 28, 1933, box 67, Library of Congress Gershwin Collection.

9. Furia, *Ira Gershwin*, 154.

10. Ibid.

11. Max Wilk, *They're Playing Our Song* (New York: Da Capo Press, Inc., 1997), 122.

12. George Gershwin, letter to Rose Gershwin, June 10, 1937, box 64, Library of Congress Gershwin Collection.

13. Paul Mueller, interview by Edward Jablonski, July 25, 1972, Harry Ransom Humanities Research Center, The University of Texas at Austin.

14. Pollack, *George Gershwin: His Life and Work*, 150.

15. Kashner and Schoenberger, *A Talent for Genius*, 180.

16. Pollack, *George Gershwin: His Life and Work*, 212.

17. Ibid., 184.

18. Kate Wolpin, interview, January 30, 1986.

19. Julia Van Norman, letter to George Gershwin, July 1, 1937, box 67, Library of Congress Gershwin Collection.

20. Kashner and Schoenberger, *A Talent for Genius*, 183.

21. Peyser, *The Memory of All That*, 284.

22. Jablonski, *Gershwin*, 320.

23. Lillian Hellman, *An Unfinished Woman* (Boston: Little, Brown and Co., 2007), 74.

24. S. N. Behrman, *People in a Diary* (Boston: Little, Brown & Co., 1972), 253.

25. Jablonski, *Gershwin*, 321.

26. Paul Mueller, in a 1972 interview with Jablonski and Stewart, said that George was "exiled" by Leonore to the Harburg house.

27. Paul Mueller, interview, 1972.

28. Peyser, *The Memory of All That*, 294.

29. "Nearing 90, Songwriter Still At Work," *The News and Courier/The Evening Post* (Charleston, S.C.), October 12, 1986, sec. 10D.

30. Kay Swift telegram to Mrs. Lou Paley, July 11, 1937, box 66, Library of Congress Gershwin Collection.

31. Katharine Weber, e-mail to the author, July 8, 2005.

189

Chapter 22. Epilogue

1. "Death of Gershwin," *Time*, July 19, 1937, 37.

2. "Gershwin Concert Has Record Crowd," *New York Times*, August 10, 1937.

3. This was not the only instance when Ira claimed to have written someone else's music. In a letter to Edith and Edward Jablonski dated August 20, 1972, Lawrence D. Stewart recalled Ira saying that Kurt Weill "had no sense of melody" and that he had to "hum to him some of the tunes for *Lady in the Dark*." (Harry Ransom Humanities Research Center, The University of Texas at Austin).

4. Feinstein, *Nice Work If You Can Get It*, 73.

5. Ibid., 285.

6. Mark Trent Goldberg, interview by the author, March 11, 2005.

7. Feinstein, *Nice Work If You Can Get It*, 76.

8. Ibid.

9. Ibid., 119.

10. Lasker, "Notes for an Autobiography."

11. Ohl, *Fine and Dandy*, 185.

12. Ibid., 211.

13. Virgil Thomson, "Porgy in Maplewood," *New York Herald Tribune*, October 19, 1941.

14. Hyland, *George Gershwin*, 173.

15. Berg, *Goldwyn*, 480.

16. Rimler, *A Gershwin Companion*, 309–10.

17. Ohl, *Fine and Dandy*, 236.

Author's Note

1. Wyatt and Johnson, eds., *The George Gershwin Reader*, 236.

2. Meredith Willson, *And There I Stood With My Piccolo* (Garden City, N.J.: Doubleday & Company, Inc., 1949), 46.

3. Lawrence D. Stewart to Edith and Edward Jablonski, March 26, 1972, Harry Ransom Humanities Research Center, The University of Texas at Austin.

4. Paul Mueller, interview, 1972.

5. Lawrence D. Stewart to Edith and Edward Jablonski, June 27, 1972, Harry Ransom Humanities Research Center, The University of Texas at Austin.

193

15–16; other composers and, 28, 31–32, 131–32, 141, 157; other songwriters and, 25, 38, 45, 87–88, 90–91, 126, 131– 34, 139, 146, 150, 155–56, 160–61; as a painter and art collector, 11, 44–45, 84, 122, 154; parents and, 26, 36, 51, 146, 156; personality, 7–8, 10, 15, 35–37, 41–42, 45, 70, 99, 104, 108, 110, 122–23, 126, 145; physical description, 7; 42; as a pianist, 10, 19; posthumous works, 167–68; psychiatrist Gregory Zilboorg and, 80–81; residences, 8, 44–45, 69, 83

Gershwin, Ira: childhood, 1, 2, 17; collaborations with other composers, 18, 66, 73, 87, 115–16, 121, 165–66, 189n3 (chap. 22); drawings and paintings, 45; after George's death, 120–21, 134, 165–67, 171; George's estate and, 163; George's fatal illness and, 153–54, 156, 158–60, 162; Leonore Gershwin and, 19–20, 45–46, 146, 153, 156, 158–60, 162, 164, 166–67, 176; mourns George, 165; parents and family, 26, 146; partnership with George, 14, 18, 23, 43, 45, 50, 57–58, 62, 97–98, 124–25, 128, 132, 137, 144–46, 153, 155, 158, 176, 187n12 (chap. 20); personality, 17–19, 108–9, 141, 146, 164; *Porgy and Bess* and, 66, 73, 96–98, 100, 106, 111; physical appearance, 18; residences, 8, 44, 69, 130; *Rhapsody in Blue* and, 4–5; "Someone to Watch Over Me" and, 20, 23; "Summertime" and, 68; William Daly and, 13

Gershwin, Leonore (wife of Ira): courtship and marriage, 18–20; death of, 167; after George's death, 164, 166–67; George's fatal illness and, 153–54, 156, 58–160, 162, 176; George's music and, 20, 96, 100, 111; Gershwin family and, 18–20, 26–27, 146, 153–54, 176, 180n9 (chap. 5); after Ira's death, 167; Kay Swift and, 26–27, 81, 136; Oscar Levant and, 46; personality, 19–20, 45–46, 146–47, 153–54, 156, 158–60, 162, 164, 167, 176–77

Gershwin, Morris (father): death and burial, 51–52, 164; as a father, 17–18, 176; as a husband, 51; personality, 8

Gershwin, Rose (mother), 8, 138–39; buys a piano, 1–2; death of, 166; George and, 26, 36, 154, 156, 158; George's estate and, 163; Ira and, 17, 163; Kay Swift and, 26, 81; as a mother, 146, 176; son-in-law and, 88; as a wife, 51

"Get Happy" (Arlen), 40

Gilbert, W. S., 23–24

Gilbert and Sullivan, 23–24, 59

Girl Crazy, 41, 43, 49, 126

Girls Dormitory (film), 136

Givoty, George, 57

Glaenzer, Jules, 8, 35

Glazunov, Alexander, 14, 110

Globe Theatre, 13

Gluck, Cristoph Willibald, 15

Goddard, Paulette, 147–49, 156–57, 176

Godowsky, Frances Gershwin (sister), 8, 29, 138, 146, 160; Leonore Gershwin and, 46, 167; Rose Gershwin and, 26, 166; as a singer, 88

Godowsky, Leopold, Jr., 88, 138

Goetschius, Percy, 15

Goldberg, Isaac: on Gershwin's boyhood, 1, 35; Gershwin's May 12, 1937 letter to, 144, 150; on Gershwin's music, 7, 40

Goldman, Sherwin M., 170

Goldmark, Karl, 3

Goldmark, Rubin, 2

Goldwyn, Frances, 152, 166

Goldwyn, Samuel: described, 151–52; George Gershwin and, 155–56, 160; *The Goldwyn Follies* and, 126, 150, 152–53; Ira Gershwin and, 164–65; Leonore Gershwin and, 166; *Porgy and Bess* (movie) and, 171–72

Goldwyn, Samuel, Jr., 166

Goldwyn Follies, The, 150, 154, 164–65

Gone With the Wind, 149

Good Earth, The (Buck), 63

Gorman, Ross, 5

Grant, Cary, 143

195

197

199

201

203

WALTER RIMLER is the author of *Not Fade Away:
A Comparison of Jazz Age With Rock Era Pop Song
Composers* and *A Gershwin Companion*. His articles
and fiction have appeared in *Midstream, Prism
International,* and other publications.

MUSIC IN AMERICAN LIFE

Way Up North in Dixie: A Black Family's Claim to the Confederate Anthem
    Howard L. Sacks and Judith Rose Sacks
The Bluegrass Reader   *Edited by Thomas Goldsmith*
Colin McPhee: Composer in Two Worlds   *Carol J. Oja*
Robert Johnson, Mythmaking, and Contemporary American Culture
    Patricia R. Schroeder
Composing a World: Lou Harrison, Musical Wayfarer   *Leta E. Miller*
    and Fredric Lieberman
Fritz Reiner, Maestro and Martinet   *Kenneth Morgan*
That Toddlin' Town: Chicago's White Dance Bands and Orchestras, 1900–1950
    Charles A. Sengstock Jr.
Dewey and Elvis: The Life and Times of a Rock 'n' Roll Deejay   *Louis Cantor*
Come Hither to Go Yonder: Playing Bluegrass with Bill Monroe   *Bob Black*
Chicago Blues: Portraits and Stories   *David Whiteis*
The Incredible Band of John Philip Sousa   *Paul E. Bierley*
"Maximum Clarity" and Other Writings on Music   *Ben Johnston, edited by*
    Bob Gilmore
Staging Tradition: John Lair and Sarah Gertrude Knott   *Michael Ann Williams*
Homegrown Music: Discovering Bluegrass   *Stephanie P. Ledgin*
Tales of a Theatrical Guru   *Danny Newman*
The Music of Bill Monroe   *Neil V. Rosenberg and Charles K. Wolfe*
Pressing On: The Roni Stoneman Story   *Roni Stoneman, as told to Ellen Wright*
Together Let Us Sweetly Live   *Jonathan C. David, with photographs by*
    Richard Holloway
Live Fast, Love Hard: The Faron Young Story   *Diane Diekman*
Air Castle of the South: WSM Radio and the Making of Music City
    Craig P. Havighurst
Traveling Home: Sacred Harp Singing and American Pluralism   *Kiri Miller*
Where Did Our Love Go?: The Rise and Fall of the Motown Sound
    Nelson George
Lonesome Cowgirls and Honky-Tonk Angels: The Women of Barn Dance Radio
    Kristine M. McCusker
California Polyphony: Ethnic Voices, Musical Crossroads   *Mina Yang*
The Never-Ending Revival: Rounder Records and the Folk Alliance
    Michael F. Scully
Sing It Pretty: A Memoir   *Bess Lomax Hawes*
Working Girl Blues: The Life and Music of Hazel Dickens   *Hazel Dickens*
    and Bill C. Malone
Charles Ives Reconsidered   *Gayle Sherwood Magee*
The Hayloft Gang: The Story of the National Barn Dance   *Edited by Chad Berry*
Country Music Humorists and Comedians   *Loyal Jones*
Record Makers and Breakers: Voices of the Independent Rock 'n' Roll Pioneers
    John Broven

The University of Illinois Press
is a founding member of the
Association of American University Presses.

Composed in 10.25/15 Adobe Minion Pro
by Jim Proefrock
at the University of Illinois Press
Designed by Kelly Gray
Manufactured by Thomson-Shore, Inc.

University of Illinois Press
1325 South Oak Street
Champaign, IL 61820-6903
www.press.uillinois.edu